Complete Handbook of
WINNING SOFTBALL

Complete Handbook of
WINNING SOFTBALL

Sharon J. Drysdale

Karen S. Harris

ALLYN AND BACON, INC.
Boston · London · Sydney · Toronto

Figures 2–2, 3–3, 6–5, 6–7, 6–8, 9–10, and 10–5 by Cheryl Haugh.
Figure 5–20 by Christie Price. Figures 9–2 and 9–3 by Susan Palmer.
Figure 9–8 by George Gabauer. All other photos by Larry Williams.

Library of Congress Cataloging in Publication Data

Drysdale, Sharon J.
    Complete handbook of winning softball.

    Includes index.
    1. Softball.   2. Softball coaching.   I. Harris,
Karen S.   II. Title.
GV881.D78   796.357′8   81–12900
ISBN 0–205–07597–5   AACR2

Series Editor: Hiram G. Howard
Managing Editor: Paul Solaqua
Production Editor: Rowena D. Dores

Printed in the United States of America

10 9 8 7 6 5 4 3 2   87 86 85 84 83

To those who play with pride, principles, and love!

Contents

FIVE
Coaching   297

Foreword

Teachers, coaches, and players have been waiting a long time for a comprehensive analysis of the skills and techniques of fast pitch softball. Until *Complete Handbook of Winning Softball,* there was no single reference source available that could accommodate the needs of both beginning and advanced players and coaches.

A strength of the book lies in the fact that the author assumes no background knowledge on the part of the reader. Therefore, in the treatment of each skill, mechanical sequence is meticulously detailed and the reader is informed of how to recognize and correct every imaginable departure from efficient execution of the task. The chapters on pitching, hitting, and individual defensive positions are particularly good in this regard.

From a strictly coaching perspective, the sections on team offense (Chapter 12) and coaching (Section Five) are excellent, especially for new high school and college coaches who would rather not learn the hard way. The generous use of high-quality sequential photographs is also tremendously helpful.

It is especially important for coaches and aspiring coaches to recognize that the critical difference between the "average" mentor and the "expert" is attention to detail and knowing the "why" behind everything you ask a player to do. The author has shown herself to be attentive to both of these requirements.

The *Complete Handbook of Winning Softball* belongs on every softball enthusiast's bookshelf and deserves to be used as a standard text in college physical instruction and professional preparation courses devoted to the sport. This is a softball book that needed to be written—I'm glad it was.

Donna Lopiano
Director of Women's Athletics
University of Texas

Preface

Complete Handbook of Winning Softball may be used in a variety of ways. Since the book covers everything from the most basic fundamentals to advanced team strategy, practicing coaches at all levels will find it useful as a general guide for developing a winning team. Coaches will also find it useful as a reference for solving specific problems, including those very serious but seldom-addressed problems that frequently arise in the areas of team management, practice organization, player assessment, and the many other nontechnical aspects of coaching.

Teachers will find that the book is especially effective in coaching methods courses. It is developmentally organized and provides the necessary depth for serious study of softball. The fundamental skills are analyzed kinesiologically as well as described. Differences between skilled and unskilled play are examined. The advantages and disadvantages of various techniques are discussed, and the importance of skills to the game as a whole is considered.

Players and students will find the book helpful, especially when neither a coach nor a teacher is available. Because of the clear presentation and the many illustrations, the book functions well as a self-instructional tool.

Drawing on their experiences as coaches, teachers, and players, the authors have attempted to provide the most comprehensive and instructive book available on the subject of softball. The book is divided into five sections. Section One provides in-depth analyses of individual defensive fundamentals, such as throwing, catching, fielding, covering, and backing up. Section Two gives practical help on position play, with particular attention paid to individual and team responsibilities. Section Three, "Individual Offensive Fundamentals," is intended to help coaches develop their players' hitting, bunting, and baserunning skills. Section Four, "Team Play," deals primarily with strategy, paying particular attention to such neglected topics as rundowns, pickoffs, and offensive plays. Section Five, "Coaching," discusses such valuable topics as team management, game coaching, assessing individual and team play, and scouting.

This book is intended for all players and coaches of softball, both male and female. However, to avoid awkward phrases such as "s/he" and "his or her," we have used the traditional masculine pronouns when referring to the player or the coach in general.

Acknowledgments

THOSE WHO MADE IT HAPPEN

Mr. & Mrs. Drysdale Mr. & Mrs. Harris Mrs. L. J. Searle	The Source—those who positively supported our play and subsequent professional endeavors
Shirley Carmichael Karren J. Drysdale Irene Kerwin Charles McCord	The Inspiration—our teachers, coaches, models
Kathryn Christiansen	The Force—a friend, critic, project manager
Natalie Hector	Typist
Larry Williams	Photographer
Cheryl Haugh	Illustrator

THOSE WHO MADE IT ALL WORTHWHILE

Our Athletes	Bishop Kelley Comets Northwestern University Wildcats University of Kansas Jayhawks Greater Milwaukee "West Allis State" Bankettes

SPECIAL THANKS

To Donna Lopiano for writing the Foreword to this book and for providing constructive criticism.

To those who read and critiqued selected parts of the manuscript—Cindy Anderson, Karren Drysdale, Brenda Gold, Jan Gulbis, Karen Swarts.

To Larry Williams, who combined his love of the game, his photographic skills, and many hours of hard work to provide the major portion of the photographs in this book. Also, to Cheryl Haugh, George Gabauer, Christie Price, and Susan K. Palmer for their photographs.

To the many amateur and professional athletes who so capably demonstrated the basic techniques of softball as pictured throughout this book: Cynthia Anderson, Debbie Biggs, Ronald Biggs, Jennifer Bridges, Karren Drysdale, Laura Frost, Deborah Gannon, Billy Jackson, William Kelley, Janet Kohl, Tony Peters, Kelly Phipps, Anne Scalet, Reatha Stucky, Karen Swarts, Marlys Taber, Carolyn Townsend, Scott Williams, and Margie Wright.

To the Northwestern University administration, athletic department, and athletes for providing an intellectually stimulating environment and the support necessary to complete the manuscript.

To those who care—friends (C.A., K.C., K.D., D.G., J.G., P.G., E.I., I.M., S.P., C.T., M.T. . . .) and readers.

Complete Handbook of
WINNING SOFTBALL

ONE

Individual Defensive Fundamentals

Throwing

Because of individual players' differences in physiological makeup, body size and structure, and conditioning, there will be intrasex and intersex differences in the maximum speed of a thrown ball and in the distance it may travel. However, the basic techniques for a skilled overhand throw will not vary with the sex of the thrower. A girl who throws with skill and proper technique is not throwing "like a boy," but rather like a skilled softball player.

Techniques for the proper execution of an overhand throw are also the same for right-handed and left-handed throwers. We will analyze procedures for throwing right-handed only, in the interest of brevity and to avoid redundancy.

Mentally Preparing to Throw

Each athlete must consider all prospective throwing possibilities in advance of a catch. Each should have an idea of where the ball should be thrown and who the receiver should be. Each should also have an idea of the speed and distance required for the throw. A nonproductive or unnecessary throw should never be made.

Gripping the Ball

It is important for a player to develop a sense of feel for the ball as it is taken out of the glove. Gripping across the seams will allow a firmer

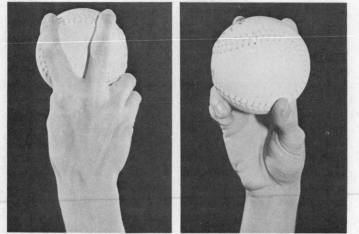

Figure 1-1. Tripod Grip

hold of the ball and will help to prevent the ball from slipping as it is released. The exchange from glove to throwing hand must be smooth, fast, and sure.

Two types of grips are possible: a tripod grip (Figure 1–1) and a three-finger grip (Figure 1–2). The type of grip used will depend upon the size of the thrower's hand. A larger hand is necessary for the tripod grip in order to cover as much of the ball's surface as possible with two fingers, rather than three.

Regardless of the type of grip used, the ball should be held securely with the fingers—not the palm of the hand. An observer should be able to look from a variety of angles and see daylight between the palm of the thrower's hand and the ball, as in Figure 1–3.

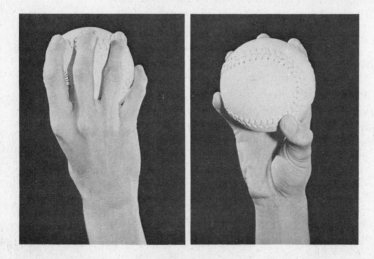

Figure 1-2. Three-Finger Grip

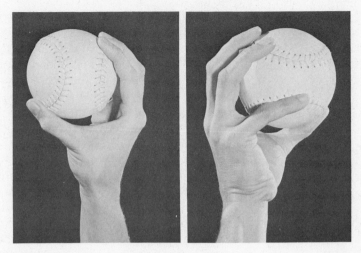

Figure 1-3. Gap Test

Assuming the Throwing Position

Figure 1–4 illustrates sound form for assuming the throwing position. Once the player has the ball securely in her grasp, she faces the target and narrows her visual field to the target area. Her body weight shifts to the rear (right) leg, with the foot pointed between 45 and 90 degrees to the target. At the same time, the left leg raises slightly as the

Figure 1-4. Assuming Throwing Position

trunk, and the shoulders twist right. Raising the left arm up in front of the body helps to maintain balance throughout this phase. As the trunk twists, the right arm, led by the elbow, drops down, back, and up, with the little finger leading the hand. When the hand has gone as far backward and as high as it will go, the wrist should be cocked. The eyes remain focused on the target, the left leg strides forward, and the tip of the left shoulder points directly at the target.

Releasing the Ball

A good strong push from the rear (right) leg initiates the action phase of the throw. As the left leg completes its stride forward and the left knee flexes, the hips twist and move forward, with the trunk and shoulders following, until they are square to the target (see Figure 1–5). The arm is held back as long as possible and is then permitted to continue its motion forward, with the elbow leading and the upper arm swinging forward horizontally. The ball is released with a strong whip-like action as the forearm extends almost completely and the wrist snaps forward. The

Figure 1–5. Throwing

Figure 1-6. Following Through

player's weight is forward, and the arm and fingers extend toward the target.

Following Through

At the completion of the throw, as in Figure 1–6, the right hand faces the target. The arm crosses over to the left side of the body, helping to reduce the momentum generated by the throw and minimizing strain on the arm and shoulder. Allowing the right leg and hip to move forward at the conclusion of the throw, and continuing to flex the trunk at the hips, also help to minimize strain.

The Differences between the Throw of a Skilled Performer and That of an Unskilled Performer

The differences between the throw of a skilled performer and that of an unskilled performer become evident when the throws are viewed from the side. Figure 1–7 illustrates an unskilled throw. Compare that figure with Figure 1–8, which illustrates a skillful throw.

Figure 1-7. Unskilled Throw

Head not in front of right shoulder.	Head not in front of right shoulder.	Head not in front of right shoulder.
Shoulders and hips remain square to target.	Shoulders and hips behind arm.	Limited elbow extension.
Elbow in close to body.	Wrist leads action forward instead of elbow.	Limited transfer of weight.
Upper arm perpendicular to ground.	Forearm perpendicular to ground and above elbow.	No hip flexion or trunk movement forward.
Wrist leads back instead of elbow leading.	Body erect—no hip flexion.	Right leg remains back.
Left arm in close to body.	Limited transfer of weight.	Arm pushes out.
Toes point directly forward.		Throw finishes with hand facing target.
Limited push from back leg.		Head and shoulders remain back.
		Little bend in left knee.
		Limited follow-through, in general.

Figure 1-8. Skilled Throw

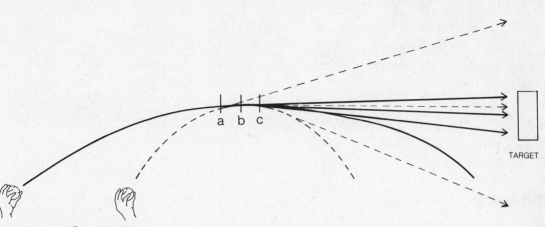

Figure 1-9. Throwing Arcs

Throwing with Accuracy

To execute an overhand throw, the hand moves in an arc. Increasing the curve of this arc decreases the possibility of an accurate throw. Control problems arise because the ball will go off on a tangent to the arc at the point where the hand releases the ball. (See Figure 1–9.) Accuracy in the overhand throw can be improved by developing consistency in the timing of the release and by flattening the path through which the hand travels. Primary action must be directed forward, toward the target.

Whenever feasible, the intent of a fielder should be to place the ball in the baseman's glove. A performer who has developed some skill should concentrate on throwing *strikes* (balls thrown between the receiver's armpits and knees, and no wider than the receiver's body). Throwing inaccuracy is often due as much to carelessness, lack of concentration, and improper response to relevant situational cues as it is to faulty technique.

Throwing with Speed and Accuracy

A performer who practices throwing at a given speed will develop accuracy at that speed. Therefore, it is imperative that performers repetitively practice each type of throw at its appropriate velocity.

The best throw for speed is a low horizontal one with as flat an arc as possible. In general, low straight-line throws are the best because they cover the distance between the thrower and the receiver in the shortest length of time. If a fielder cannot get a low horizontal throw to the target on, at *most*, one bounce, a relay should be used. A properly executed relay, with two quick throws, is faster than, and preferable to, one slow looping throw or a throw that bounces repeatedly and is slowed by friction each time the ball hits the ground.

Figure 1–10. Sidearm Throw

SIDEARM

A sidearm throw allows a more rapid arm action than the overhand pattern, but sacrifices some ball speed in the process. Still, it is particularly useful when quickness, rather than speed over distance, is the critical factor; and it does provide more speed than the underarm pattern. After fielding a bunt or grounder, for instance, the fielder can save time by remaining low and using a sidearm throw to release the ball from the height at which he fielded the ball. The major points of the sidearm throw are demonstrated in Figure 1–10.

A primary distinguishing feature of the sidearm throw is the position of the throwing arm and the horizontal plane in which the arm movements are made. Because the hand moves through a horizontal arc, left-right inaccuracies will be more prevalent with the sidearm throw than with either the overhand or the underhand throw. Some of the errors will be due to inconsistency in the timing of the ball's release, perhaps compounded by allowing the hand to travel through a more curved arc or path. Moving the shoulder girdle and the body forward by rotating the hips and trunk, and striding into the throw, will help to flatten the arc and increase tolerance for errors in timing of the release.

Another distinguishing feature of the sidearm throw is increased reliance on hip action as a contributor to the velocity of the throw. Another is fuller extension of the right elbow at release.

In executing the sidearm throw, the player must not allow the forearm to supinate as the little finger leads the hand. Supination, coupled with an elbow snap and no follow-through, can lead to elbow injury.

UNDERHAND TOSS

The underhand toss is effective when a quick release is imperative and the distance to the target is fifteen feet or less.

Figure 1-11. Underhand Toss

Assuming Tossing Position

Figure 1–11 illustrates the execution of an underhand toss. Once the player has fielded the ball, she begins the toss by moving her glove away and exposing the ball to the receiver. It is important that the thrower "show" the ball as soon as possible because of the limited time and distance the receiver has in which to react. The thrower's body, low and flexed at the hips, pivots to face the target in forward stride position. At the same time, the throwing arm and hand drop to a position almost perpendicular to the ground, with the fingers behind the ball and the palm of the hand squarely facing the target. The ball is thus in clear view of the receiver as soon, and for as long, as possible.

Releasing the Ball

The toss is executed with a stiff wrist and a forward pendulum swing from the shoulder. The ball leaves the hand as the arm reaches directly *out* toward the target. The arm stops between waist and chest height, with the fingers extended toward the target and the palm of the hand facing the receiver. The ball must be thrown firmly and with little arc. Allowing the body to continue forward as the ball is released adds a little momentum to the ball, emphasizes the follow-through in the direction of the toss, and assists in reducing high-low inaccuracies.

The underhand toss cannot be delivered with as much speed as the sidearm or overhand throw because there is a very limited backswing, little trunk rotation, minimal wrist action, and, in summary, fewer body parts contributing to the action, each to a lesser degree. The advantage of this throw lies in the speed with which the ball can reach its target receiver and in the greater ease with which the ball can be followed and handled by the receiver.

BACKHAND FLIP

The backhand flip is used when a short, quick throw must be made to a receiver who is located on the right side of a right-handed thrower's body. The flip may be used for a force-out at second or third, to start a double play, or to catch a player leading off base following a caught line drive. Like the underhand toss, the backhand flip is usually executed when the receiver is within fifteen feet of the thrower. This distance must be covered rapidly, but the ball cannot be thrown too hard or the receiver will not be able to handle it and the throw will not accomplish its objective. Rather than saving time through the speed of the throw, the backhand flip saves time through a quick release.

Assuming Flip Position

The backhand flip is frequently quicker than the underhand toss because the fielder's body remains in position behind the path of the batted ball and does not turn to face the targeted receiver of the throw. When fielding a batted ball, the player's feet are usually in side-stride position, or the foot on the throwing side of the body is back. Weight is evenly distributed on the balls of both feet, the body is bent forward at the waist, and a line through the left and right shoulders remains perpendicular to the target receiver.

As the fielder's arms give with the catch, the right hand grips the ball, and the glove is drawn away so that it doesn't interfere with the receiver's focus on the ball. The throwing hand and forearm turn in and down (pronate) as the elbow points toward the target receiver and the back of the hand is brought in to the chest, toward the midline of the body. The wrist is stiff, the head is turned toward the target, and the eyes are focused on the receiver's glove. (See Figure 1–12.)

Figure 1-12. Backhand Flip

Executing the Flip

The ball is released as the elbow extends and the palm of the hand moves directly toward the receiver in a pushing action. The arm stops between waist and shoulder height, with the elbow fully extended, the palm of the hand perpendicular to the target, and the fingers pointed toward the target.

The backhand flip is more difficult to control than the underhand toss and requires a great deal of practice. Because the forearm and hand sweep toward the target in a horizontal-oblique path, left-right inaccuracies are most common. During practice, players must be afforded the opportunity to experiment with release timing and with varying delivery speeds.

2

Catching and Fielding

CATCHING THROWS

Preparing to Receive a Throw

The first thing a potential receiver must do while awaiting a throw is to develop the proper mental set. This means developing a psychological readiness for the expected and the unexpected. Too often a receiver anticipates that the ball will be thrown within easy reach and therefore relaxes to a lesser or greater extent. If the unexpected does occur, the unprepared receiver must rely on quick reactions to save the play and sometimes cannot react in time. By placing the mind and muscles on alert, the player is better able to respond to any or all of the following: (1) a high, low, or wide throw; (2) an unreasonably hard throw or (less frequent) an unusually slow throw; and (3) a change in the flight of the ball (curve, rise, drop).

The receiver must also prepare physically to catch the ball. (Figure 2–1 illustrates the correct preparatory position.) First, the potential receiver should face the thrower with her feet comfortably apart and her glove-side foot slightly in front. Weight should be distributed evenly on both feet so that movement in any direction is possible without compensatory action. It is also important that the knees be bent. Even if movement is not necessary, the flexed position will help to stabilize the body. Next, the arms should extend toward the thrower, with the glove chest

Figure 2-1. Catching a Throw

high and the pocket facing the thrower. The open glove provides a small, specific target. If the thrower succeeds in hitting the chest-high target, the receiver is in the optimal position to relay the ball elsewhere.

Having prepared mentally and physically to catch the ball, the receiver should call to the thrower. This will indicate to the thrower that the receiver is ready, and it will also provide a cue for target location.

Watching the Ball

As the thrower releases the ball, the receiver's eyes should be focused directly on the release point rather than in the thrower's general direction or on the thrower's face, body, etc. The release will provide the receiver with the important initial cues used to judge the flight of the throw.

The receiver must watch the approaching ball as closely as possible and try to follow its flight all the way into the glove. The head and shoulders should bend slightly toward the glove. This action allows the receiver to view the ball for the maximum length of time and thus provides the greatest opportunity to see any directional changes in the flight of the ball. In addition, should the ball start to pop back out of the glove after the catch, recovery can be made quickly because the receiver's head is already turned toward the ball, and the eyes are focused on it.

Receiving the Throw

Whenever possible, the receiver's body should be positioned in direct line with the approaching ball and both hands should be involved in making the catch. Both arms will be extended, with the thumb of the bare hand in contact with the back of the thumb of the glove. The fingers of the bare hand should be slightly flexed and somewhat relaxed, with the palmar surface of the hand facing the ball.

The actual catch will be made in the pocket of the glove, with the fingers of the bare hand closing over the ball *after* its entry into the glove. The padded glove absorbs some of the force of impact, increases the catching area, and increases the area that absorbs the force of impact.

The receiver should reduce the shock of the ball's hitting the glove

Figure 2-2. Catching Balls That Are (a) High, (b) Middle, (c) Low, (d) Wide (Forehand), and (e) Wide (Backhand)

by flexing the elbows and allowing the arms to give to some extent as the impact occurs. The appropriate amount of give is dependent upon the force of the approaching ball. Sometimes referred to as *soft hands*, this technique reduces the chance that the ball will pop out of the glove and also protects the hand from bruises. Near full extension of the arms before the catch provides maximum time and distance over which to absorb the force of the ball.

Figure 2–2 illustrates correct form for catching balls that are high, middle, low, and wide. If the ball is to be caught above the waist, the fingers should be pointed upward, thumbs toward each other. If the ball is to be caught below the waist, the fingers should be pointed downward, little fingers toward each other. When the receiver is fielding line drives and catching throws, the palms of the hands should always face the approaching ball. This position provides a maximum surface area for catching the ball and absorbing impact force; allows the player the mobility necessary for making unexpected last-second adjustments; and prevents jammed fingers, which result from impact force at the tips of the fingers.

Both hands should be involved in the catching process. The bare hand aids in trapping the ball and decreases the probability of its rebounding out of the glove or being dropped. Also, a player who has used two hands for the catch can throw the ball more quickly because no time need be wasted in bringing the throwing hand to the ball after the catch.

FIELDING

Assuming Ready Position

By assuming a side-stride position and distributing his weight evenly on the balls of his feet, the player is stable, balanced, able to move quickly in any direction, and prepared to shift to meet any change in the course of the ball. (Allowing the weight to rock back on the heels, placing the weight primarily on one leg, or moving one leg in back of the other may facilitate a player's movement in one direction, but makes the player vulnerable to a hit or throw requiring quick movement in other directions.) Pointing the toes slightly outward readies the fielder for lateral movement. Bending at the knees and hips, in addition to preparing the player for movement, allows the arms to hang freely in front of the body and allows the glove to touch the ground. From this position the player is able to rise with the ball and to give with it as he brings it in toward his chest or into throwing position. Opening the pocket to the expected approach of the ball eliminates the need for any glove manipula-

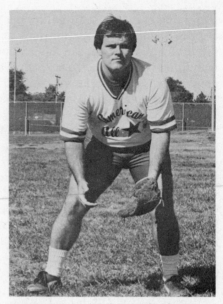

Figure 2-3. Infielder's Ready Position

Figure 2-4. Outfielder's Ready Position

tion before fielding a grounder in front, or to the left, of the body. As a result, the player is better prepared to handle hard hits, as well as unexpected hops that require quick reaction time and immediate response. (Figure 2–3 illustrates the infielder's ready position.)

The outfielder's ready position, as Figure 2–4 demonstrates, is almost identical to that of the infielder. The basic differences are that the outfielder's body is slightly more erect, his arms hang freely in front of his body, and his glove is held at approximately knee level rather than on the ground. The hands of the outfielder, like those of the infielder, must *not* be on his knees as the pitcher delivers the ball to the batter.

The fielder's stance—legs in a side-stride position, with toes even and pointed slightly outward—permits movement in all directions, but it is more conducive to lateral movement than to forward-backward movement. It is sometimes referred to as a square stance.

On occasion, it may be advisable to drop one leg back on the side of the expected hit. This adjustment favors forward-backward movement rather than lateral movement. The type of stance to be assumed will depend upon the anticipated path of the ball, as judged by the fielder.

Anticipating the Path of the Ball

Once the pitcher begins the windup, the fielder should watch the batter. The fielder should concentrate on the ball as it comes off the bat, trying to judge the future flight of the ball from its initial direction and speed. General direction and speed can be determined by listening to the sound as the bat hits the ball; by watching the speed, direction of movement, and angle of the bat as it strikes the ball; and by observing the angle and speed of the ball as it leaves the bat. Players who get a good jump on the ball use this initial information to direct their first steps toward the ball. If the fielder waits, more directional information becomes available as the ball continues its flight, but less time is left to react and to move into position to catch the ball. Quick initial action is, therefore, highly desirable. If a player is starting at the proper time, some physical move will be made toward every batted ball.

Fielding Ground Balls

Moving to the Ball

The fielder should charge, or move toward the ball, whenever possible, positioning his body in direct line with it. By going to meet the ball swiftly, with the body under control, the fielder reduces the number of bounces the ball will take, limiting the chance that it will take a bad hop. Charging also saves time by decreasing the distance over which the ball will travel and by permitting a quicker throw. Positioning squarely in front of the ball allows the body to act as a barrier, protecting against the possibility that the ball will take a bad hop or otherwise be missed. Balls that are not caught cleanly should rebound off the body and remain playable.

Handling the Ball

As the ball nears, the fielder should stop his approach and assume a stationary *set position* that deviates from the *ready position* only in that the left foot is forward for a right-handed thrower. As Figure 2–5 shows, this position provides a firm base of support; affords room for the momen-

Figure 2-5. Preparing to Handle a Ground Ball

Figure 2-6. Fielding the Grounder

tum of the ball to be absorbed into the backswing of the subsequent throw; and facilitates hip and spinal rotation for a strong, balanced throw. The chin tucks as the eyes follow the ball closely all the way into the glove. (Any head movement up or away from the ball as it approaches will lift the body and may allow the ball to pass under the glove and to escape between the legs.) The arms hang freely in front of the body, and weight is centered on the balls of the feet. The glove remains on the ground, with fingers down and the pocket facing toward the approaching ball. The fingers of the bare hand, adjacent to the glove, also point down, and the palm is perpendicular to the path of the ball.

The bare hand, as in Figure 2–6, closes over the ball *after* it bounces into the glove at a point approximately opposite the forward foot. Both arms flex and bring the ball back up, and in to the body as the throwing hand grips the ball and the give becomes the backswing for a throw. Two hands should be used whenever possible to ensure that the ball does not rebound out of the glove and to permit transferring the ball from glove to hand quickly and cleanly as the arms give with the catch.

Every attempt should be made to smother the bounce of the ball, or, in other words, to catch the ball as soon after it leaves the ground as possible. This increases the chance of covering a bad hop on the rebound.

Fielding a Grounder to the Side of the Body

When a ground ball is hit to either side of the body, the fielder should first get in front of the ball and then set or, if there is time, charge it. Many fielders, particularly beginners, take the shortest and most direct route when charging a ground ball hit to the side of the body. They follow a diagonal path rather than a semicircular path, as illustrated in Figure 2–7. The semicircular approach to the ball has three advantages:

1. The ball may be caught at several points along the approach path.

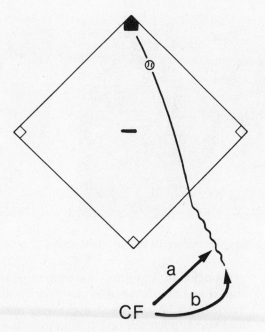

Figure 2–7. Two Approaches to a Ground Ball Hit to the Side of the Body: *a*, Diagonal Path; *b*, Semicircular Path.

2. The momentum of the body is forward, through the ball, and in the direction of the impending throw.
3. The body is in a more stable and balanced position from which to compensate should the ball take an unexpected hop, or should the ball's or body's approach speed be misjudged.

Whenever possible, the semicircular approach should be used for charging and fielding all ground balls hit to the side of the body. If the ball is hit hard and far enough to the side of the body that quick lateral movement is necessary, a cross-over step or a straight step may be used. To execute a cross-over step, the fielder pivots on the foot closest to the ball before bringing the back foot through and reaching with the glove for the ball. By turning the right foot (when the ball is hit to the right) to face the direction in which the body will move, the legs do not literally cross over. The initial movement becomes a running step forward with the left foot. The body remains balanced. Figure 2–8 illustrates the use of a cross-over step to field grounders hit to the forehand and backhand sides of the body. Note that the fielder's eyes are on the ball, the body and the glove are low, and the pocket of the glove is open to the approaching ball.

For a straight step, the fielder's initial movement is a step sideward with the foot closest to the ball. The right foot would initiate the movement if the ball was hit to the right side of the fielder.

Difference of opinion exists regarding the use of a straight step or a cross-over step. For reach and for maximum distance on the first step, the

Figure 2-8. Fielding Grounders to the (a) Right and (b) Left of the Body

cross-over is superior. For quickness, however, the straight step is superior. Less distance is covered by the striding foot, but time is saved accordingly. Also, the straight step places the body in a more balanced and stable position, and it is more advantageous when moving back and to the side for a ball or when adjusting to a bad hop. In summary, it appears that the best method to use is dependent upon the speed of the ball as it approaches, its distance from the body, and the resultant priorities—a slower, longer reach or a quicker, shorter reach.

Fielding Fly Balls and Pop-Ups

Judging the Path of the Ball

The ball's flight will depend upon the speed, spin, and approach angle of the pitched ball; the speed, direction of movement, and angle of the bat as it contacts the ball; and the effects of air resistance and gravity on the ball. Unfortunately, these factors combine to make judging the flight of the ball difficult, particularly for beginners. It will help if the fielder, in ready position, concentrates on the ball as it comes off the bat, trying to judge the future flight of the ball from its initial direction and speed.

There is no substitute for experience in learning to judge the flight of fly balls under ideal and difficult (windy, sunny, night light) circumstances. Repetitive practice is necessary for players of all skill levels.

Moving to the Ball

As soon as the ball leaves the bat, the fielder should be off and running, with arms pumping, to the spot where he expects to catch the ball.

While moving toward this position, the player's eyes remain on the ball. Running on the toes rather than on the heels minimizes the up-and-down movement of the body so that the ball is easier to follow.

Calling for the Ball

A fly ball or a pop-up that is hit high into the air often provides time for more than one player to be in position for the catch. Couple this possibility with the necessity of each player to look up in order to follow the flight of the ball, and the potential for collisions, injuries, and mix-ups becomes readily apparent. A fielder cannot be focusing on the ball and looking around for teammates at the same time. This potentially dangerous situation can be handled only through communication. A player, as soon as he decides that he definitely intends to try for the ball, must call for it by repeatedly yelling, "I've got it!" "Mine!" or "I have it!" A waving off or sweeping action with the throwing hand may be used as a supplemental visible cue, but it is not a substitute for calling for the ball aloud.

Once a player has repeatedly called for the ball, he must follow through with the attempt. Teammates should move away, preferably to a back-up position behind the fielder, and give plenty of room for the catch.

Assuming Fielding Position

Having called for the ball, the fielder should assume a balanced, forward-stride position and face the approaching ball with the right foot (in

Figure 2-9. Fielding a Fly Ball

a   b

the case of a right-handed thrower) forward and the knees slightly flexed. Figure 2–9 illustrates proper positioning. The fielder's eyes are focused on the ball, and her body is positioned far enough back that she can see the ball when it descends in front of her forehead. When a fielder is in doubt about the distance of the hit, or when a subsequent throw must be made, it is best to be further back than is deemed necessary. It is much easier to move in on a ball at the last second than it is to move back. The forward movement also provides added momentum for the throw.

Both arms, although partially extended above and in front of the head, should be relaxed. The back of the glove (backhand) faces the eyes and is positioned in front of the throwing shoulder, thereby crossing the midline of the body. The pocket of the glove is open and directly faces the approaching ball, with fingers of the glove pointing up at an oblique angle. The thumb of the bare hand is braced behind the thumb of the glove, and the palm faces the path of the approaching ball.

Handling the Fly Ball or Pop-Up

The ball is caught above eye level on the throwing side, and with both hands, whenever possible. (See Figure 2–9b.) The glove actually catches the ball, and the bare hand assists in closing the glove around the ball so that the ball is trapped and cannot rebound out. The bare hand is also close by to permit quick removal of the ball from the glove for a subsequent throw.

With the catch, the arms give as the elbows flex to absorb the force of the ball, and the throwing hand grips the ball. If no throw is imminent, the fielder should squeeze the ball with both hands as she brings it in to the body. If a subsequent throw is necessary, the bare hand grips the ball, and the give becomes the backswing for the throw. The fielder should allow the give that occurs on the catch to move across the ear on the same

Figure 2-10. Fielding a Short Fly Ball before It Touches the Ground

side as the throwing arm in order to reach the cocked arm throwing position and to enhance a quick release.

When a *high* fly ball is hit and the fielder has plenty of *time* to position *under* it, it is advantageous to make the catch with the left shoulder pointing in the direction of the target. When a ball is dropping in a fairly vertical path, the direction the fielder's body faces does not appreciably alter the player's perceptions or increase the difficulty of the catch. Turning and moving in the direction of the target before making the catch will save time, and the added momentum gained by the forward motion of the body will contribute to the force of the throw. This throwing technique should be used whenever it is practically feasible.

Fielding a Short Fly Ball or Pop-Up

If a fly ball is falling in front of a player, as in Figure 2–10, she should keep her body low, head down, and glove extended toward the ball. Keeping the head down and the chin tucked as the ball approaches the ground is extremely important because if the head is lifted, the body raises as well, and the ball can slip beneath the glove as the glove pulls up. The back of the glove faces the ground, the fingers point away from the body, and the pocket is open to the ball as it descends. The player's eyes remain clearly focused on the ball until it enters the glove.

As the catch is made, the wrist and arm give a little and the bare hand, adjacent to the glove, assists in closing over the ball to prevent a rebound. The ball is then brought in to the chest as the body straightens up.

If the ball falls to the ground before it can be caught, the player must remain low to the ground, keep her head and glove down, maintain eye contact with the ball, and field it on the short hop. She should do everything possible to keep the ball from going past her, including blocking it with her body.

If the ball is falling in front and to the side, the player should first attempt to get her body behind the ball, as when charging and fielding a grounder. If this is impossible, body position and extension of the arm should be similar to that assumed when catching throws to the side and low.

Fielding a Long Fly Ball

As soon as it appears that the ball will be coming down behind her present position, the player must begin to move backwards. Unless only one or two steps are necessary, back pedaling should be avoided. Not only is it slow, but it also causes balancing problems that can lead to a fall. In order not to back pedal, the player must turn. The decision about which way to turn must be based on the direction and speed of the ball.

Figure 2-11. Fielding a Long Fly Ball Hit over the Right Shoulder

To field a ball hit over the right shoulder, the player should pivot and jab step (see Chapter 10) to the right, rear, and then run toward where she projects that the ball will come down. The player's feet point in the direction of the run, while her eyes look back over her left shoulder to check the ball's flight. She must make every attempt to get behind the ball and to be waiting for it, in throwing position, when it comes down. If this is not possible, and the ball must be fielded on the run, the player extends her left (glove) arm across her body and uses a backhand catch, as in Figure 2-11. The extension should occur during the last four or five steps—not at the last moment—so that the glove will be in position to give with the catch, and to pull the ball in to the body, immediately. Once the catch is made, the player stops her momentum by bracing against her bent right leg. She then pivots back to the left, and throws.

To field a ball hit over the left shoulder, the player pivots and jab steps to the left, rear, and then runs toward where she projects that the ball will come down. Her feet point in the direction of the run, while her eyes look back over her right shoulder to check the ball's flight. If the player has time, she gets behind the ball, stops, turns back to the right, and assumes the catching-throwing position. If the player cannot get behind the ball, she simply extends her left arm to make the catch on the run, as in Figure 2-12. Again, extension of the glove should take place during the last four or five steps, and not at the last moment. To get into position for a throw, the player first allows her momentum to continue in the direction of the run. Then, at the earliest opportunity, she checks this momentum by bracing her right leg. The body completes its rotation to the left, and the player throws.

Figure 2-12. Fielding a Long Fly Ball Hit over the Left Shoulder

It is possible to check the body's momentum by bracing the left leg. If that is done, the player steps back and pivots to the right before throwing. This technique is not recommended, however, because the turn of the body is away from the direction of the throw. Therefore, it wastes time and energy.

Occasionally, balls will be hit so that they pass directly overhead. These are probably the hardest fly balls to judge because of the difficulty of determining their velocity. In these cases, the direction the player turns depends upon how far the ball is hit. If the ball is shallow enough to allow the player to get behind it, she should pivot to the right. This places her body in the proper throwing position with minimal turning of head and trunk. If the ball is hit deep, however, the player may need maximum extension of the glove arm and should, therefore, turn to the left.

If the ball is hit so hard that the player anticipates no chance of catching it on the fly, she should turn 180 degrees and run directly toward the spot where she believes the ball will come down. She should run as fast as she can and without glancing back at the ball. This procedure assumes that she will be able to see the ball come down ahead of her and allows maximum speed for the pursuit.

Fielding in the Sun Field, in the Wind,
and Near a Fence or Other Obstacle

Players should familiarize themselves with the effect of natural or artificial light on the visibility of balls that they can expect to receive while playing their respective positions. When players know that they will be looking into natural or artificial light while catching fly balls and pop-ups, they can prepare and respond accordingly. They may wear flip-down sunglasses, for instance, to reduce the glare from the sun. Most players use their glove to shield their eyes. Some place their glove on the sun as the ball is pitched, sighting the ball above or below the glove as the ball follows its flight path. Others choose to sight the ball from an angle. They turn their body so that they no longer face directly toward the light source. This position frequently means watching the ball from the side, and perhaps catching it in less than ideal throwing position. It is better than being blinded, however, and guessing at the ball's position. When two players are capable of fielding the ball, the one least likely to be bothered by light should make the catch, whether or not he is in the best throwing position.

Strong wind can drastically affect the velocity and direction of a ball hit into the air. Fielders should, therefore, always be aware of wind speed and direction. A handful of grass clippings or dust or a ball thrown high into the air will provide this information. The player must then incorporate this knowledge and use it to estimate the ball's flight pattern. Periodic checks must be made throughout the game, as wind conditions can change.

When fielding a fly ball or pop-up near a fence, the player should move to the fence quickly, alternately checking the position of the fence and the position of the ball. When time permits, it is usually best to go to the fence first, and then come off the fence into the path of the ball.

RECOVERING A FUMBLED BALL

If a fielder drops or blocks the ball, the fielder must immediately react and attempt to recover it. The first place to look is in front of the body. Once the ball has been located, the eyes of the fielder must remain focused on it until it is securely within grasp. Looking around to see where runners are, or what is happening, will slow the approach to the ball and will likely lead to subsequent fumbling. The ball cannot be thrown until it is caught, so the fielder's first priority must be the retrieval of the ball.

It is very important, at this point, that one error not lead to another. Speed in regaining control of the ball is critical, but only the body must hustle and move quickly. The mind, on the other hand, must keep things in perspective—cool and controlled. Tenseness and rushing often compound the problem and lead to more bobbles.

As the fielder bends to pick up the ball, the feet should be spread and the knees bent to increase balance and stability. Weight is on the balls of the feet, the trunk is flexed, the arms hang freely, and the head, whenever possible, is directly over the ball. *Both* hands should be used, particularly if the ball is moving or spinning in place. The glove hand blocks the path of the ball by sweeping in from one side, and the bare hand closes in from the other side—both hands moving through the same plane as the ball. The bare hand sweeps the ball into the pocket of the glove, and both arms flex as the ball is brought back, up, and into throwing position.

Catching/Fielding and Throwing

THROWING FROM VARIOUS BODY POSITIONS

The catch and the throw are component parts of a whole play. Each part must be executed successfully, and the transition between the two must be clean, fast, and smooth. After catching/fielding the ball, a player may use any one of nine throws: the pivot, the jump shift, the drop shift, the pivot step, the weight shift, the running step starting on the left leg, the running step starting on the right leg, the crow-hop starting on the left leg, and the crow-hop starting on the right leg.

PIVOT

The player, without taking a step, twists her hips and pivots on the balls of her feet until the tip of her nonthrowing (left) shoulder faces the target. (See Figure 3–1.)

Figure 3–1. Pivot Throw

A pivot throw is often used by the second baseman to start a double play. It may also be used by the first baseman for a play at second or by the shortstop for a play at third. Usually, a pivot throw is used when a quick release is more important than throwing force; when the distance to the target is relatively short; and when the receiver is to the throwing side of the fielder's body. The ball can be easily followed by the receiver.

JUMP SHIFT

The player fields the ball off her right knee, jumps into the air from both feet, and twists to the right so that her nonthrowing shoulder and the foot on the same side of the body move forward to face the receiver. The right foot lands slightly before the left, and the throw is made while pushing against the right leg and stepping forward onto the left foot, in the direction of the receiver. (See Figure 3–2.)

A jump shift permits a more forceful throw than the pivot throw. It is sometimes used by first or second basemen to start a double play or otherwise throw to second base. The pitcher, too, may need to employ a jump shift to get into position for a throw to second or third.

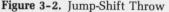

Figure 3-2. Jump-Shift Throw

Figure 3-3. Drop-Shift Throw

DROP SHIFT

The player fields the ball, plants her weight on her left leg, drops her right foot back behind the left, and steps off the right foot in the direction of the receiver. (See Figure 3–3.)

A drop shift may be used in place of a jump shift. It is commonly used by third basemen and shortstops who range to their forehand side for a grounder and must then check their momentum and shift position for a throw to first base. It may also be used by outfielders when a ball caught to their left must be thrown back toward second, third, or home plate.

PIVOT STEP

The player pivots on his rear (right) foot and steps in the direction of the throw with his forward (left) foot, shifting his weight onto his left leg. (See Figure 3–4.)

Figure 3-4. Pivot-Step Throw

A pivot-step throw is usually made following a backhand catch when the target and the body's momentum are in opposite directions. When necessary, a step or two may be taken to control body momentum following the catch. The pivot and throw are made off a braced right leg. Infielders, who must reach far to their right for the ball and then throw it back across the diamond, need to employ this throw. Outfielders, ranging to their backhand side to cut off the ball, may also use this throw, to get the ball back into the infield quickly and to prevent runners from taking extra bases. A pivot-step throw is appropriate when time does not permit a run or crow-hop before the throw and when the back leg has ultimately checked body momentum and is supporting body weight.

WEIGHT SHIFT

The player, without taking a step, simply shifts her weight from her rear (right) leg, furthest from the target, to her forward (left) leg. By keeping her hips open, the fielder needs only a minimum of preparatory action before the throw, so the ball can be released quickly. Because the feet are apart as the ball is caught, they provide a firm base for a controlled, accurate throw. (See Figure 3–5.)

The weight-shift throw should be used by the shortstop, whenever possible, to start a double play. It may also be used by the second baseman for a play at first. In addition, the pitcher or third baseman may use this throw for a play at first base after fielding a slow roller or bunt.

Figure 3-5. Weight-Shift Throw

Figure 3-6. Running-Step Throw Starting on the Left Leg

RUNNING STEP STARTING ON THE LEFT LEG

The player throws from a running approach, stepping onto her left leg while fielding the ball and stepping onto her right leg while releasing the ball. (See Figure 3–6.)

This catch-and-throw sequence requires much practice before it can be executed with control and accuracy, because it involves an off-balance throw from fielding position and from the foot on the same side of the body as the throwing arm. It is not a technique for beginners. Once mastered, it is an asset to third basemen, in particular, since they must frequently field bunts and charge slow rollers. Shortstops and second basemen may also need to use a running throw occasionally. Sometimes it is the only technique that can be executed quickly enough to retire a batter-baserunner at first base.

RUNNING STEP STARTING ON THE RIGHT LEG

The player throws from a running approach, stepping onto her right leg while fielding the ball and stepping onto her left leg while releasing the ball. (See Figure 3–7.)

This running step and throw is primarily used by players who have fielded the ball on the run and with the body weight centered on the right foot (if they are right-handed throwers). Executed properly, this technique

Figure 3-7. Running-Step Throw Starting on the Right Leg

permits the quickest release of a strong throw. The glove moves from the catch in front of the right shoulder directly back past the ear into throwing position. The transition from catch to throw must be extremely fast and clean, however, or the timing will be off and the effectiveness of the throw will be reduced. In addition, it is not as natural a movement sequence for most athletes as that involving a crow-hop. Consequently, it is not used as often as the crow-hop throws illustrated in Figures 3–8 and 3–9.

CROW-HOP STARTING ON THE LEFT LEG

The player places his weight on his forward (left) leg as he fields the ball; closes the right leg to the heel of the left foot with a hop; and then transfers the weight forward again with a step on the left leg in the direction of the throw. The sequence is lean, hop-close, and step. (See Figure 3–8.)

This crow-hop throw is frequently used by fielders as they make the transition from the catch of a ground or fly ball to the throw. With practice, the fielder develops a rhythmic pattern that can help to improve the accuracy and distance of the throw. Sometimes, however, time will not permit a crow-hop before the throw. The fielder must, therefore, be able to make plays with and without a crow-hop, as necessary.

Figure 3-8. Crow-Hop Throw Starting on the Left Leg

CROW-HOP STARTING ON THE RIGHT LEG

The player places her weight on her forward (right) leg while fielding the ball, hops on the right foot, and then transfers the weight forward with a step on the left leg in the direction of the throw. The sequence is step, hop, step. (See Figure 3–9.)

This crow-hop, like the one that starts on the left leg, is useful when throwing distance and rhythm are needed. It is used by outfielders to make plays on advancing baserunners.

Figure 3-9. Crow-Hop Throw Starting on the Right Leg

Of the nine maneuvers described, the running approaches and the crow-hops provide for the most forceful throws. The crow-hops also take more time to execute, however, because of the extra steps.

POSITIONING THE BODY FOR A CATCH THAT FAVORS A QUICK RELEASE AND A STRONG THROW

Maneuvering the body so that a catch can be made with both hands, well out in front of the right shoulder, serves several purposes. First, it allows the athlete to give with the ball and to bring it in to the body, thus increasing the time and distance over which force is absorbed and reducing the shock of impact. Second, the give (from the catch in front of the right shoulder directly back past the ear) can become the backswing of a throw, thus saving time by reducing the number of body movements necessary to get the ball into throwing position. Third, it provides more time and space for a smoother transition of the ball from glove to hand. Fourth, it provides some margin for error should the ball be mishandled or misjudged.

When continuous throws are necessary, as in double plays and relays, the ball should be thrown to the right shoulder of the receiver. This eliminates the need for the receiver to maneuver his body into optimum position for the throw.

Taking a hop, step, or run before throwing allows the momentum of the body to be added to that of the throwing movement, thus increasing speed. Therefore, a catch that can be made on the run toward the target, and well out in front of the right shoulder, will permit the quickest release of the strongest throw.

4

Covering and Backing Up

Each player will have a role to play following the delivery of the ball to the batter. It will be to field or catch the ball, to cover a base, or to back up. Covering is the act of positioning to receive a throw to a base. Backing up is the act of positioning behind the front line of players, thereby providing physical as well as psychological support to retire the batter-baserunner or to limit his advance.

COVERING

The procedure followed by a fielder covering a base will vary, depending on whether the player is preparing for a tag play or for a force play.

Tag Play

Any baserunner not in contact with a base may be put out if, while the ball is in play, he is legally touched with the ball when it is in the hand or glove of a fielder. The tag-play procedure followed by most fielders is as follows (see Figure 4–1):

1. The fielder/receiver moves to the base as quickly as possible and sets, with the lower body one quarter facing the ball and three

Figure 4-1. Covering a Base for a Tag Play

quarters facing the runner. The lateral aspect of the knee should never be presented to an oncoming runner.

2. The fielder/receiver straddles the corners of the base with her weight evenly balanced over the balls of both feet. The fielder/receiver's feet are near the back of the base, and her chin is above the front edge. This position permits mobility in any direction, as well as movement of the glove to either side of the base. It also reduces the danger of interference or accidental spiking. Some fielders/receivers (particularly shortstops and second basemen covering a steal of second) prefer to anchor one foot to the base, on the side from which the throw is coming, rather than straddling the base. The advantage of this method is that the baseman is closer to the thrower and receives the ball sooner, thereby saving some time. Also, the path of the ball from thrower to receiver is clear, so there is less chance of body contact with the runner, whether he slides or not. From this position, however, the outside corner of the base is harder to reach, and a runner who executes a hook slide or fall-away to the outside corner may be able to evade the tag. The straddle technique provides for better coverage of all sides of the base.

3. The fielder/receiver crouches low and turns her upper body to face the oncoming ball. By staying low the player ensures that her eyes will be more level with the hops, should the ball bounce, and the path of the ball will be easier to judge. Also, the ball is more likely to be stopped by the body even if the ball is misplayed. The

fielder/receiver provides a low target, with the pocket of the glove open to the path of the ball, stationary, and about knee height. This placement saves time by decreasing the distance the ball must be lowered for the tag.

4. The fielder/receiver anticipates a bad throw. She is prepared to leave the base, if necessary, to make the catch.

5. The fielder/receiver keeps her eyes on the ball, concentrating first on the catch and then on the tag. She does not reach out for the throw, but lets the ball come to her.

6. After catching the ball, with both hands whenever possible, the fielder/receiver faces the runner and lowers her glove to the side of the base the runner is approaching. She holds the glove on the ground with the outer surface of the webbing, or back of the glove, facing the runner. (Some players prefer to make the tag with the palm of the glove facing the runner, but this increases the chance of the ball's being kicked out of the glove and is not recommended.) The fielder/receiver looks for the runner's foot or hand, squeezes the ball, and allows the runner to slide into the glove, thereby tagging herself. The fielder must keep the glove on the ground rather than reaching for the runner, as reaching would commit the body weight and make it easier for the runner to evade the tag. The tag itself is usually made with the glove hand only. If both hands are used, the throwing hand should be protected by the glove. The fielder gives with the glove and ball at contact with the runner in order to protect the ball, and she clears out of the base area immediately following the tag. She must be alert for a continuation of play elsewhere.

If the ball is thrown wide, the fielder/receiver shifts her feet to the side of the base from which the throw is coming and leans back into the base for the tag. When necessary, as with a high, wide, or late throw, the fielder makes a sweeping motion, snapping the ball down to the ground in front of the base and in front of the runner's foot or hand as it is about to touch the base. Some fielders prefer to use a sweep tag all the time because they believe it provides the runner with less opportunity to knock the ball out of the glove. Others prefer a quick downward-upward motion. The important point is to protect the ball as much as possible and pull it away from the runner as soon as the tag is made to eliminate the chance of its being jarred loose by contact.

The fielder/receiver leaves the base, if necessary, to catch an erratic throw. When it is obvious that the runner is going to beat the throw to the base, the baseman should leave the bag and advance toward the ball, catching it on the fly and getting into position to make a play on the batter or another runner who may be attempting to advance on the throw.

Force Play

The potential for a force-out exists when a baserunner loses the right to the base that he is occupying because the batter becomes a baserunner. To effect the out, the fielder must either touch the runner with the ball or, holding the ball, tag the base to which the baserunner is forced to advance, before the runner reaches the base. There are a variety of ways to tag the base.

1. As Figure 4–2 illustrates, the baseman may anchor one foot to the side of the base to which the throw is coming. A stationary target, with outstretched glove, is presented to the thrower, and the receiver's body is balanced over both feet. A bad throw is anticipated and the baseman is prepared to shift, leaving the base if necessary, to make the catch. A stretch may be used if the play is close.

   This method of covering a base for a force-out shortens the distance of the throw, thereby saving time. The path of the ball from thrower to receiver is clear, and potential contact between the receiver and the runner is minimized.

2. The receiver may present a moving target to the thrower. The ball is caught as the baseman moves across the base. For best results, the ball should be thrown to the baseman before he reaches the base so that he can concentrate fully on catching the ball before

Figure 4-2. Covering a Base for a Force-out with a Stationary-Foot Tag

concerning himself with locating and touching the base. If time permits, the baseman should approach the bag in line with the throw. Timing is critical, and the throw must be accurate.

   This technique is primarily employed at second base by the second baseman or shortstop for the first out of a double-play attempt or for the third out of an inning. It is also used frequently by the second baseman or pitcher for a force-out of the batter-baserunner at first when the first baseman has been pulled off the bag by the hit.

3. A player who fields the ball close enough to a base for an unassisted putout should take advantage of the opportunity to avoid a throw. He should wave off a teammate who may be moving into covering position and touch the base himself, as quickly as possible. He may then continue across the base in the direction of his approach or step back from the bag.

   Regardless of the method used, the base area must be cleared as soon as the force is complete. The fielder should *not* remain at the base, as this position increases the chance of contact that may lead to injury, dropping the ball, or inability to participate in continuous play. As the player clears out, he should check other runners to be sure they remain where they are, and he should be alert for a continuation of play elsewhere.

   Any player, regardless of position, may be called upon to cover a base. Specific assignments, under varying game circumstances, are discussed in Part 2.

BACKING UP

   If a play is made and a fielder is not either going after the ball or covering a base, he should move into position to back up the hit or a subsequent throw. When backing up a batted ball, a player must allow the fielder plenty of room for the catch. The back-up fielder should assume a ready position in line with the oncoming ball, but about five to ten yards behind the play. He should block the ball, if necessary, but keep it in front of his body. Few runners will try to advance when a back-up fielder is close to the ball. When backing up a throw, a fielder should cooperate with teammates to cover a variety of angles.

   Most players have more than one base to back up and must anticipate to which base the throw will be made. As a rule, the backup should initially move in the general direction of the anticipated play and then, as the play develops, adjust accordingly and move to the most appropriate spot.

   Every fielding and throwing play should be backed up. With runners on, infielders should be alert to back up any throw back to the pitcher. Errors cannot be eliminated, but the resultant damage can be greatly limited by good back-up play.

TWO

Position Play

Battery

The pitcher and the catcher are referred to as a battery. They must work together very closely.

The margin of victory in softball is one run. Consequently, the fewer the number of runs an opponent scores, the fewer the number of runs a team must generate to win. The extent to which an opponent's run production will be limited depends largely upon the pitcher.

Area of Responsibility and Position

The shaded area in Figure 5–1 represents that portion of the infield that the pitcher can reasonably be expected to cover. The X indicates the pitcher's usual position. Depending upon the fielding ability of the pitcher or the philosophy of the coach, the size of the pitcher's domain may be increased or decreased. If the pitcher is a good fielder, for instance, he may assume responsibility for bunts, pop-ups, or grounders that might otherwise be handled by teammates. Some coaches, however, do not want their pitchers to field any batted balls. Others limit them to fielding balls that are hit or bunted directly back up the middle of the diamond. Still others extend the pitcher's area of responsibility to include

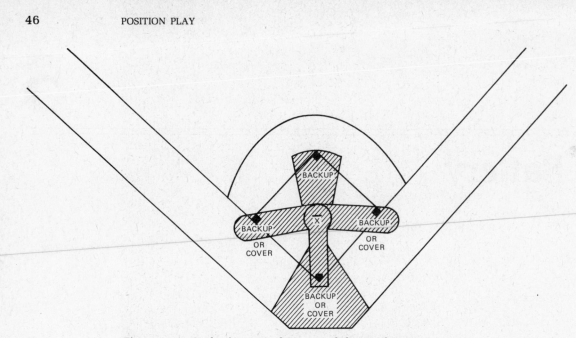

Figure 5-1. Pitcher's Area of Responsibility and Position

one or both base lines. The area shown in Figure 5-1 is recommended because it is restrictive, helping to eliminate confusion among the pitcher, catcher, first baseman, and third baseman about who should play the ball. The lines are the responsibility of first and third, and the catcher fields balls directly in front of the plate. The pitcher stays back and is in position to field push or slug bunts.

It is to the pitcher's advantage to be close to, or within, an eight-foot radius of the pitcher's plate following delivery of the ball to the batter. A base runner who is off base after a ball or strike call, or after a batter completes his turn at bat, is forced to commit himself if the pitcher has the ball within the eight-foot radius. The runner must immediately proceed to the next base or return to his base. If he fakes or changes direction, he will immediately be called out by the umpire.

Characteristics

A pitcher's performance is affected by his physical endowment, level of fitness, skill, and psychological state. Tall pitchers, with long arms and legs, benefit from increased leverage. They gain speed. Heavy pitchers, too, can throw faster than their lighter counterparts if they use their greater mass to advantage. In addition, a pitcher with size can be imposing—even intimidating—to a batter.

Much strength and endurance are required to withstand the rigors of an entire game and to put forth the physical exertion necessary to throw hard, repeatedly. Pitchers are sometimes called upon to pitch two games in one day or several games within a few days.

Flexibility is also important. When a pitcher increases his range of motion, the ball travels a greater distance, more momentum is developed, and the potential velocity of the pitch is extended.

Most coaches generally agree that a good pitcher must have fair speed. A *live* fastball—one that moves—is an even greater asset, as are an off-speed (change-up, knuckleball) pitch and a breaking (riseball, drop, curve) pitch. By being able to throw a variety of pitches on command and by making the ball do the unexpected, the pitcher can keep the batter off balance. Each pitch must be controlled, however, and thrown to a spot where it is difficult to hit.

Psychologically, a good pitcher is usually confident, emotionally stable, aggressive, and challenging to a batter. In addition, a quality pitcher is disciplined. He is able to focus on the game and to concentrate on the task at hand. Concentration is essential; it must be emphasized.

It takes years to develop the skill to throw a variety of pitches, on command, to selected spots. The difficult and time-consuming learning process will test the drive and determination of any athlete. Beginning pitchers must recognize this. Patience, a positive attitude, and the ability to place victories and defeats in proper perspective are invaluable assets.

Individual Responsibilities

Once the pitcher has delivered the ball to the batter, he must prepare to function as an infielder. This responsibility necessitates a follow-through that will leave the pitcher in a balanced position, facing the batter, with glove out in front of the body. At this point, the pitcher is less than forty feet from the batter. Consequently, alertness, physical preparedness, and quick reactions are necessary if hard-hit grounders and line drives back through the middle of the diamond are to be caught.

Fielding Grounders and Throwing to Bases

If the catch has pulled the pitcher away from his target base (first), he should recover his balance by bracing against his right (front) foot, pivot to the left, sight the glove target of the covering baseman (receiver), and throw. When a ball is hit directly back to the pitcher, or to his left, he has two alternatives after fielding the ball: (1) He may pivot to his left; show the ball to the receiver while taking a few running steps toward first; and throw the ball with an underhand toss and follow-through toward the chest of the receiver. (2) He may pivot to his left; turn to face the receiver while getting set and waiting for the receiver to get into position; and throw the ball with a strong, controlled overhand toss and follow-through toward the chest of the receiver.

Fielding Bunts and Throwing to Bases

One of the primary defensive challenges for a pitcher is fielding a bunt. As soon as the batter declares his intent to lay the ball down, the pitcher must move quickly toward home plate. As the ball approaches, the right-handed pitcher should set directly in front of it with his feet spread and his right foot slightly ahead of the left. His eyes must remain on the ball until it is secure, because it is usually spinning, and its course can be changed by rocks, clumps of dirt, etc. By bending forward at the waist, the pitcher brings his head directly over the ball so that he can field the ball in front of his body, with both hands. The bare hand scoops the ball into the glove, as when recovering a fumbled ball (see Chapter 2). Weight is placed on the right foot as the ball is caught, and the throw to first is made with a rear pivot and step back on the left foot in the direction of the receiver. The turn is toward the glove side of the body, and the target is sighted just before the ball is released with a short step toward first. The right foot follows through. The throw, directed toward the chest of the receiver, is executed with an overhand motion. The same procedure is followed when throwing (right-handed) to second and third, although the pivot may be to the right if the pitcher, when fielding the ball, is partially turned in that direction.

A left-handed pitcher should try, whenever possible, to field the ball off his left foot, pivoting to his right (toward his glove side) for the throw to first, second, or third base. The only exception to this rule is when the pivot would be shorter in the opposite direction. If, for instance, the left-hander is partially facing first as he fields the ball, he should turn to his left to throw.

When a squeeze play is being attempted, the pitcher must move quickly to handle the ball in normal fielding position. An underhand toss should be used in this situation because of the short distance to home and the need for a quick release. (See Chapter 1.)

Fielding Pop-Ups

The catcher normally indicates who should catch an infield pop-up, and the pitcher must yield if called off the ball. As a rule, the pitcher fields only the pop-ups that descend within about an eight-foot radius of the pitcher's plate or those (such as popped-up bunts) that will not be in the air long enough to be reached by a teammate.

For the most part, the pitcher's role in dealing with pop-ups is to encourage and direct the fielder, warning him about obstacles. Occasionally, the pitcher must cover the base of a teammate who is fielding a pop-up.

Checking Runners

Any runner who has rounded a base without stopping, or who is legitimately off the base after a pitched ball or after a hitter has completed his turn at bat, must be considered a threat to advance and must be dealt with accordingly. As soon as the pitcher receives the ball from the catcher or a fielder, he must check the progress of runners. Otherwise, he may be the victim of a delayed steal, or a runner who receives a base on balls may successfully continue running to second base. By causing a runner to stop after rounding a base, and by holding the ball within an eight-foot radius of the pitcher's plate, the pitcher forces the runner to proceed immediately to the next base or return to his base. The runner cannot delay, fake, or reverse his direction in an attempt to draw a throw. He must commit himself immediately, in full view of the pitcher. Once he returns to his base, he cannot legitimately leave it again until the ball is delivered to the batter, a play is made on him or another runner, or the pitcher no longer has the ball in the eight-foot radius. Timely use of the eight-foot-radius rule takes the pressure off the defense and allows the pitcher to devote full attention to the batter.

Team Responsibilities

Covering

First base. The pitcher covers first when a *hit* pulls the first baseman out of position, away from the bag. In this situation, the pitcher should follow a rounded path to first—one that will allow him to approach the bag by running parallel to, and one or two feet from, the foul line. He should receive the ball a couple of strides ahead of the base. This timing gives him the opportunity to concentrate on the catch first, while still leaving him time to locate the bag and to tag the front, inside corner of it, preferably with the right (inside) foot.

Home plate. The pitcher covers home whenever there are runners in scoring position and the catcher must leave the plate area to retrieve a passed ball or wild pitch, to catch a foul fly, or to field an errant throw. The pitcher should hustle to a balanced fielding position directly in front of, and a step or two from, home plate. The pitcher's knees bend, and both arms extend toward the catcher, with the pocket of the glove open to the anticipated path of the ball and directly over the plate. Neither the head nor any other part of the body (except the hands) should extend over the plate. The pitcher calls to the catcher, thus indicating readiness to receive the ball and providing a cue for target location. The pitcher should concentrate on the ball until it is caught. Receipt of the ball is paramount. The next step is to grip the ball in the bare hand, cover it with the glove, turn to the right, and *crouch* to meet the approaching runner on the third-base side of home plate. Allowing the runner to tag himself out, giving with the contact, and withdrawing the hands immediately, preferably pulling them in toward the body, all help to prevent the ball from being knocked loose.

Unguarded bases. Sometimes a player is pulled away from the base that he normally covers, and it is left unprotected. This situation most frequently occurs when more than one infielder goes after a fly ball with a runner, or runners, on base. The pitcher often assumes temporary responsibility for the vacated base.

Backing Up

It is the responsibility of the pitcher to back up throws to infielders from the outfield and all throws to the catcher. Although the back-up technique itself is not complicated (see Chapter 4), it is sometimes hard to determine which base to back up. Most coaches suggest that the pitcher move into the back-up position at least one base ahead of the lead runner.

Rundowns

As a rule, when a runner is caught off base between first and second, it is the pitcher's responsibility to assume a back-up position at first base. When a runner is caught in a rundown between second and third, the pitcher covers third; and any time the rundown is between third and home, the pitcher backs up the catcher at the plate. The pitcher participates in the rundown, if necessary. (The technique for executing a rundown is described, in detail, in Chapter 11.)

PITCHING

Pitching involves a number of steps. Before actually releasing the ball, the pitcher must (1) mentally prepare for the task, (2) assume position on the pitcher's plate, (3) receive the signal from the catcher, (4) present the ball to the batter, and (5) grip the ball for the type of pitch to be thrown. The next step is to deliver the ball to the batter.

Mentally Preparing

Mental preparation for pitching begins with physical conditioning. A pitcher who is in shape gains confidence in the knowledge that he is capable of meeting any physical demands that may be placed upon him through the course of a game. The development of a positive attitude is also important. A pitcher who expects to fail, or enters a game with apprehension and self-doubt, is fighting himself. A wise pitcher sets realistic game goals and limits his focus to the game at hand.

Before the game, the pitcher and the catcher review the strengths and weaknesses of individual batters, developing a plan of attack for each hitter. (Specific recommendations related to pitch selection and target placement are given later in this chapter, under "Catching.") The pitcher and catcher also warm up together before the game. They determine what *stuff* the pitcher has and work out any kinks. When the umpire calls, "Play ball!" the pitcher should know what he is up against, what he has going for him, and what he must do to accomplish his goals for the day.

Assuming Pitching Position

There are a variety of ways to attain the *presentation* position that a pitcher is required to assume before delivering any pitch to a batter. Many involve personal idiosyncrasies and are unique to the individual pitcher. Following are two of the more common methods.

Figure   5-2. Assuming   Pitching Position

1. The right-handed pitcher assumes a comfortable position on the pitcher's plate, with the weight primarily centered over the left (rear) foot and the arms hanging freely at the sides. The ball may be held in either the glove or the bare hand. The catcher's sign is flashed at this time. Having accepted the sign, some pitchers simply bring both hands together at about waist level and present the ball. Others, however, choose to use a preliminary windup, as in Figure 5–2. The trunk is bent forward at the waist as the weight is shifted to the right (front) foot, and the arms extend backward for balance. The body then rocks backward as the arms swing forward and upward in a pendulum motion. The hand and glove join each other somewhere along the circular path that may extend beyond head height, and by the time the hands drop back down to waist level, in presentation position, the weight is once more centered over the left (rear) leg. The ball is presented and the pitch is delivered.
2. The pitcher assumes a comfortable position on the pitcher's plate, with the weight centered over the right (front) foot. The right leg is usually extended, and the upper body is bent forward from the waist. The left (rear) leg is bent at the knee, and the heel is raised off the ground. The arms usually hang freely at the sides, with the ball in either the glove or the bare hand. Sometimes the ball is held in the hand, behind the back, while the glove hangs at the side. This is the position in which the catcher's sign is received. Once a sign has been agreed upon, the arms swing forward and upward to join each other in a circular motion as the weight shifts backward. The ball is presented and subsequently delivered to the batter.

Pitchers who use a windup before presenting the ball do so for a variety of physical and psychological reasons. Some find that it helps to relieve tension, establishes rhythm, or loosens the clothing for more freedom of movement. Others believe that it improves their concentration, narrows their focus, and causes tension in some batters. Pitchers who do not use a windup tend to believe that the extra movements can interfere with control or decrease their stamina through the course of a game. While it is true that a windup can be distracting during the initial stages of learning, this effect will diminish as the windup becomes a habit. It need not affect control. In summary, the use of a pre-presentation windup is a matter of personal preference.

Presenting the Ball

Before the ball can be legally delivered, it must be *presented* to the batter. The pitcher's body must come to a complete stop—with the

Figure 5-3. Presenting the Ball

shoulders in line with first and third base and with the ball held in both hands in front of the body—for at least one second and not more than ten seconds. The arms hang freely from the shoulders, the elbows are flexed, and the ball is held at about waist level and directly in front, or slightly to the right, of the midline of the body. The head is up and motionless, with the eyes focused on the target.

The pitcher should present the ball as comfortably as possible, while still complying with the rules of the game. *Both feet must be firmly on the ground and in contact with, but not off the side of, the pitcher's plate.* This does not mean, however, that the feet must be together. On the contrary, the pitcher should stand with the toe of the left foot on the rear edge of the pitcher's plate and with the heel of the right foot on the front edge, with both feet a little less than shoulder distance apart. (See Figure 5–3.) This is a more natural and effective starting position, as it provides greater distance over which to generate momentum, plus a firm base of support for better balance. The toes of both feet point directly toward home plate so that the force of the push off the pitcher's plate will be straight backward and downward. Consequently, all the force will be useful in moving the body forward, and there will be no waste of energy.

The upper body leans back slightly. This position centers the weight primarily over the left (rear) leg and further increases the distance over which momentum can be developed. The left (rear) leg is extended and slanted slightly forward, so the body's center of gravity remains within the base of support, and balance is maintained. The right (front) leg, on the other hand, is relaxed and somewhat flexed, with the toe pointing toward the ground.

The presentation of the ball and the initial stance are basically the same whether using a windmill or a slingshot style of delivery.

Gripping the Ball

The particular grip used will depend upon the type of pitch to be delivered, the size of the pitcher's hand, and the pitcher's delivery style (windmill or slingshot). It is possible to vary the firmness of the grip, the surface area of the hand that contacts the ball, and the position of the seams relative to the hand and the air as the ball is released. Through control and manipulation of these variables, the speed and direction of the ball's flight are determined. For instance, to attain maximum speed, a pitcher should use the following technique.

1. Grip the ball firmly so that maximum force can be transferred to the ball in the desired direction.
2. Grip the seams of the ball. Because they are rough and elevated, they increase the friction between the fingers and the ball, reducing slippage and permitting greater ball control.
3. Grip the ball near the ends of the fingers to maximize the length of the lever and increase the potential contribution of the wrist and fingers to the ball's velocity.
4. Hold the ball between the thumb and first two fingers of the hand, with the third and fourth fingers against the side of the ball. If the hand is too small to control the ball with a tripod (two-finger) grip, hold it between the thumb and the middle three fingers, with the little finger against the side of the ball.
5. Grip the ball so that the smallest surface area of seams is at right angles to the desired direction of flight. Because seams create air resistance, this grip will retard speed the least.

When change in the direction of the flight of the ball is desired, the pitcher should use this technique:

1. Hold the ball deep in the hand so that there is maximum surface area contact between the hand and the ball. This grip shortens the length of the lever and *limits* the speed of *wrist snap*, thereby decreasing potential speed. At the same time, however, the distance the ball can roll before leaving the hand is increased. Consequently, greater spin can be imparted to the ball. Increased

spin further decreases forward speed and produces greater direction change. Decreased spin increases forward speed and produces a sharper, but less pronounced, direction change.

2. To maximize the breaking effect, hold the ball so that the greatest number of seams and the greatest length of seams are placed across the desired line of flight of the ball. The seams create air resistance and, in conjunction with spin (or lack of spin), cause the ball to rise (go up), drop (go down), curve (go right or left), or float.

The particular grip used can indicate to opponents the type of pitch to be delivered. For this reason, it is important to establish the grip for a specific pitch while the ball is within the confines of the glove, out of the opponent's sight.

Types of Deliveries

A specific type of delivery should not be forced on a pitcher. Each pitcher should be allowed to use a delivery that feels natural and is productive. Although some pitchers will develop their own style, most will use either the windmill or the slingshot. These styles have been employed, with equal effectiveness, by top-flight amateur and professional pitchers.

Windmill

Winding up. The windup for the windmill style of delivery starts with the forward inclination of the trunk from the presentation position, as shown in Figure 5–4. The head is up and the eyes remain focused on the target as the shoulders move forward, the weight shifts toward the

Figure 5-4. Start of Windup for Windmill Delivery

right (front) foot, and both arms begin a descent toward the right (throwing) side of the body. The weight shift to the right foot during the wind-up phase allows a subsequent weight shift forward during the pitching phase, so the momentum generated can be added to the ball as it leaves the hand. The right (front) foot begins to turn outward, and the knee is flexed, but the hips and shoulders are still fairly square to the target. The outward rotation of the right foot ultimately permits greater body rotation and places the right leg in a better position to provide force in a horizontal direction when it later pushes backward against the pitcher's plate and drives the body forward in the direction of the pitch.

The center of gravity moves ahead of the right (front) foot as the left knee flexes, the left heel raises off the ground, and the left foot strides forward vigorously in the direction of the pitch. The hands have separated, and the ball hand continues along a path down and back until the pitching arm reaches full extension toward the rear of the body, with the back of the hand facing the target. By extending the ball toward the rear of the body, the arm will follow a counterclockwise, circular path of more than 360 degrees before the ball is released. By increasing the distance through which the ball travels, the pitcher develops greater momentum and increases the potential velocity of the pitch. The left leg continues to stride forward as the back of the right hand leads the pitching arm through a wide and circular path forward and upward. The left (glove) arm assists with balance by moving up toward the front and midline of the body.

At the midway point of the upswing (see Figure 5–5), both arms are extended toward home plate and are approximately parallel to the ground. The left (striding) leg is also well out in front of the body, although the knee and ankle remain flexed, the toe points toward home, and the

Figure 5-5. Midway Point of Up-swing for Windmill Delivery

Figure 5–6. Top of Backswing for Windmill Delivery

foot is still above the ground. The ball is held with the palm of the hand facing the ground, directly in line with the right shoulder. The upper body leans into the pitch to assist in the transfer of momentum toward home plate and to increase the range of motion. The knee and ankle of the right (rear, supporting) leg are still flexed.

The right shoulder and hip are pulled back, away from home plate, as the pitching arm swings close by the right ear and approaches full extension at a position approximately perpendicular to the ground, so the ball is held high above the right shoulder, hip, and knee. (See Figure 5–6.) By holding the ball with the fingers, laterally rotating the upper arm, and turning the ball toward third base, the pitcher can hyperextend his shoulder and hold the ball higher and farther back. The longer the lever, the greater the distance over which momentum can be developed, and the greater the potential velocity of the pitch. At this point, the trunk has rotated until the left shoulder and hip face home plate, the eyes look directly over the left shoulder to the target, the upper body is erect, and the glove arm remains extended at about chest height for balance. Both knees and ankles are flexed, and the center of gravity has moved well out in front of the right (rear) supporting foot. The left (lead) leg is about to plant, and the right (rear) leg is ready to extend against the pitcher's plate and to thrust the body forward.

Releasing the ball. The action phase of the pitch begins as the right (pitching) arm extends back and starts the downswing. (See Figure 5–7.) The upper body also extends backward, and the wrist cocks. All of these

Figure 5-7. Positive Action Phase of Windmill Delivery

actions, combined with hip, trunk, and shoulder rotation away from home plate, move the ball and body away from the release point and increase the distance through which the ball travels. Consequently, more force can be applied to the ball over a greater distance. The slight backward lean of the upper body also checks forward momentum and helps keep the body weight behind the left (lead) leg.

When the pitching arm reaches a point almost horizontal to the ground, the left (striding) foot plants. Although planting the foot in alignment with home plate would permit greater rotation and the development of more momentum, most good pitchers establish ground contact slightly to the right of a direct line to the plate, with the toe and knee turned slightly inward. This position may vary somewhat, depending upon the type of pitch to be thrown and the placement of the pitch (inside or outside). Some pitchers make initial ground contact with the heel of the left (striding) foot, but the jarring caused by this action can lead to foot or back problems, as well as difficulty in keeping the eyes on target. By lifting the left knee high and plantar-flexing the foot (pointing the toe), the pitcher can make a more advantageous toe-heel contact. The left knee and ankle joints flex immediately upon ground contact to lower the center of gravity, assist in absorbing the landing force, and lower the center of the arc of the throw, thereby helping control. A strong extension of the right (rear) leg against the pitcher's plate turns the right knee inward and forces the right hip to move forward against the flexed, but braced, left (front) leg. The right (rear) hip pulls the weight of the body and the right shoulder into the pitch, thereby producing a powerful rotary, counterclockwise action.

As the hips, trunk, and shoulders approach a position square to the target, the scapula abducts, the right shoulder flexes, and the upper arm moves directly down and forward in a vertical plane. The line of force through the ball must be directly toward home plate. The right elbow is still slightly bent, though extending; the lower arm is abducted slightly; and the wrist is cocked so that the ball hand trails the forearm until the final wrist snap. The shoulder, upper arm, and forearm pull the ball through the downswing. (Note: Emphasize a perfect windmill circle in the line of force toward home plate to maximize centrifugal force and length of the lever.) As the elbow of the right (pitching) arm stretches, extends, and moves down and forward, the left (glove) arm moves down and inward to assist with balance. There is a very slight lean laterally to the right that drops the right shoulder, clears the hip out of the way, and provides more space for the pitching arm to move through.

The ball is released from the right (pitching) hand somewhere between the knee and hip joints, when the upper arm is about perpendicular to the ground. (See Figure 5–8.) The lower arm is still abducted slightly, so the wrist is a little farther from the body than the elbow. The right shoulder is lower than the left, as a slight lateral lean to the right is still present. The trunk is almost square to the target and moving forward, though still behind the heel of the left (lead) foot, when the elbow flexes; the upper and lower arms rotate either medially or laterally, depending upon the type of pitch to be thrown; and the wrist flexes vigorously.

To keep the center of gravity within the base of support, to

Figure 5-8. Releasing the Ball (Windmill Delivery)

Figure 5-9. Following Through (Windmill Delivery)

counteract the action of the pitching arm, and to maintain balance, the right (rear) knee flexes and the foot swings to the back left of the support leg as the pitch is released. The right (rear) foot extends, and the toes sometimes drag along the ground as the foot moves forward. The left (glove) arm extends downward, to the left of the body, to further counterbalance the pitching action.

Following through. The left (striding) foot remains planted following the release of the ball, as the weight continues to move forward. (See Figure 5-9.) The pitching arm, following the release of the ball, also continues forward, but its specific direction will vary, depending upon the type of pitch being thrown. By allowing the arm to continue along its path, the pitcher ensures that the speed of various body parts will slow down over a greater distance, and the risk of injury will be reduced. Completing the full range of motion also assures that there will be no interference with the application of force to the ball before it is released. The head remains up, eyes on the target, as the hips and trunk complete their rotation. The right shoulder may even point toward home plate. The left (glove) arm moves in toward the waist as the pitcher prepares to assume fielding position as quickly as possible in case the pitch is hit back to him. The right (rear) knee may alter the direction of the trailing leg by leading it toward the throwing side of the body. Ideally, both legs should be in a parallel, flexed, and balanced position at the conclusion of the followthrough. The trunk should be slightly bent forward at the waist, with both arms out in front of the body in fielding position.

Figure 5-10. Start of Windup for Slingshot Delivery

Figure 5-11. Approaching Top of Backswing for Slingshot Delivery

Slingshot

Winding up. The windup for the slingshot style of delivery, like that for the windmill, starts with the forward inclination of the trunk from the presentation position. (See Figure 5-10.) As the head and shoulders move forward, both arms begin a descent toward the right (pitching) side of the body—an action that pulls the left shoulder out in front of the body and down. Accompanying this initial twist is the outward turn of the right (front) foot. As a result of this movement, greater body rotation is possible, force can be developed through a greater distance, and the potential velocity of the pitch is increased. In addition, the right leg is in a better position to provide force in a horizontal direction when it later pushes backward against the pitcher's plate and drives the body forward in the direction of the pitch. Both knees flex slightly as the center of gravity continues to shift forward and downward, and the body continues to bend at the waist. The hands separate at about the point where the glove reaches past the right side of the body. At this point the weight is primarily centered over the right (front) foot. The eyes remain focused on the target.

As Figure 5-11 illustrates, the right shoulder and hip are pulled back as the ball hand moves along a circular path toward the rear of the body (back, up, and away), with the back of the hand facing the target. The glove hand assists with balance by moving toward the front of the body (down, front, up, and away). Simultaneously, the knee of the left (rear) leg bends, the heel raises off the ground, and the foot pushes backward, assisting the transfer of weight forward in the direction of the pitch. The left leg strides past the pitcher's plate and the right foot as the right (pitching) arm approaches full extension at a position approximately perpendicular to the ground, so the ball is held high above the right (rear) foot. By holding the ball with the fingers, outwardly rotating the upper arm, and facing the ball toward third base, the pitcher can hyperextend her shoulder and can hold the ball higher and farther back. The longer the lever, the greater the distance over which momentum can be developed, and the greater the force potential of the pitch. (Be sure to keep the ball directly in the line of force toward home plate, however.) At this point the glove arm has raised to an extended position, almost horizontal to the ground, in front of the body; and the trunk has rotated until the left shoulder and hip face the target. Both knees are flexed, and the center of gravity has moved well out in front of the right (rear) supporting foot. The body is still bent at the waist, the head and shoulders are beyond the right hip, and the eyes are on the target.

Releasing the ball. The action phase of the pitch begins as the right (pitching) arm starts downward. (See Figure 5–12.) At the same time, the right (supporting) knee bends, lowering the center of gravity. The left (striding) leg plants slightly to the right of a direct line to the plate, with the toe turned slightly inward. The left knee and ankle joints flex to further lower the center of gravity and to reduce the force of the landing impact. A strong push forward off the inside of the right (rear) foot turns the rear knee inward and forces the hips to open. The left (front) leg, though flexed, is braced to withstand the force of weight thrust against it.

The action of the hips is critical, as they must lead the power thrust of the delivery. Failure to use hip action in proper sequence, with proper timing, will reduce the power input to what can be generated by the arm

Figure 5–12. Positive Action Phase of Slingshot Delivery

Figure 5-13. Releasing the Ball (Slingshot Delivery)

and wrist, severely limiting the effectiveness of the delivery. It also puts excessive strain on shoulder muscles.

The right (rear) hip pulls the weight into the pitch. It also pulls the right shoulder through and produces a powerful rotary action. The right (pitching) shoulder drops and, along with the elbow, leads the ball hand down and forward. The elbow is flexed, the wrist is extended, and the trunk leans a little laterally to the right. The left shoulder is higher than the right, and as it is pulled back, it moves the glove across the body, to the left.

The ball is released between the knee and hip joints, with a strong whiplike action as the elbow extends almost completely and the wrist snaps. (See Figure 5–13.) Speed results from the sequential extension of all flexed levers. The arm is approximately perpendicular to the ground, and the hips are almost open, but still behind the heel of the left (front, planted) foot. Because the center of gravity is still moving forward, the right (rear) knee flexes and swings to the back left of the support leg. The right (rear) foot extends, and the toes sometimes drag as the foot moves forward. This action is necessary to keep the center of gravity within the base of support and to help maintain balance. The extension of the glove hand to the left of the body also helps to counterbalance the pitching action. The upper body is in an erect position.

Following through. The left (striding) foot remains planted following the release of the ball, as the weight continues to move forward. (See Figure 5–14.) The right (pitching) arm also continues to move, but its direction will vary, depending upon the type of pitch being thrown. A complete follow-through is necessary to reduce the momentum generated

Figure 5-14. Following Through (Slingshot Delivery)

by the pitch and to minimize strain on the arm and shoulder. It also ensures completion of hip and trunk rotation, and it often places the pitcher in better fielding position. The follow-through with a slingshot delivery is similar to that with a windmill delivery.

Pitching with Speed versus Accuracy

The more speed a pitcher has, the faster the ball reaches home plate, and the less time the batter has in which to decide whether or not to swing. Without enough time to assess the pitch, the batter is more apt to misjudge the ball and to swing at a bad pitch. He is also more likely to be late swinging, thereby losing power. On the other hand, the fastest pitch possible is not effective if the batter takes it and it's a ball. A balance between speed and accuracy seems necessary. Unfortunately, however, there is no direct relationship between the two. A pitcher who achieves accuracy at a slow speed will not necessarily have the same control at an increased speed. Furthermore, decreasing the speed of a fast pitcher will not necessarily improve his accuracy. It may, in fact, compound the problem, for a pitch, like an overhand throw, will be most accurate at the speed at which it was practiced. It is strongly recommended, therefore, that coaches and teammates alike refrain from yelling such things as: "Just get it over," "Let them hit it," "Lob it in, we'll back you up," "Take it easy."

Coaches generally agree that beginners should work to produce consistent speed before becoming concerned with control. Of course, coaches must recognize that beginning pitchers who are being developed according to this philosophy are not going to be ready to pitch to batters for some time. Initially, in fact, they will benefit from throwing without a catcher. By throwing to a fence or wall, they will be under no pressure to be in control; they will be free to let their pitches go without reservation. By practicing at a given speed, in this case fast, the pitcher will eventually develop accuracy at that speed.

Once a pitcher has reasonable control of a good fastball, he is ready to experiment with different grips and various types of pitches.

Types of Pitches

There are basically six types of pitches: fastball, change-up, drop, riseball, curveball, and knuckleball. Although a pitcher's success will be related to the number of these that he can throw well, it is better for a pitcher to master two or three different pitches than to throw five or six pitches poorly. Frequently, in fact, a young pitcher can find success with a simple repertoire of a fastball and a change-up.

As a rule, it is advisable for a young pitcher to learn to throw with maximum speed first, and then to move on to other types of pitches one at a time. We recommend that youngsters, after learning to throw hard, learn, *in order*, change-up, drop, rise, curve, and knuckleball. This sequence requires minimal technical change from pitch to pitch. For example, the fastball and change-up differ only in grip, while the rise and curve differ only in the point and direction of the release and follow-through. The knuckleball differs the most from any of the others.

Techniques for Throwing the Basic Pitches

Fastball. The grip is illustrated in Figure 5–15a. The step is of medium length and directly toward home plate. (See Figure 5–15b.) To

a   b

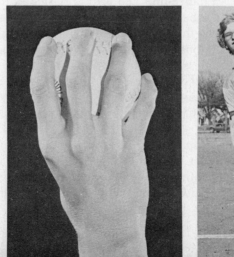

Figure 5-15. Fastball: *a*, Grip; *b*, Release

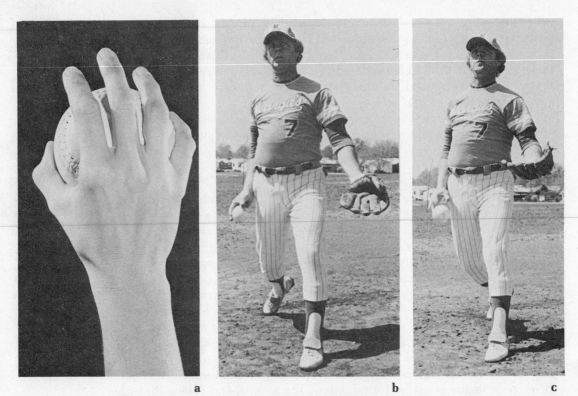

a   b   c

Figure 5-16. Change-up: *a*, Grip; *b* and *c*, Release

release, the pitcher snaps her wrist up and rolls the ball off her fingertips. Much of the pressure of the ball, as it leaves the hand, is exerted toward the index side of the middle finger. Early in the season, many hard-throwing pitchers develop a blister at this point. Later it becomes a callus.

Change-up. The grip is basically the same as for a fastball, except that the ball is pushed back into the palm of the hand and is held tightly with the thumb and little finger. (See Figure 5–16*a*.) The other fingers are placed loosely on the ball, and they come off before the pitch is released. The ball is thrown with the same pattern and velocity of arm motion as the fastball, but the grip for the change makes it impossible to throw the ball as hard as a fastball. (See Figure 5–16*b* and *c*.) If the wrist is rotated over (to the left) as the pitch is released, the ball will "die" and drop.

Drop. The grip is the same as that for a fastball. (See Figure 5–17*a*.) The wrist leads the fingertips and ball through the downward, forward phase of the delivery. For an active drop the thumb comes off the ball just before release, and the wrist snaps over the top of the ball. The fingers roll

Figure 5-17. Drop: *a*, Grip; *b*, Release

a   b

over the top of the ball and press down. For a passive (natural) drop, the thumb is lifted and the ball is allowed to roll off the fingers. (See Figure 5–17 *b*.) The pitcher's step is shortened, and weight is placed on the toes. The shorter step reduces the speed of the pitch, but increases the amount of drop. Thus, there is a trade-off between speed and movement of the ball. If the drop is thrown too slowly, some batters will be able to detect the movement and still hit the ball solidly. Each pitcher should attempt to find a stride that optimizes both ball movement and speed.

Riseball (Riser). The grip is illustrated in Figure 5–18*a*. The motion of the arm for the riseball is similar to that of a baseball pitcher throwing a curve, except that the arm follows an underhand pattern. While the overhand curve requires a wrist turn over and a snap forward and *downward* in relation to the body, the riseball requires the same type of snap and relative arm motion, but from *under* the ball. As the arm comes down from the top of the backswing, the elbow is brought in toward the side, and the lower arm is extended to form an L. (See Figure 5–18 *b*.) The forearm rotates so that the hand is brought under the ball. The release involves a vigorous lifting and a snapping of the wrist from underneath the ball so that the ball rolls over the inside of the middle finger and the first joint of the index finger. (Some pitchers may need to bend the wrist inward toward the body in order to obtain backward rotation for the rise.) The stride is long, and the follow-through of the body and arm is an upward movement.

a   b

Figure 5-18. Rise: *a*, Grip; *b*, Release

Curve. The grip is illustrated in Figure 5–19*a*. When thrown by a right-handed pitcher, the curve usually breaks out, away from, a right-handed hitter. The arm motion is similar to that for a riseball, except that the wrist snap occurs later, and in a horizontal plane—under the ball, but across the body. (See Figures 5–19*b* and *c*.) The step and follow-through are toward the left.

Figure 5-19. Curve: *a*, Grip; *b* and *c*, Release

a   b   c

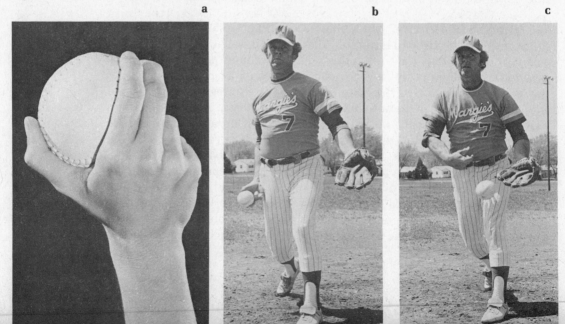

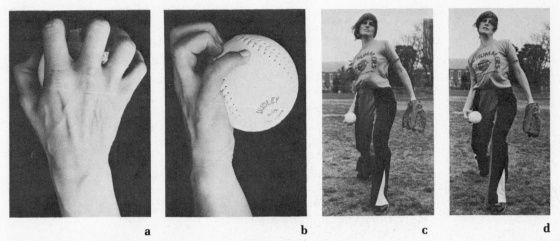

Figure 5-20. Knuckleball: *a* and *b*, Grip; *c* and *d*, Release

Knuckleball. The ball is gripped by the thumb and fingertips, with the nails digging into the ball, as shown in Figures 5–20*a* and *b*. As the arm comes down beside the body, the wrist is already flexed and *firm*. (See Figures 5–20*c* and *d*.) The ball is pushed out of the hand. There is no wrist snap. The pitching arm is brought forward quickly, the right leg and foot push off the plate to produce forward momentum, and the follow-through is either exaggerated or curtailed, whichever works best for the individual pitcher.

Developing Variations

Experienced pitchers usually experiment with pitches they've mastered, and they frequently develop variations. Slow curves, slow drops, curving riseballs, and dropping change-ups further help to keep batters off balance. Because the techniques for each pitch differ, however, learning a new one may cause problems with those pitches already mastered. For example, it is common while learning a new pitch to lose control of an established one because of *kinesthetic confusion*. It becomes important, therefore, to continually practice old pitches while learning a new one, in order to distinguish the differences in feel.

Common Problems Associated with Various Pitches

A pitcher may encounter a number of problems when attempting to throw various types of pitches. Following are the most common problems associated with each pitch, along with the possible causes of each problem.

I. Fastball
    A. Too slow. Causes include
        1. Aiming.
        2. Holding the ball too deeply in the palm of the hand.
        3. Gripping the ball too loosely.
        4. Taking too fast a backswing.
        5. Taking too short a backswing.
        6. Limiting drive from the pitcher's plate.
        7. Not completing rotation of trunk and hips.
        8. Overstriding.
        9. Keeping right leg (right-handed pitcher) stiff.
      10. Keeping elbow stiff.
      11. Not completing follow-through.
    B. Not controlled. Causes include
        1. Aiming.
        2. Changing finger pressure on the ball—too loose or too tight.
        3. Using inconsistent stride length—too long or too short.
        4. Using inconsistent stride direction.
        5. Using inconsistent release point—too early or too late.
        6. Keeping lead leg stiff.
        7. Not completing arm extension and follow-through.

II. Change-Up
    A. Too fast. Causes include
        1. Having too many fingers on the ball at the time of its release.
        2. Having too much wrist snap. May not be holding the ball firmly and deeply in the palm of the hand.
    B. Too low. Causes include
        1. Releasing the ball too soon.
        2. Taking too short a stride.
    C. Doesn't fool the batter. Causes include
        1. Telegraphing the pitch by reducing the speed or range of the backswing or windup.
        2. Throwing too slowly. (The batter can hold his swing, re-set, and still hit the ball effectively.)

III. Drop
    A. Doesn't drop. Causes include
        1. Taking too long a stride.
        2. Keeping the thumb on the ball too long.
        3. Turning the wrist over, or lifting, as the ball is released.
        4. Releasing the ball too late.
    B. Too low. Causes include
        1. Releasing the ball too soon.
        2. Gripping the ball too loosely.
        3. Using too short a stride.

C. Too slow. Causes include
1. Pushing off the pitcher's plate weakly.
2. Using too short a stride.

IV. Rise

A. Doesn't rise. Causes include:
1. Keeping the elbow too far from the body.
2. Keeping the wrist insufficiently cocked.
3. Not keeping the hand under the ball.
4. Using a wrist snap that is not vigorous enough to obtain backward rotation for the rise.
5. Using too short a stride.
6. Not flexing the rear leg enough.
7. Not completing follow-through.
8. Delivering to a catcher's target that is being held too low.

V. Curve

A. Doesn't break. Causes include
1. Having a strong wind at one's back or in opposition to the ball's break.
2. Using a premature wrist snap.
3. Using a forward-backward snap rather than a horizontal one with the arm moving across in front of the body.
4. Executing the stride and follow-through in the wrong direction.

B. Too slow. Causes include
1. Pushing off the pitcher's plate weakly.
2. Using a weak wrist snap.
3. Gripping the ball too loosely.

VI. Knuckleball

A. Spins. Causes include
1. Having uneven finger or knuckle pressure on the ball.
2. Using unwanted wrist snap.
3. Not completing follow-through.
4. Failing to push the ball from the hand and to follow through toward the target.

B. Doesn't break. Causes include
1. Throwing the ball too hard. A slow knuckleball is more apt to react to shifts in air currents.

When to Throw Each Type of Pitch

The following list suggests when various pitches might be thrown. The catching section of this chapter contains additional information regarding pitch selection and target placement.

Fastball

1. To a sweep hitter
2. To an opposite-field hitter
3. To a weak hitter
4. To a late swinger
5. To a hitcher
6. To an uppercutter
7. To a batter who stands up in the box
8. To a batter who holds the bat high or low
9. In a bunt or steal situation

Change-Up or Knuckleball

1. To a pull hitter
2. To a hyper-anxious or highly activated hitter
3. To a long- or over-strider
4. To a batter who stands up in the box
5. To a batter who stands away from the plate
6. To a batter who pulls away from the plate during the swing
7. When the count is 2–0 or 3–1

Drop

1. To a chopper
2. To a batter who stands tall and erect
3. To a batter who stands back in the box
4. To a batter who holds the bat high
5. When runners are in scoring position, especially on third

Riser

1. To a hitcher
2. To a chopper
3. To an uppercutter
4. To a croucher
5. To a long- or over-strider
6. To a batter who stands up or deep in the box
7. To a batter who holds the bat high or low
8. To a batter who holds his hands low
9. In a bunt situation

Curve

1. To an opposite-field hitter
2. To a batter with an open or closed stance
3. To a batter who stands back in the box
4. To a batter who crowds the plate
5. To a batter who stands away from the plate
6. To a batter who pulls away from the plate during the swing

Tips for Pitchers

1. Throw the same kind of ball in practice that you will use in games.
2. Keep your arm loose and warm, stretching out between innings and wearing a jacket, as necessary.
3. Take time between pitches on a hot, muggy day.
4. Take time between pitches when a teammate has run hard or far to play a ball. Give the player time to rest and to get into position.
5. Be sure that all teammates are in proper position before you present the ball.
6. Find out early what pitches are working, and rely most heavily on them.
7. Use one pitch to set another one up and to make it more effective.
8. Keep the batter off-balance by changing spots and speeds, but do not fall into a predictable pattern.
9. Vary pitching rhythm (time between pitches, length of time of the ball's presentation to the batter).
10. Work with the umpire. For instance, if the umpire seems to have a short strike zone, do not rely on a fastball at the armpits. Frequently throw at, or just below, the knees.
11. Try to maintain emotional control and an outward appearance of self-confidence—even cockiness—regardless of the situation. Fear, doubt, and anger can be seen by the opponents and can give them a psychological lift.
12. Recognize that game conditions (wind, temperature, sun) and ball parks vary. Pitch selection and placement may need to be adjusted accordingly.
13. Use rosin to improve your grip on a hot, muggy day.
14. Recognize that every hitter is dangerous. Treat each with respect, regardless of his position in the batting order.
15. If the batter is taking a lot of time to get set, step back off the pitcher's plate. Do not wait on the rubber for the batter, as waiting can increase tension and upset rhythm.
16. Take a deep breath before each pitch.
17. Throw a variety of pitches, but with the same motion—a consistent windup.
18. Keep the ball in the line of force toward home plate on the downward swing of the pitch (regardless of the type of delivery). Taking the ball out of this line with *any* windup is dysfunctional.
19. Hide the ball as long as possible throughout the delivery.

20. Release the ball the same way each time for a specific pitch.
21. Do not attempt to increase control by reducing the speed of the pitch or by aiming. Both actions are counterproductive.
22. Experiment with various grips, types of delivery, and stride lengths.
23. Keep the ball low when runners are in scoring position.
24. Usually throw fastballs high and tight, slow balls low and outside, risers high, and drops low.

Relief Pitching

A relief pitcher, who must be physically ready to enter a game at a moment's notice, requires a different warm-up routine than that used by a starter. Before the game, a relief pitcher must loosen up well; but once the game has started, he must balance work and rest. Otherwise, when called upon, he will be either too tired or too tight to pitch effectively. Most relievers throw frequently enough that they can throw hard after about ten warm-up pitches. By keeping an eye on the game and considering the inning, the number of outs, the score, and the pitcher's and team's performance, the relief pitcher can gauge when he is most likely to be needed and can adjust his warm-up routine accordingly. Adjustments may also be made for weather conditions (hot, muggy, cold, windy, rainy) and for how the individual pitcher's arm feels on a given day.

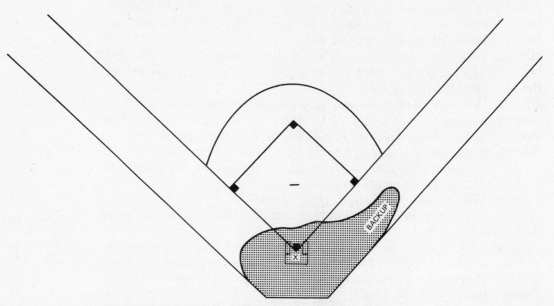

Figure 5-21. Catcher's Area of Responsibility and Position

Maintaining psychological readiness throughout a game is not easy for a relief pitcher. There may be numerous occasions when it appears that he will be needed, and he prepares accordingly; but an opponent's threat is removed, and the starter is able to remain in the game. The reliever must fight the peaks-and-valleys syndrome that might result from such false alarms, striving to maintain a relatively consistent and productive activation (readiness) level.

When a relief pitcher is pressed into service, his team is usually in trouble. There is little margin for error, so the reliever must bear down on every pitch. He has no opportunity to warm up with a couple of batters; nor can he waste a pitch or two, either to feel a batter out or to get his head into the game. A relief pitcher, upon entering a game, is not psychologically ready unless he knows the situation, is confident and poised, and is able to approach his task with intensity and concentration. Although even one mistake may be devastating, the relief pitcher must have a positive attitude. He must focus on what he can do and will do—not on what he can't do or what might happen if . . . !

CATCHER

Area of Responsibility and Position

The dotted area in Figure 5–21 represents the catcher's territory. The X indicates where the catcher most frequently positions. While receiving the pitch, the catcher must remain in the catcher's box, the ten-foot–by–eight-foot-five-inch outlined area behind the plate. More specifically and practically, the catcher should take a position two to three feet behind the batter's back leg. Positioning too close to the hitter puts the catcher in danger of getting hit with the bat and being injured, or being called for interference. Positioning too far behind the batter decreases the chances of catching foul tips and increases the throwing distance to bases. It also increases the pitching distance, which may be disturbing to the pitcher.

Characteristics

As the name of his position implies, the catcher is expected to catch the ball—pitched balls, bunts, foul tips, foul balls, and throws. Catching requires *quick reaction time, agility, muscular strength* and *endurance,* and *coordination.* Exceptionally strong legs are necessary to withstand many innings of crouching to receive the pitch and of rising quickly, often unexpectedly, to throw, catch errant pitches, or field the ball. Throws from the outfield will sometimes bounce close to home plate, so the catcher should be skilled at picking up short hops. Because such throws, as well as pitches in the dirt, must be blocked by the body, a catcher *cannot be afraid* of the ball.

Good size can be an asset to a catcher. Coupled with sufficient upper body strength, it helps a catcher to block a runner from the plate. Size is also advantageous in that a catcher with height and long arms can reach high or wide pitches. A larger catcher also presents a more visible target for throws to home plate. Smaller catchers must compensate for lack of size with quickness.

A catcher should have a *strong, accurate* throwing *arm* and a *quick release* in order to prevent runners from stealing and taking extra bases. Being right-handed is often advantageous because the majority of hitters are right-handed, so the batter is out of the way for throws to first and second base. Good *peripheral vision* is also desirable because it enables a catcher to keep track of runners while watching the pitch.

The catcher, from behind the plate, has the whole field in view, so he can give directions to teammates, keep them alert, and coordinate defensive efforts. Therefore, a catcher with *leadership* qualities is invaluable.

One of the most important responsibilities of the catcher is handling pitchers. Because a pitcher's emotional state influences his performance, the catcher's ability to help a pitcher develop and maintain a positive attitude is particularly significant. A strong and steady catcher who is willing to study hitters and to take partial, or in some instances complete, responsibility for pitch selection and placement provides valuable support to the pitcher. The pitcher and catcher form the battery. They must work together as a team.

Individual Responsibilities

Receiving Pitches and Throwing to Bases

In normal catching position, the left foot is slightly ahead of the right, for increased balance and stability; the heels are closer together than the toes, for increased lateral mobility; and the toe of the right foot faces toward first. This stance provides a firm foundation for a throw to any base.

The catcher has to throw to another base (1) after fielding a fair ball in front of the plate, (2) when a baserunner is attempting to steal, and (3) when a baserunner has led off far enough to be picked off the base. In each case, a quick, snap throw is necessary. There is no time for a big backswing or a step-hop to get more power into the throw. It is very important, therefore, that the catcher have a strong arm.

Figure 5-22. Snap Throw

To execute a snap overhand throw (Figure 5–22), the catcher receives the pitch, immediately pivots to the right, and shifts her weight onto her right foot. Simultaneously, the right elbow leads the glove and ball *directly up and back toward throwing position.* Along the way, the catcher removes the ball from the glove and continues to bring back the ball hand (palm facing the target) until the right arm is cocked (with the elbow extended back at shoulder level) and the ball is held behind, and close to, the right ear. The body has raised from a crouch; but the knees are still flexed, and the left shoulder points toward the target. The eyes remain focused on the base to which the throw is to be made.

The action phase of the throw begins as the left leg strides forward in the direction of the target, and the left knee flexes. The glove arm swings across the body, helping to pull the shoulders and hips square to the target; and the right (rear) leg completes a strong forward push. The right elbow leads the throwing arm forward; and the ball is released with a vigorous forward snap of the arm and wrist. The follow-through begins as the throwing arm continues forward and downward and the trunk flexes.

Catchers with weaker arms may need to take a short step forward, into the ball, with the right foot, as they receive the pitch. They can then step left and throw with a little more momentum. Others might find it helpful to throw with a jump shift, as described in Chapter 3. This is basically a quarter-turn jump and throw.

The catcher must get rid of the ball quickly during pick-off and steal situations. The type and location of the pitch received by the catcher will determine, to some extent, how quick the release can be. For instance, a pitchout (shoulder-high, outside fastball) naturally brings the catcher up into throwing position, and away from the batter, to receive the ball.

Since a pitchout is a very difficult pitch to hit, the catcher is free to concentrate on the impending throw. When a pitchout is not called, but a throw is necessary, the catcher may receive the ball in a position that is not as conducive to throwing with speed and accuracy. Also, the hitter, positioned in the batter's box, may be blocking the throwing path to a base. In those cases, the catcher will have to shift his feet before throwing.

Snap throwing to first base. When a right-handed batter is at the plate, the right-handed catcher has a clear throwing path to first base. If the pitch is over the middle of the plate, the catcher need only shift his body weight to his right foot as he receives the pitch, push off the right foot, and step onto the left foot in the direction of first base. This throw has the quickest release, but requires a strong arm. If the pitch is over the middle of the plate or to the catcher's right, he can step out toward first base with his right foot as he receives the ball. This step generates momentum for the throw. The ball is released, as usual, with a push off the right foot and a step onto the left foot in the direction of first base. If the pitch is received to the catcher's left, a drop-step throw may be used (see Chapter 3). The disadvantages of a drop step are that (1) it is time consuming and (2) it shifts the body weight away from the direction of the throw, adversely affecting throwing speed and accuracy. An alternative to the drop-step throw is a jump-shift throw (see Chapter 3). Some catchers, when receiving a pitch to their left, find it easiest to step to the left with their left foot to catch the ball and then to shift their weight back to their right foot for the throw. Others step to the left with the left foot to receive the ball, step forward onto the right foot, and step toward first base with the left foot. All throws to first should be to the inside of the base line, between knee and waist height.

When a left-handed batter is at the plate, his position in the box and the location of the pitch will determine the footwork necessary for the pick-off throw to first. Ideally, the throw should be made to the inside of the foul line, from in front of the batter. If the batter stands deep in the box, the catcher may be able to reach this ideal and employ the same techniques used for a right-handed batter. If the batter stands in the front of the box, however, those techniques might be time-consuming and difficult to apply. The catcher might need to throw from behind the batter, particularly if the pitch is inside. The catcher should receive the pitch with a sideward step to the right with the right foot, in order to clear the batter's body. The ball is then thrown from behind the batter with a push off the right foot and a step onto the left foot in the direction of first base.

Snap throwing to second base. Assuming that the pitcher ducks, or moves to the side, the catcher has a clear throwing path to second base. The batter's position is not particularly significant, except that if the batter stands up in the box, the catcher can move closer to the plate, thereby decreasing throwing distance to second. The location of the pitch will dictate the footwork necessary for the throw. Techniques are similar to those for a throw to first base with a right-handed batter at the plate. The major difference is that the push off the right foot and step onto the left should be in the direction of second base, rather than first. All throws to second should be over the base, at knee height.

Snap throwing to third base. When a left-handed batter is at the plate, the catcher has a clear throwing path to third base. If the pitch is over the middle of the plate, the catcher need only shift his body weight to his right foot as he receives the pitch, push off the right foot, and step onto the left foot in the direction of third base. If the pitch is over the middle of the plate or to the catcher's right, he can step out with his right foot as the ball is received; push off the right foot; and step onto the left foot in the direction of third base. If the pitch is received to the catcher's left, a crow-hop throw may be used. (See Chapter 3.) The sequence is lean, hop-close, step.

When a right-handed batter is at the plate, his position in the box and the location of the pitch will determine the footwork necessary for the throw to third. Ideally, the throw should be made to the inside of the foul line, from in front of the batter. This positioning is particularly imperative with a pick-off throw to third, because the runner is likely some distance down the third-base line, in foul territory. A throw from behind the batter would have to cross the runner's path to reach the covering baseman. If the batter stands deep in the box, the catcher may be able to employ the same techniques used for a left-handed batter and still throw from in front of the hitter. If the pitch is over the middle of the plate or to the catcher's right, he should step out toward the pitch with his right foot, push off the right foot, and step onto the left foot in the direction of third base. If the pitch is to the left of the catcher, he should step to the left with his left foot to receive the ball; step forward onto his right foot; and step toward third base with his left foot, throwing from in front of the batter. Some catchers, if they're tall and strong enough, simply throw over or around the batter's head.

Pick-off throws to third should be to the inside of the base line, between knee and waist height. Throws on steals should be over the base, at knee height.

Dealing with Wild Pitches, Passed Balls,
and Overthrows

Catchers should always check the backstop before the game to determine how a ball will rebound off of it—if the ball rebounds at all. This knowledge can be used in retrieving wild pitches, passed balls, and overthrows. In each of these cases the catcher's first task is to secure the ball as quickly as possible. The pitcher can help by providing early directional cues—"Straight back," "First," or "Third." If the ball passes to the catcher's right, he turns right and runs directly to the ball. If it passes to his left, he turns left. Once the ball has been located, the catcher must focus on it until it is securely within his grasp. Looking around to see where runners are, or what is happening, will slow his approach to the ball and will probably lead to subsequent fumbling. The technique used by the catcher to pick up the ball is the same as that used by any fielder to recover a fumbled ball. It is described, in detail, in Chapter 2.

As the catcher picks up the ball, his back will probably be toward the play, and he will need to be told if he should throw, and where. By calling for the ball, a covering baseman provides a cue for target location and indicates that he is prepared to receive the ball. If target information is received early enough, the catcher can plant his feet in position for the throw as he picks up the ball. By bracing body weight against the right leg and turning back toward the diamond, the catcher can use a snap sidearm throw, from fielding position, to get the ball back into play quickly. If the throw is to home plate, care must be taken not to throw too hard. The distance is usually not great, and the receiver must have time to react and to move his glove into position for the catch. If no putout is possible, or is highly unlikely, the covering baseman should yell, "No play!" at the earliest possible moment. The catcher should then hold the ball, check runners, and run the ball back to home plate.

Handling Pitchers

The catcher can significantly affect a pitcher's performance. Consequently, he should always be positive and encouraging. Even in warm-up, comments like "Good shot!" or "The curve's really moving" can help to build up a pitcher's confidence. If the pitcher is throwing low, the catcher can give him a higher target. The catcher can also help if the pitcher eases up or loses concentration. At times, simply pointing out the undesirable behavior is enough. At other times, the catcher may have to become stern and demanding. The strategy used should be dictated by the pitcher's personality and the situation. Obviously, the catcher must know the pitcher pretty well, including how he tends to react in given situations. Careful observation of, and communication with, the pitcher will lead to better rapport and greater understanding.

When a pitcher is having difficulty, it does little good to make comments like "Don't walk him" or "Don't hang one." Such comments, while providing no helpful information, serve to remind the pitcher of the possibility of walking the batter or hanging a pitch. Thinking of the possibility can cause the pitcher to let up or become anxious, which may lead to loss of control or flattening of a pitch—the opposite of the intended effect. There are other options for correcting a pitcher, but again their effectiveness depends on the pitcher's personality and state of mind. Encouragement, reprimand, and technique analysis are different ways of approaching the situation.

Rhythm is important in pitching and can be thrown off by working too slowly or too fast. The catcher helps to control the pitcher's rhythm by the way he gives signals and gets ready to receive the pitch. He may slow down the tempo of the game by taking time before returning the ball to the pitcher. The catcher may even call a conference—going out to the pitcher to talk *with* him. This not only slows down the tempo of the game, but also provides an opportunity to discuss pitching strategy and to steady the pitcher. The catcher can speed up the pitcher's rhythm by remaining in a crouch between pitches, throwing back to the pitcher from a crouch, and putting a little extra oomph on the return throw.

Fielding Bunts and Throwing to Bases

As soon as the catcher reads the batter's intent to bunt, he must prepare to move out in front of the plate quickly. He stays low to the ground in order to save time, reach the ball sooner, waste less movement, and expend less energy. The feet are spread in the direction the ball is moving, with the knees, hips, and shoulders squarely facing the line of the ball's path. As the catcher bends to field the ball, weight is on the balls of the feet, the knees and trunk are flexed, the arms hang freely, and the head, whenever possible, is directly over the ball. The glove hand blocks the path of the ball as it sweeps in from one side and the bare hand closes in from the other side—both hands moving through the same plane as the ball. The bare hand sweeps the ball into the glove, and both arms flex as the ball is brought back, up, and into throwing position.

When the ball is bunted directly out in front of the plate or toward first, the ball is approached from the left, as in Figure 5–23. The right foot

Figure 5–23. Fielding a Bunt toward the First-Base Line and Throwing to First

is placed as close to the ball as possible so that there is room to field the ball as it continues rolling to the left. The weight shifts to the left foot as the ball is brought into throwing position, and a snap throw is made with a crow-hop (see Figure 3–8). This procedure can also be used when fielding a bunt down the third-base line, but the catcher must circle the ball to get into proper position. This movement takes time, but keeps the play in front of the catcher. At no time will her back be toward any base to which she might have to throw.

When the ball is bunted down the third-base line, most catchers prefer to approach the ball as quickly as possible, as in Figure 5–24. Rather than circling to the left of the ball, the catcher moves directly to it with her back toward first base. The left foot is placed as close to the ball as possible so that there is room to field the ball as it continues rolling to the right. The weight shifts to the right foot as the ball is brought into throwing position, and the throw is made with a body pivot to the left on the right foot and a step toward first with the left foot.

Bunts close to home plate, especially toward the first-base line, are the catcher's responsibility. The catcher is moving toward the ball, and in the direction of the throw, while the first baseman and pitcher have their backs to the play and must turn to throw. Because the third baseman is in better fielding position to handle bunts down the third-base line, the catcher should only take the very short bunts on that side. When time permits, a snap overhand throw should be used. With no time to straighten up, the catcher should throw from the fielding position with a snap sidearm motion.

When not directly involved in the play, the catcher calls the base to which the ball should be thrown. If a putout is impossible, or unlikely, the

Figure 5-24. Fielding a Bunt toward the Third-Base Line and Throwing to First

catcher yells, "No play!" and the ball is held. If the ball is rolling close to a foul line the catcher may shout, "Let it roll!" in hopes that it will go foul. This technique is not advised with runners on base, however, as they might seize the opportunity to advance farther.

Fielding Pop-Ups

As soon as the catcher realizes that the ball has been popped up, he must stand up and turn toward the ball. The pitcher can provide valuable assistance at this point by shouting "Up," "Back," "First," or "Third" to indicate the ball's general direction. If the ball is hit over the catcher's right shoulder, he turns to his right. He pivots left if the ball passes over his left shoulder. Usually, an outside pitch is fouled off to the catcher's right, and an inside pitch is fouled off to the catcher's left. Once the ball has been located, the mask is thrown in the opposite direction or is dropped on home plate so that the catcher knows where it is and it will not interfere with the catch. Some catchers will leave their mask on—particularly if it is lightweight and provides good visibility.

Although some catchers prefer to use a basket catch, the majority favor an overhead technique. In general, the above-the-head technique is easier for most players to master, provides more room in which to recover the ball should it be bobbled, and is more conducive to a quick throw following the catch.

Catching pop-ups is particularly difficult for a catcher because the ball spins and drifts, usually toward the infield. Certain environmental variables (sun, wind) can add further difficulty. Consequently, it is recommended that infielders handle such balls whenever possible.

Checking Runners

Any runner who has rounded a base without stopping, or who is legitimately off the base after a pitched ball or after a hitter has completed his turn at bat, must be considered a threat to advance and must be dealt with accordingly. The catcher, because he has a full view of the field and can see all aspects of a play as it develops, is in position to keep his teammates informed of the status of runners and to alert them when changes occur.

With runners on base, the catcher must always expect, and prepare for, a steal. As soon as he receives the ball from the pitcher, he must check the progress of runners. By focusing intently on runners, and by being prepared to throw, he may discourage both straight and delayed steals. If no immediate throw is necessary, the ball should be returned to the pitcher.

Team Responsibilities

Covering

The catcher almost always covers home plate. When out of position and unable to cover home, for whatever reason, he gets help from the pitcher and the first baseman, depending upon the situation. The catcher may need help in covering home plate when he has left his position (1) to field a pop-up with a runner on third base or (2) to retrieve a wild pitch, passed ball, or errant throw to home with runners in scoring position.

The catcher may cover first if the first baseman has left his position to field a ball hit down the right-field line and there are either no runners on base or a runner on first. He may also cover third when a bunt or slow roller is fielded by the third baseman with a runner on first. Usually these bases are covered by others, however, with the catcher establishing a back-up position or returning to cover home plate.

Blocking home plate and tagging runners. As a runner comes into home, the catcher must be prepared to catch the ball, block the plate, and tag the runner out. Technically, the catcher cannot block the plate without the ball, but on many plays the ball and runner arrive almost simultaneously. Obstruction is rarely, if ever, called on a close play.

Figure 5-25. Covering Home Plate (Tag Play)

Figure 5–25 shows the position of the catcher upon receipt of a throw to home. Note that the catcher's feet are in front of home plate, in fair territory. The heel of the catcher's left foot is on the third base side of the plate, toe pointing toward third, so the *leg directly faces the runner*. The lower body is turned so that three quarters faces the runner and one quarter faces the ball. The lateral aspect of the knee should never be presented to an oncoming runner. (Note: Some catchers prefer to move a foot or two down the line toward third, catching the ball and making contact with the runner at that point.) The feet are in side-stride position, with weight evenly balanced over the balls of both feet. This position permits mobility in any direction. The catcher's knees and hips are flexed. By staying *low*, the catcher ensures that his eyes are more level with the hops, should the ball bounce, and his body is in position to block the path of the ball should it be misplayed. The pocket of the catcher's glove is open to the path of the ball, stationary, and held away from the body. Ideally, the ball should be received at about knee height. This positioning saves time by decreasing the distance the ball must be lowered for the tag. The catcher's eyes are focused on the ball, because it must be caught before a tag can be applied to the runner.

The catcher should anticipate a bad throw and should leave the plate, if necessary, to make the catch. He should let the ball come to him, however, rather than unnecessarily reaching, or moving out, for the throw.

Once the ball has been caught, *with both hands*, the catcher turns to face the runner and lowers both his body and his glove to block everything but the rear pointed section of the plate (see Figure 5–26). The back of the fingers of the catcher's glove faces the runner and serves as a protective buffer between the ball—held in the catcher's bare hand within the pocket of his glove—and the runner. The catcher looks for the

Figure 5-26. Blocking the Plate and Tagging the Runner

runner's foot or hand, squeezes the ball, and allows the runner to slide into the glove, thereby tagging himself. The catcher then gives with his glove and the ball to absorb impact force and protect the ball from being jarred loose.

If it becomes apparent that the runner is not going to slide, the catcher should shift his weight to his right foot, use it as a pivot, and swing the left foot to the rear, thereby clearing a path for the runner. The tag is made with both hands, and the ball is immediately pulled away to decrease the chance of its being jarred loose by contact.

When it is obvious that the runner is going to beat the throw to the plate, the catcher should yell "Cut!" and the base to which the ball may be thrown. The cutoff player then intercepts the throw. If there is no cutoff, the catcher should rush the ball, catch it on the fly, and get into position to make a play on the batter or another runner who may be attempting to advance on the throw. If the throw is erratic, the catcher must leave home plate to play the ball.

Forcing runners at home plate. The simplest technique that can be used to force a runner at home is to anchor one foot to the plate, on the side from which the throw is coming. A stationary target, glove outstretched, is presented to the thrower, and body weight is balanced over both feet. The catcher anticipates a bad throw and is prepared to shift, leaving the plate if necessary, to make the catch. A stretch may be used if the play is close. The plate area is cleared as soon as the force is complete, and other runners are checked to be sure that they stay where they are.

Backing Up

When a ground ball is hit to an infielder and there are no runners on base, or a runner is on first and a double play is possible, the catcher should back up the throw to first. As soon as the ball is hit, the catcher rises from crouch position and runs toward first base—parallel to, and about ten to fifteen feet from, the base line, in foul territory. Ideally, the catcher should establish a back-up position about ten to fifteen feet behind the first baseman, in line with the throw. Standing nearer would not be effective, as there would be little time to react. When it is not possible to get behind the throw, the catcher should move into position to field the ball off the dugout or fence and to prevent the runner from taking an extra base. With runners in scoring position, the pitcher can back up first while the catcher covers home.

The catcher should back up throws to the pitcher from second or short when there are runners on base. An errant throw, without alert back-up play, could allow a runner to advance. Special care must be taken not to stray too far from home plate, however, when there is a runner on third base.

Relay and Cutoff

When a direct or relay throw is headed toward home with a runner or runners in scoring position, it is the catcher's responsibility to direct the cut-off player to a position directly in line with home plate and the outfielder making the throw. It is also the catcher's responsibility to determine the possibility of a putout at the plate. If an out is likely, the catcher says nothing or yells, "Let it go!" This means that the cut-off player, usually the first baseman, should let the ball go through to the catcher. If an out is unlikely or impossible, the catcher yells "Cut!" and the base to which the ball may be thrown. Having conceded the run at home, the cut-off player intercepts the throw and makes a play on a back runner or, at the very least, checks the runner's advance.

Pickoff

A baserunner who takes a big lead on the pitch, or who is not alert when returning to base after the pitch, is a candidate for a pick-off attempt. The catcher, who has a full view of the field and can see all aspects of a play as it develops, is in an ideal position to call for a pickoff of lead or back runners at first, second, or third base.

Once a pick-off play has been called, the catcher's responsibility is to receive the pitch and to throw the ball to the appropriate base. Care must be taken to concentrate first on the catch, and then on the throw. The throw itself must be quick, accurate, and unexpected. If these criteria cannot be met, for whatever reason, the ball should be held. An indiscriminate throw, with little chance of retiring a baserunner, only enhances the possibility that the baserunner may advance.

If a pick-off opportunity arises, and there is adequate defensive coverage, the catcher may make a play on a runner even though it has not been prearranged. If there is no one in position to receive the throw, a fake throw may be used to force the runner back to his base, or farther off base. If a runner is more than ten feet from the nearest base, the catcher should be alert for a delayed steal. The best way to deal with this situation is to force the runner to commit himself by running directly toward him. No throw should be made until the runner is definitely committed in a given direction. If he fails to commit, the catcher should be able to tag the runner for the putout or trap the runner in a rundown. At the least, the runner should be forced to return to his original base.

Rundowns

The catcher takes part in the play on a runner caught off base between third and home. The responsibility of the catcher is to be the rundown player. This requires receiving the ball and running full speed toward the trapped runner, thereby forcing him to retreat toward third. Once the runner is committed to third, a soft toss to a receiver waiting near third base should result in a tag-out. If the runner fails to commit himself toward third, he may be tagged out by the catcher. (The technique for executing a rundown is described in detail in Chapter 11.)

The catcher assumes a back-up position at first base when a runner is trapped between first and second and there are no other runners on base. Should the runner manage to reach second base safely, or advance beyond second, the catcher must immediately return to cover home plate.

CATCHING

Preparing to Catch

Catchers are most apt to use their bodies to block pitches in the dirt, short-hop throws, and sliding runners if they are well equipped (mask, chest protector, leg guards). Confidence is gained with the knowledge that they have maximum protection against injury, and that they are physically prepared to handle any situation that might arise. Each piece of equipment must fit properly, however, to protect without inhibiting.

Choosing Pitches and Glove Placement

Choosing what type of pitch to throw and where to throw it depends upon the following factors:

1. Batter's position in the box (e.g., up, back, crowding, or away from the plate)
2. Batter's grip and hand position on the bat (e.g., end, semi-choke, choke)
3. Position of the bat relative to the ground (e.g., straight up, slanted, parallel)
4. Batter's stance (e.g., open, closed, upright, crouched)
5. Batter's length and direction of stride
6. Batter's swing (e.g., uppercut, sweep, hitch, chop)
7. Batter's bat and foot speed
8. Batter's apparent psychological state (e.g., determination, anxiety, aggressiveness)
9. Batter's performance history (what, how, and where the batter hits)
10. Game situation (e.g., score, inning, number of outs, count, position of runners)
11. Pitcher's condition (e.g., speed, stuff, control, best pitch)

Before a game, all of these bits of information are consolidated, and a basic plan of attack is developed for each hitter. For example, an inside pitch might be thrown to a batter who uses a closed stance and who positions close to the plate. It is important to note, however, in which direction the batter strides. Even with a closed stance a batter may hit an inside pitch if he steps away from the plate as he swings. Table 5-1 is presented as a guide to pitch selection and target placement.

Table 5-1. Pitch Selection and Target Placement

Factors	Pitch and Location
Batter's Bat Position and Grip	
Holds bat high	Rise—high; fastball—high, inside; drop—low
Holds bat low	Rise or fastball—high
Holds bat parallel to ground, hands low	Rise—high; fastball—high, inside
Holds bat at end, arms away from body	Fastball—inside
Batter's Foot Position	
Stands up in box	Rise—high; fastball—on corners; change—low, outside
Stands back in box	Stuff: drop—low; rise—high; curve—on corners
Stands away from plate or pulls away during swing	Fastball—outside; change—low, outside; curve—outside
Batter's Stance	
Crowds plate	Fastball or curve—inside
Uses open stance	Fastball or curve—low, outside
Uses closed stance	Fastball or curve—low, inside
Crouches	Fastball—high, inside or outside; rise—high
Batter's Stride	
Short stride	Drop, curve, or change—low
Long stride, overstride	Fastball—high, inside; rise—high; change—low, outside
Batter's Swing	
Late	Fastball—inside; no change-up
Hitch	Fastball—high, inside; rise—high
Chop	Drop—low; rise—high
Uppercut	Fastball—high, inside; rise—high
Sweep (very little wrist action)	Fastball—high, inside

Table 5-1. Pitch Selection and Target Placement (*continued*)

Factors	Pitch and Location
Type of Batter	
Pull hitter	Change—low, outside; curve—outside
Opposite-field hitter	Fastball—inside; off-speed curve—low, inside
Weak hitter	Anything except change-up
Bunter or slasher	Fastball—high, inside; rise—high; curve—inside
Hyper-anxious or highly activated hitter	Change—low (delay between pitches; long presentation time)
Situation	
Bunt	Fastball—high, inside; rise—high
Steal	Fastball—pitchout or high, outside
Runner in scoring position	Drop or curve—low; best pitch that day
Double-play possibility	Fastball, drop, curve, or change—low
Intentional walk	Medium fastball—middle, outside

The rise pitch should be thrown high. If it begins low, it will rise into the middle of the strike zone and be easier to hit. The rise can be an effective pitch against many free-swingers and batters who uppercut or "golf" swing.

A dropball, on the other hand, should be thrown low. Because of the way a drop is released, a low target is necessary. A high target will cause the pitcher to lift or snap the wrist up too early, which will cause the ball to go straight rather than to drop. Batters who chop down on the ball can have particular difficulty attempting to hit a drop.

A change-up is most effective when thrown low and outside, because that's the first area passed by the bat, and the batter has little time to react to the pitch. It is a good idea to throw the change early in the game to let opponents know that it is within the pitcher's repertoire, and to make them wonder if and when it will be thrown again.

A curve that breaks outside to a right-handed batter can be an effective strike-out pitch. For pitchers with fairly good control, the curve may also be effective to a left-handed batter because it will break in on his wrists. The same pitch can be thrown inside to a right-hander, but it cannot be thrown very often. If the batter is not fooled, the curve is an easy pitch to hit.

As a rule, it is best to avoid a consistent pattern when pitching to a particular batter. One way this can be done is to mix the type and speed of pitches. Another is to spot pitch. A pitcher who cannot throw a variety of pitches on command can still be effective if he hits the catcher's target. The "theory of opposites" may be applied—throw low/inside followed by high/outside, and so on.

If a pitcher is having trouble with a certain pitch, he should not eliminate that pitch, but use it as a waste pitch (e.g., when ahead of the hitter). The pitch may start working later in the game. If a pitch is working well, it should be used frequently, but not exclusively.

Obviously, a catcher can have a great influence on a pitcher's performance. Some pitchers prefer that the catcher take complete charge of the pitching strategy, while other pitchers prefer to have some input into the plan. Either way, the battery must cooperate. Pitchers pitch better when they are comfortable with their catcher; and catchers call a better game when the pitcher isn't constantly shaking the call off or, worse yet, throwing something that wasn't called. The best batterymates are those with mutual confidence and respect.

Giving Signals

Once the catcher has determined the type of pitch he thinks should be delivered, the suggestion must be communicated to the pitcher. The quickest and easiest way to transmit the information is through a prearranged set of signals. The simpler the signals, the better. For example:

1. One finger extended—fastball
2. Two fingers extended—riseball
3. Three fingers extended—dropball
4. Five fingers extended—change
5. Fist—pitchout

The number of signals corresponds, of course, to the number of pitches within the pitcher's repertoire. If the pitcher has more than six pitches, combination signals can be given. For instance, a fist followed by one finger might call for a slow curve.

The advantage of signals is that the catcher knows what he can expect to receive and can prepare accordingly. Without signals the possibility of injury to the catcher's hands and fingers is increased, as is the likelihood of passed balls. In addition, the catcher is more apt to be out of position for a throw following the catch. Another advantage of catcher's signals is that the pitcher is free to concentrate specifically and fully on the selected pitch and its delivery. The catcher is in better position to identify those pitches that are working for a pitcher on any given day and to remain objective when analyzing the situation and determining the best

Figure 5-27. Giving Signals

pitch to throw. Catcher's signals are suggestions, however, and they can be shaken off by the pitcher. The pitcher knows how he feels and the condition of his arm. Some shake-offs can be expected through the course of a game, but a lot of them signifies trouble.

If signals are to be effective, they must not only be simple, but also hidden from opponents (batter, baserunners, first- and third-base coaches) as illustrated in Figure 5–27. To keep the signals hidden, the catcher sits on her heels and flashes the signal over her right leg, near the upper, inner part of the thigh. Holding the glove down by the left leg further helps to shield the signal from the third-base coach.

With a runner on second base, normal precautions may not be sufficient to prevent the runner from stealing signs and transmitting them to the batter. In this case, multiple signs may be used. A series of three signals may be flashed in succession, with a predetermined one signaling the desired pitch. The indicator that determines which signal in the series to accept may be the game inning. For example, the first sign in the series may be used in odd numbered innings (1, 3, 5, 7), with the second sign being used in even innings (2, 4, 6). The indicator may be a piece of the catcher's equipment, rather than innings. For example, touching the mask might indicate that the first signal flashed is to be followed, while touching the chest protector would indicate the second sign. The pocket of the glove could serve as the indicator for the third sign. With this system, a catcher who adjusted his mask, extended one finger (fastball), extended five fingers (change), and made a fist (pitchout), would be calling for a fastball. The mask is an indicator telling the pitcher that the first sign flashed (in this case, one finger extended) identifies the pitch to be thrown.

Signals can also be given by the catcher to call for pickoffs. These may be physical signs (adjusting the mask, protector, or leg guard in a certain way; touching a specific ankle, knee, or hip when assuming position to give routine signals to the pitcher; brushing dirt off a specific part of the body or emptying it out of the glove), or they may be verbal signs (using players' last names or team name when shouting out encouragement, e.g., "Let's go, *Bears*"; standing up or walking out in front of the plate to call and signify the number of outs). These signals must also be simple.

Since a pickoff requires a coordination of defensive effort, the player who is to receive the throw should acknowledge the catcher's signal. The receiver might respond by tapping his bare hand in his glove, wiping his forehead, or picking up dirt.

A catcher may occasionally want to call for a pitchout, usually when the catcher believes that a runner intends to steal on the pitch. By calling for a pitchout, the catcher can receive the ball in better throwing position. The call also allows fielders to move into covering and back-up position as the ball is released from the pitcher's hand, since there is no danger that the ball may be hit or bunted. A pitch-out signal may, or may not, follow that for a pickoff. Fielders should not leave their position early unless a pitchout is called.

Assuming Catching Position

The catcher assumes position to receive the pitch as soon as the pitcher has accepted the signal and is ready. It must be a comfortable stance that provides for balance and maximum mobility. It must also permit the umpire full view of the plate and the ball. Figure 5–28 shows the catcher's body position for receiving the pitch.

Both feet are slightly more than shoulder width apart, with the left foot slightly ahead of the right for increased balance and stability. The heels are closer together than the toes, and the toe of the right foot faces toward first base for increased lateral mobility. Weight is fairly evenly balanced and slightly forward, on the balls of the feet, but the heels remain as close to the ground as possible. The knees are bent a little more than ninety degrees, but the hips are up. Catchers who tend to sit on their heels will have trouble moving for bunts, pop fouls, and erratic pitches. They will also have trouble getting into throwing position.

Figure 5-28. Catcher's Stance

The upper body of the catcher is inclined forward so that the shoulders are above the toes. The arms are relaxed and extend from the shoulders so that the elbows, though flexed, are out in front of the knees. The glove is extended toward the pitcher, with the wrist of the glove hand flexed slightly so that the top part of the glove, rather than the perpendicular face of the pocket, points toward the pitcher. The bare hand is close to the glove, but must not be exposed. Most catchers form a relaxed, loose fist with their bare hand and protect it by gently pressing the thumb or the back of the curled fingers against the back of the glove, or behind and along the thumb of the glove. (Some coaches teach catchers to hold their bare hand behind their back or down by their leg. These positions are not recommended, however, as they cause unnecessary delay in bringing the throwing hand to the ball after the catch.) The catcher's head is up, facing the pitcher, and the eyes remain on the ball until it is securely caught.

The catcher's stance should be assumed as close to the hitter as possible without interfering with his swing. This position decreases the catcher's throwing distance to bases. It also makes foul tips and pitches in the dirt easier to catch because the rebound angles off the bat and ground, respectively, can be smothered. Furthermore, the catcher is closer to fair territory and can reach bunts quicker. Another advantage of positioning close to the hitter is that pitched balls are caught sooner and nearer to the striking zone, so they may look better to the umpire.

With runners on base, many catchers spread their feet a little farther apart so that they have a wider base of support and a more stable position from which to throw, if necessary. They also raise their hips slightly for a quicker start.

Giving a Target

After calling for a specific type of pitch and assuming catching position, the catcher must give the pitcher a target. The target will tell the pitcher where to throw the ball. It should be as large as possible, and it must be held stationary until the pitch has been released. Some catchers assume position directly behind the center of home plate and reach from there to provide a high, low, inside, or outside target. Others initially assume a catching position slightly to the right of the plate's center for a pitch over the outside corner to a right-handed batter, or to left of center for an inside pitch to a right-handed batter. By starting off-center, the catcher places his body directly behind the glove, presenting a larger target to the pitcher. The glove of the catcher is extended toward the pitcher, but it is not held so far out in front of the body that it interferes with any part of the batter's swing or upsets the balance of the catcher.

Receiving the Pitch

The catcher must focus intently upon the flight of the ball from the moment it leaves the pitcher's hand until it is either secure within his grasp or is hit. This takes concentration and self-control, particularly if the batter swings and misses or hits a foul tip. The catcher must also be careful to stay low in order to give the umpire full view of the plate and the ball. Umpires dislike catchers who jump up as the pitch crosses the plate, and they may call pitches balls simply because they cannot see the strike zone.

As a rule, the catcher should always try to keep his body in front of the ball. If, for example, the ball is moving to the catcher's right, he should take a step to the right with his right leg rather than remaining in place, reaching out, and trying to backhand the ball.

The fingers of the glove point up to catch high pitches and down for low ones, with the pocket of the glove facing the ball. If the ball cannot be caught, it should at least be blocked. Even if there are no runners on base, the catcher should make every attempt to keep the ball from getting past him. This effort can help a pitcher to maintain confidence.

Figure 5–29 shows a catcher dropping one knee to the ground to block a low pitch. Notice that the body weight of the catcher is forward, and that her shoulders and body are square, facing the pitcher. If the ball does hit the catcher, it will most likely bounce out in front, where it can be recovered easily. Note, too, that the catcher's chin is tucked and that her eyes are focused intently on the ball. The fingers of the catcher's glove point down, the pocket is directly in line with the path of the approaching ball, and the bare hand is close by, ready to grip the ball in preparation for a throw once the ball is secure.

Figure 5-29. Handling a Low Pitch

If the pitched ball is in the dirt to the side of the body, the catcher should lean to that side and drop the opposite knee first, twisting as necessary to keep her shoulders and body square to the ball. Once the ball is secure she must get to her feet quickly in preparation for subsequent play.

Many catchers today try to catch the ball cleanly, but with their body in position to block its path should it be missed. When necessary, both knees may be dropped to block any holes that the ball may pass through. Dropping both knees is advised with a runner on third, although the catcher will probably be out of position to throw following the catch. The first priority is to stop the ball.

Giving, with a relaxed arm and hand, is important when catching any pitched ball. It is this action that helps to absorb the force of impact, thereby reducing the chance that the ball will pop out of the glove and protecting the hand from bruising. Giving in toward the center of the body as the pitch is caught may also help the pitch to look more like a strike than a ball. When catching a borderline pitch, the catcher may even choose to hold the ball momentarily so that the umpire gets a good look at it.

Tips for Catchers

1. Get to know each pitcher's strengths, weaknesses, and typical reactions to given situations.
2. Wear a mask, chest protector, and leg guards when catching—even when warming up the pitcher in pre-game practice.
3. Keep count of how many pitches the pitcher delivers between innings. Do not exceed the allowable number.

4. Do not assume catching position until fielders are properly aligned.
5. Throw the ball back to the pitcher in an accurate, consistent manner.
6. Check the speed of runners and consider this information when determining if, and where, to throw the ball in a given situation.
7. Do not throw the ball indiscriminately. Throw when a putout is possible.
8. Block the plate when necessary, but try to minimize body contact.

6

Infield

FIRST BASEMAN

Area of Responsibility and Position

The shaded area in Figure 6–1 represents the first baseman's domain. The X indicates where the baseman is most frequently positioned, although situational adjustments will be made throughout the course of a game. From this position the baseman can handle bunts and slow rollers and still has time to get back to cover first if the ball is hit elsewhere. The location, toward and away from home plate, is a compromise between two conflicting factors. First, the farther the baseman is from home plate, the longer it will take for a batted ball to reach him, and the more time he will have to react to it and to catch it. On the other hand, the farther back he is, the greater his vulnerability to a bunt or slow roller. The distance from the foul line is fixed, to a large extent, by the baseman's quickness, lateral mobility, and ability to make a backhand catch. If he stands too close to the line, particularly if he is a right-handed thrower, he is likely to be troubled by balls hit into the hole between him and the second baseman. If he positions too far away, he may have difficulty in guarding the line. A ball that is hit past the baseman and down the line will frequently result in extra bases for the batter–baserunner. Also, confusion may arise between the first and second basemen about who will field balls in the hole, and first base may be left uncovered.

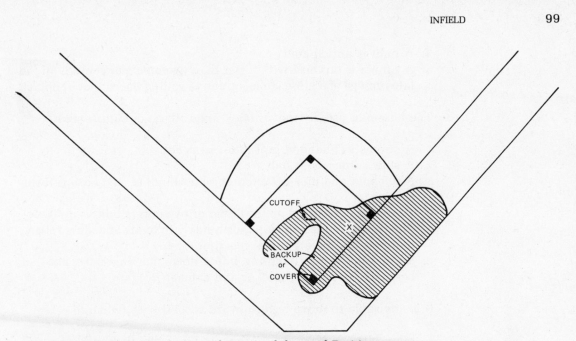

Figure 6-1. First Baseman's Area of Responsibility and Position

Because the first baseman is responsible for covering first base on the majority of plays, his fielding territory is limited to a relatively small area around the bag. The specific area can change slightly, however, depending on the particular situation and the batter. For example, a batter who usually hits up the middle may force the second baseman to shade toward second, thereby adding area for the first baseman to cover. A poor fielding pitcher may force the first baseman to make plays farther toward the mound, while an excellent fielding pitcher will considerably reduce the first baseman's area of fielding responsibility.

If a sacrifice bunt is expected, the first baseman may move in farther, but he must be careful because his vulnerability to a push or slug bunt increases. When the chances of a bunt are minimal (two strikes, two outs, or opponents far behind in late innings), the baseman may play even with, or behind, the bag. Playing behind the bag is particularly advantageous for a pick-off attempt because the baseman can move toward the throw, rather than away from it, while keeping the runner in sight at all times. The runner is at a disadvantage because he can't watch the ball and the baseman at the same time.

In summary, the first baseman generally moves in (toward home plate) under the following circumstances:

1. The infield is wet and soft.
2. A weak, but fast-running, hitter is at bat.

3. A bunt is anticipated.
4. A runner is on third with fewer than two outs, particularly in the late innings of a close game (option of getting the runner at home).

The baseman usually moves *back* under these circumstances:

1. A strong, left-handed pull hitter is at bat.
2. A slow runner is at bat.
3. A pitchout and pick-off attempt on a runner at first base is forth-coming.
4. There are two strikes on the batter or two outs (a bunt is unlikely).
5. The fielder reads and responds quickly to bunts and slow rollers, but does not have a quick reaction time.
6. Responsibility for handling bunts down the first-base line has been assigned to the pitcher and catcher.

It is advisable to move *right* (toward second base) when

1. More hits are expected up the middle of the diamond.
    a. A strong, right-handed pull hitter is at bat.
    b. A left-handed, late-swinging, or opposite-field hitter is at bat.
    c. The pitcher is slow, tiring, or throwing a change-up.
2. The fielder is a right-handed thrower with a weak backhand catch.

A shift *left* (toward the first-base line) is recommended when

1. A strong, left-handed pull hitter is at bat.
2. A bunt is anticipated.
3. The team is in the late innings of a close game (guard the line against extra-base hits).
4. The pitcher is exceptionally fast and overpowering, and opposing right-handed hitters are swinging late—going to the opposite field.
5. The fielder is a left-handed thrower with a weak backhand catch, but good reach to his right side.

Characteristics

Good size can be an asset to first basemen. Tall and rangy players, with long arms and legs, can reach farther for high or wide throws. They also present a larger, more visible target. Smaller players must compensate for lack of size with *quickness*. Being *left-handed* is often advantageous because:

1. Bunts and hits can be fielded and thrown to second or third without the time-consuming pivot that right-handed throwers must use.
2. The hole between the first and second baseman is to the forehand side. A right-handed thrower must have a good backhand to cover this area.
3. The baseman's glove is to the inside of the diamond to receive throws. This makes a pick-off play a little easier. In addition, upon receipt of the ball, the left-hander is more mobile and better able to give with contact if it should occur.

Although first basemen must react and move quickly, running speed is not essential, as the area the basemen cover is relatively small. They must be able to respond quickly, however, to bunts and slow rollers. Such response frequently requires either charging, catching, and throwing in one continuous motion or returning quickly to first base and positioning to receive a throw. The ability to get to the bag quickly is essential to the success of first basemen. It requires *agility* and *mobility*. First basemen must maneuver their bodies into many varied positions to catch good and bad throws while keeping the bag covered. *Footwork patterns* must be practiced until they become automatic (conditioned responses). A strong arm, though desirable, is not as essential to first basemen as to players in other positions.

Individual Responsibilities

One of the most common, yet difficult, decisions a first baseman must make is whether or not to go for a ball hit in the hole to his right. If he ranges too wide, there may be confusion regarding first-base coverage. Even if the ball is fielded, there may be no one in position to receive the throw. It is very important, therefore, that the first baseman carefully and objectively evaluate his second baseman's range. Knowing whether or not the second baseman is likely to make a catch allows the first baseman to determine quickly what he should do. Generally, if the first baseman feels he can field the ball and reach first base ahead of the runner for the force-out, he should try to make the play. If not, he should cover the bag and give the second baseman or right fielder full responsibility for fielding the ball. It is almost always an easier play if the first baseman is able to cover first. The primary exceptions are bunts and slow rollers, which the first baseman must move away from the bag to field, and unassisted plays by the second baseman. There may be rare instances when both the first and the second basemen are out of position and the pitcher must cover the bag; however, this situation—usually the result of confusion or physical error—is undesirable and should be a last resort.

Fielding Bunts

First basemen are usually responsible for bunts down the first-base line and must, therefore, pay careful attention to mannerisms and actions of the batter that might indicate a bunt. Particular attention should be focused on the batter's hands and feet. Changes in customary grip (choke, split, or sliding of hands up the handle), stance (square-around), or bat position are noteworthy. When such cues are presented, the first baseman moves toward home plate, but maintains body control. Charging wildly, and before the batter is committed to bunt, will greatly increase the fielder's vulnerability to a slug or punch bunt.

A left-handed first baseman has an advantage over a right-hander when fielding bunts—he may range farther to the right, toward the pitcher, because he is in better position to throw once the ball is secure. As the ball approaches, a left-handed first baseman should set in forward-stride position—left foot forward. Weight is placed on the left foot as the ball is caught, and the throw to first, second, or third base is made with a clockwise pivot (to the right) and a step on the right foot in the direction of the receiver.

Figure 6–2 illustrates a right-handed first baseman's position for fielding bunts and slow grounders. To be in proper position to throw to first or second, the player angles her body toward the first-base foul line. Weight is placed, ideally, on the right foot as the ball is caught, and the

Figure 6–2. Positioning of a Right-Handed First Baseman to Field a Bunt and Throw to First or Second

throw is made with a rear, counterclockwise pivot (to the left) and a step on the left foot in the direction of the receiver. If the bunt is to the baseman's right, she may use a front, clockwise pivot (to the right) to get into position for the throw. To throw to third the player should field the bunt with weight on her lead (left) leg. A jump shift (Figure 3–2), drop shift (Figure 3–3), or crow-hop (Figure 3–8) throw may be used. An underhand toss is recommended only for a short throw home.

Whenever possible, bunts should be fielded with two hands, as described in Chapter 2. If a bare-hand catch is necessary, the baseman approaches to the glove side of the ball. The open palm, with fingers extended at right angles to the ground, is placed directly in line with the path of the oncoming ball. The ball is allowed to roll into the hand and is then squeezed tight. Because the ball is rather large for the hand size of most players, the one-handed fielding technique should be used only as a last resort, and when the ball is almost motionless on the ground.

Bunts near the pitcher or home plate sometimes raise a question as to who should play the ball. If teammates are in proper position, the first baseman should not field the ball, because the third baseman, the catcher, and, sometimes, the pitcher are in better position to make the throw. If the first baseman has been drawn in too far and cannot recover quickly enough to cover first, he should clear a throwing path to the bag by moving to the side or ducking, and the second baseman should assume primary coverage of the bag.

The catcher normally calls the direction in which the ball is to be thrown. A hard-hit bunt, fielded cleanly, is usually thrown to second for a force-out if a runner is on first base with fewer than two outs. It may be thrown to third or home if runners are on other bases. A slow rolling or mishandled bunt is usually thrown to first. The first baseman should always be aware of the option to tag the batter–baserunner, particularly when the bunt is close to the foul line or when the first baseman is trying to limit the advance of other runners. The baseman can watch the other runners while he moves toward the base line to tag the batter–baserunner. If no play is possible at any base, and the ball is close to the foul line, it should be left to roll, with hope that it will go foul. The wait cannot be too long with runners on base, however, as they may advance while the ball is rolling. If the bunt is clearly foul, it should be touched immediately as a precaution against its curving, hitting a stone or clump of dirt, and entering fair territory.

Retiring Batter–Baserunners Unassisted

When the first baseman fields a batted ball and can retire the batter–baserunner unassisted, he should do so. By personally handling the play, the baseman eliminates the exchange with the second baseman or pitcher, thereby reducing the chance of error.

Receiving Throws

The ability to catch thrown balls is essential for the effective performance of a first baseman. Throughout the course of a game, the first baseman will almost invariably receive more throws than any other player, excluding the battery.

Establishing position. The first baseman should break to cover the bag as soon as it is evident that the ball has not been hit or bunted within his area of fielding responsibility. If the bag is not very far away, the baseman can sidestep to the bag while keeping track of the ball. The back of the heels can be used to locate the bag, eliminating the need to reach or look for it. If the bag is far away, or the baseman is unsure about the location of the base, it is faster to pivot and run directly to the bag, then turn and look for the ball. By moving to first as quickly as possible the baseman usually has time to set to receive the throw. He can then devote full attention to the catch, can present the thrower with a stationary target, and is prepared to shift quickly in any direction to handle an erratic throw.

The set position that the first baseman assumes at the bag may vary. There are three common options:

1. Same-foot tag. The left foot (of a left-handed thrower) or right foot (of a right-handed thrower) touches the middle of the edge of the bag that is closest to, and parallel to, second base. The other foot is slightly ahead.
2. Heel-contact-shift tag. The backs of the heels touch the corners of the bag that are closest to second base. The back of the right heel is against the outfield corner, while the left heel is against the infield corner. The toes of both feet point outward at approximately forty-five degrees.
3. Shift-step tag. The back of the heels are about six inches from the corners of the bag that are closest to second base. The back of the right heel is near, but not in contact with, the outfield corner; and the left heel is near, but not in contact with, the infield corner. The toes of both feet point outward at approximately forty-five degrees.

Option 1 is frequently selected by beginners, in particular, because they find it easier to tag the base with the same foot all the time. (See Figure 6-3.) They needn't worry about shifting or about losing the bag.

a   b   c

Figure 6-3. Right-Handed Baseman Receiving a Throw to the (a) Right, (b) Middle, and (c) Left of the Bag—Using a Same-Foot Tag

The only adjustment they need make is to slide to the appropriate corner of the bag to receive a wide throw. The stretch to meet the ball will always be with the leg on the glove side of the baseman's body, thereby assuring maximum reach regardless of the ball's direction.

Option 2, placing the backs of the heels against the inside corners of the bag, allows the baseman to know and to feel exactly where the base is at all times. When receiving a throw that is wide to his right, the baseman slides his left foot to the right until it touches the inside of his right foot. The right foot serves as a guide, telling the baseman how far he can and should go in that direction. The ball of the left foot then assumes body weight and presses against the outfield corner of the bag closest to second base. The left foot turns sideward (with the inside of the ankle pointing toward the ground) to push against the bag, as the right foot strides out in the direction of the throw. To catch a throw that is wide to the left, the baseman uses the reverse procedure.

When a baseman uses this technique to position for wide throws, it makes no difference whether the baseman is right- or left-handed. The procedure is the same. If the throw is directly to the base, however, a right-handed baseman places the ball of his right foot against the center of the edge of the bag closest to the thrower and steps forward with the left foot in the direction of the throw. A left-handed baseman tags the bag with his left foot.

The heel-contact method of covering first allows the baseman to move smoothly from one side of the bag to the other while maintaining base contact. Although the tag foot changes, depending upon the direction of the throw (right foot for throws to the left, and left foot for throws to the right), there is no need for the cross-over step and backhand catch that is necessary when using the same-foot-tag technique (option 1) to receive balls thrown to the right if right-handed or to the left if left-handed. The difference between the same-foot technique and the heel-contact-shift technique for receiving a throw that is wide to the right is evident in

Figure 6-4. Right-Handed Baseman Receiving a Throw to the Right of the Bag—Using a Shift Tag

Figures 6–3a and 6–4. Notice that the baseman's body, as shown in Figure 6–4, faces the approaching ball and is directly in line with its flight path. This catch is the easier of the two, although the player will not be able to stretch or reach as far as she can in Figure 6–3a. To attain maximum stretch, she must stride toward the ball with the leg on the glove side of her body.

Option 3 (shift-step tag) is recommended for use by experienced first basemen who have a mental picture of the bag and know where it is at all times. Because the baseman's heels are near, but not in contact with, the edge of the base that is closest to the thrower, the baseman must step back to tag the bag. The procedure for handling a throw that is wide to the right is as follows:

1. Step back and to the right with the left foot until it is in contact with the outfield corner of the bag that is closest to second base.
2. Assume body weight on the ball of the left foot and turn it sideward (with the inside of the ankle pointing toward the ground) to push against the bag as the right foot strides out in the direction of the throw.

The procedure is reversed to catch a throw that is wide to the left. If the throw is directly to the base, a right-handed baseman places the ball of his right foot against the center of the edge of the bag that is closest to the thrower and steps forward with the left foot in the direction of the throw. A left-handed baseman tags the bag with his left foot.

The shift-step technique of positioning to receive a throw minimizes the chance of contact with the batter–baserunner by reducing the time the baseman is in contact with the bag. It also frees the baseman from the constraining influence of the bag, enabling him to move about with greater ease and flexibility.

When the baseman is set to receive the throw, he should be in contact with, or very near, the part of the bag that is closest to the thrower. His feet should be comfortably apart (straddle or forward stride), with his weight evenly balanced over both feet so that movement in any direction is possible without compensatory action. His knees should be bent slightly in anticipation of movement in some direction, and to help stabilize his body. The upper body of the baseman should be inclined forward so that his shoulders are above his toes. His arms should be relaxed and extended toward the thrower, with the glove chest high and the pocket open to the path of the ball. The open glove will serve as a target for the thrower; therefore, it must be held stationary until the ball is released.

At this point the baseman should be both mentally and physically prepared to shift to receive all types of throws. By placing his mind and muscles on alert, he reduces the necessity of relying on last second reactions. The baseman is now ready to call for the ball. The call will indicate to the thrower that the baseman is ready, and it will also provide a cue for target location.

Catching the ball.   As the thrower releases the ball, the receiving baseman should focus on the release point. Once the baseman has determined the direction of the throw, he may stride out to meet the ball. Stretching is critical on close plays. By turning the tagging foot sideways so that the inside of the ankle is toward the ground, and the toe touches the bag, the baseman increases his flexibility and the length of his stretch. Extending his glove target and his body as far as possible, while maintaining contact with the bag, further increases the length of his stretch. The farther the reach, the sooner the catch, and the better the chance of achieving a putout. When there are two outs or no runners on base, and the play at first is expected to be close, the first baseman should stretch as far as he is physically capable. If, however, there are runners on base and fewer than two outs, the baseman must not stretch so far that he can't get into throwing position quickly enough to participate in subsequent play. He must also be careful not to stretch so far that he pulls his foot and loses contact with the base before he receives the throw.

The eyes of the baseman watch the approaching ball as closely as possible and try to follow its flight all the way into the glove. If a subsequent throw is necessary, a crow-hop step will put the baseman into position for a quick release.

The first baseman should try to receive most throws with two hands for a surer catch and a quicker exchange from catching to throwing position. The major exceptions are erratic throws and close plays that necessitate a stretch. The baseman can reach farther with one hand than with two. Once the ball has been caught, the base area must be cleared immediately to minimize the possibility of contact with the batter—baserunner.

Handling high, low, and wide throws. A cardinal rule for the first baseman is *ball first, then the base*. If a throw is erratic, the baseman must go after it, even if it pulls him off the bag. It is better to leave the base when necessary to catch the ball than to allow a runner or runners to advance.

If a throw is *high*, the baseman should rise up on his toes and stretch high to make the catch while maintaining contact with the bag. If the throw is too high to be reached in this manner, but is over the bag, the baseman should jump straight up into the air, make the catch, and land with one foot on the bag. If the throw is both high and wide, it would probably be best to leave the bag to make the catch and then to try to tag the runner as he passes by.

If a throw is *low*, the baseman should stretch to reach the ball before it contacts the ground or when it is as close as possible to the contact point. By keeping the body low, level with the hop, the player can judge the ball's position more easily.

If it is unlikely that the throw can be caught and held for a putout, the baseman should do everything possible to keep the ball from going past him, including blocking it with his body or leaving the bag to catch the ball in the air. Fewer chances should be taken with a runner in scoring position and fewer than two outs.

If a throw is *wide* to the *left*, it may cause special problems for the baseman, as it is in the direction of the approaching batter–baserunner. If the throw arrives before the runner, the baseman may be able to make the catch, tag the bag, and continue on across the base into foul territory. If time permits, and the baseman can control his momentum following the catch, he may push back off the bag into fair territory. If the ball and the runner are expected to arrive at about the same time, it might be best to leave the bag, make the catch, and attempt to tag the runner as he passes by.

If the throw is *wide* to the *right*, and the baseman cannot make the catch while maintaining contact with the base, he should leave the bag. Once the ball has been caught, the baseman's best chance for the putout will most likely be to dive back to the bag.

Tagging batter–baserunners. When a high, wide, or low throw pulls the first baseman off the bag, a putout may still be possible. If the ball is caught before the runner arrives, the baseman should

1. Hold the ball in his bare hand, but within his glove
2. Keep both hands at waist level, close to his body
3. Give with his hands and arms, and pivot back toward first base as he makes the tag
4. Make the contact with the runner as brief as possible

If the ball and the runner arrive at almost the same time, the baseman should squeeze the ball firmly and sweep his glove toward the runner to make the tag. If it's not possible to tag the runner, the baseman may be able to dive back to the base before the runner arrives. This is a dangerous play, however, and must be used only as a last resort.

Team Responsibilities

Covering

The first baseman is responsible for covering first base on the majority of plays. Included are the following:

1. Ground balls to infielders.
2. One-base hits to outfielders. A force-out may be effected at first following a sharply hit grounder to right field. In addition, a runner who rounds first and takes too big a lead may be caught off base and tagged out.
3. Bunts to the catcher, pitcher, or third baseman.
4. Fly balls or line drives caught in the air, with a runner on first base.
5. Pick-off attempts on a runner at first.
6. Dropped third strikes with first base unoccupied, or with a runner on first and two outs.
7. Bases on balls.

When out of position and unable to cover first, for whatever reason, the first baseman may get help through cooperation with the second baseman, pitcher, or right fielder, depending upon the situation. Assistance in covering first base may be needed in the following instances:

1. A tag or force play at first when the first baseman has left his position to field a ground ball, pop-up, or bunt.
2. A double play (second to first) when the first baseman has fielded the ball and made the initial throw.

In these situations, the first baseman may be able to recover quickly enough to assume primary covering responsibility. If not, he should make every attempt to establish a back-up position.

The first baseman may be assigned to cover home plate when there are runners in scoring position and the catcher has left his position to field a pop foul or to recover a wild pitch, passed ball, or erratic throw to home. For force- and tag-outs, techniques described in Chapter 4 are used.

Backing Up

The first baseman is responsible for backing up the following throws:

1. Throws from third base or shortstop to the pitcher. Backup of such throws is particularly important when runners are on base. An erratic throw, without alert back-up play, could allow a runner to advance.
2. Throws from the catcher to the pitcher covering home on wild pitches or passed balls with a runner or runners in scoring position. If the coach prefers, the first baseman may be assigned to cover home, with the pitcher backing up.
3. Throws from left and left-center field to second base.
4. Throws to the relay on extra-base hits, when the first baseman is functioning as the cutoff.

The technique for backing up is described, in detail, in Chapter 4.

Cutoff

Some coaches assign the third baseman to serve as the cut-off player on throws to home plate from left field when there is little chance of a play at third—for example, a single to left field with a runner on third base. This assignment frees the first baseman to cover first in case the batter–baserunner can be caught off base between first and second. Under all other circumstances, however, the first baseman serves as the cut-off player, and the third baseman covers third.

Other coaches designate the first baseman as the cutoff for *all* plays. This eliminates potential communication gaps and coverage mix-ups between the first baseman and the third baseman, but it also allows a batter–baserunner to take a larger turn when rounding first.

Under some circumstances, it may be easier and more effective to use the pitcher as the cutoff, with the first baseman backing up the catcher. This is particularly true at lower levels of play, where the pitcher is generally one of the better all-round athletes. The pitcher does have the shortest distance to move to get into cut-off position.

Cut-off position and technique are described in Chapter 11.

Pickoff

A first-base runner who takes a big lead on the pitch, or is not alert when returning to first after the pitch, is a candidate for a pick-off attempt. The first baseman steps back with the right foot, pivots toward sec-

Figure 6-5. Pick-off Attempt at First Base

ond base, executes a cross-over step with the left foot, and runs back toward first base. The eyes of the baseman remain focused on the ball in the catcher's hand; and the baseman's glove provides a target for the catcher's throw to the inside of the base line. As Figure 6–5 shows, at no time does the baseman's back turn completely toward either the catcher or the runner. The ball is clearly visible to the baseman at all times. The player makes the tag at the earliest possible moment, keeping in mind that the runner will usually head for the back of the base.

Some coaches recommend that the first baseman turn toward the first-base line and attempt to tag the runner by sweeping back with the glove. The disadvantage of this technique is that the baseman's back is to the runner, making him extremely vulnerable to a delayed steal. Also, an erratic throw to the glove side of the baseman will very likely enter foul territory down the right-field line. If this should happen, the runner may advance farther—to third.

If the catcher gives a pick-off signal, and the pitcher is going to pitch out, the first baseman may establish ready position a little farther back than usual. He may also move back as the pitcher delivers the ball to the batter, but that move may tip off a smart baserunner.

As a surprise tactic, when the first baseman is pulled in toward the plate in anticipation of a potential bunt, the second baseman may cover first, receive the throw, and attempt the tag-out. Usually a pitchout is called in this case so that the second baseman can break early to cover first and to cut the runner off. The first baseman ducks to provide a clear path for the throw.

Rundowns

The first baseman takes part in the play on a runner caught off base between first and second. The responsibility of the first baseman is to receive the throw and to apply the tag to the runner. If tagging is not possible, and the runner breaks for second, the first baseman should immediately throw to second and clear out of the base line so that no contact with the runner can take place. The runner is again forced back toward first, while the first baseman goes to the end of the back-up file at either first or second, depending on the procedure adopted by the team.

The first baseman also takes part in the play on a runner caught off base between third and home. In this case, however, the responsibility of the first baseman is to back up the catcher at home plate and to participate in the rundown, if necessary. The technique for executing a rundown is detailed in Chapter 11.

Tips for First Basemen

1. Check the fence before each game to determine how a ball will rebound off it.
2. Block hard-hit balls and stay with them, because an out may still be made at first base on the batter-baserunner.
3. Make the putout unassisted if you field the ball near the bag.
4. When attempting a double play (second to first) after having fielded the ball, throw to the infield side of second base.
5. Cooperate with the second baseman for coverage of first base in bunt situations.
6. If you have fielded a bunt near the base line, tag the batter-baserunner advancing to first base.
7. When fielding a bunt with runners on base, and when functioning as the cutoff, listen to the catcher's instructions as to where to throw the ball.
8. Use an underhand toss after fielding a squeeze bunt.
9. When catching throws, attempt to position so that your eyes look over the top of your glove or mitt, directly at the ball.
10. Get to know how each fielder throws and how his ball moves.
11. Anticipate an erratic throw and prepare accordingly.

SECOND BASEMAN

Area of Responsibility and Position

The shaded area in Figure 6–6 represents the second baseman's domain. The X indicates where the baseman is most frequently positioned, although situational adjustments will be made throughout the course of a game.

It is to the second baseman's advantage to position as far from home plate as his arm and fielding ability permit. By playing deeper he will have more time to react to the ball, will have a better angle to cut off ground balls up the middle and in the hole, and will be in better position to assist with pop flies. The distance from second base is fixed, to some

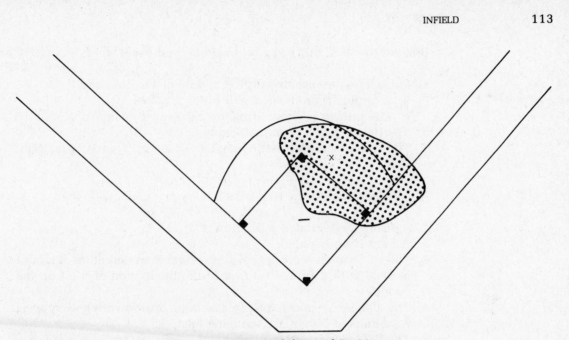

Figure 6-6. Second Baseman's Area of Responsibility and Position

extent, by the baseman's quickness, lateral mobility, and ability to make a backhand catch. If he positions too far toward first, he is likely to be troubled by balls hit through the middle of the diamond. If he stands too close to second, he may experience difficulty covering the hole to his left. Confusion may also arise between the first and second basemen concerning who will field balls in the hole, and first base may be left uncovered.

Generally, the second baseman moves *in* (toward home plate) under the following circumstances:

1. The infield is wet and soft.
2. A weak, but fast-running, hitter is at bat.
3. A bunt is anticipated, or a double play is possible.
4. A runner is on third with fewer than two outs, particularly in the late innings of a close game (option of getting the runner at home).
5. The fielder is slow charging the ball or has a weak throw, especially with runners on second or third.

The baseman usually moves *back* under these circumstances:

1. The infield is hard and fast.
2. A strong, left-handed power hitter is at bat.
3. A slow runner is at bat.
4. The fielder charges grounders and slow rollers well and has a strong throw.

It is advisable to move *right* (toward second base) when

1. More hits are expected up the middle of the diamond.
    a. A strong, right-handed pull hitter is at bat.
    b. The pitcher is slow, tiring, or throwing a change-up.
2. The fielder has a weak backhand catch.
3. The first baseman is left-handed and has good reach to his right side.

A shift *left* (toward the first-base line) is recommended when

1. A strong, left-handed pull hitter is at bat.
2. A bunt is anticipated.
3. The shortstop has moved toward second in anticipation of a bunt or steal with a runner on first or in anticipation of a hit up the middle.
4. The pitcher is exceptionally fast and overpowering—opposing right-handed hitters are swinging late.
5. The fielder has a strong backhand catch.

Characteristics

Forward, backward, and lateral *ranges* are important assets to second basemen, as they are responsible for most hits to the right side of the infield. They must be able to charge slow grounders, field short flies, catch pop-ups in shallow right field and behind first base, and handle balls hit up the middle of the diamond or in the hole between the first and second basemen. *Speed, quickness,* and the ability to get a good *jump on the ball* are characteristic of second basemen with good range.

Also characteristic of quality second basemen is *agility*—mobility, maneuverability, or the ability to effect quick changes in positions of the body and its parts. Agility is required to throw with appropriate speed and accuracy from a variety of positions while moving to the right of, to the left of, away from, or toward, the target receiver. It is also important when covering a base and when pivoting to complete a double play attempt.

A great variety of throws are required of second basemen, each depending on the situation and the purpose of the throw. An accurate, snap throw, with a *quick release*, is often more essential than a strong throw, as the distance between the basemen and their target is usually short. A second baseman's arm must be strong enough, however, to execute a double play and a relay throw.

Second basemen must frequently receive and execute throws despite potential body contact with an approaching runner. In such cases size is less important than *courage, aggressiveness,* and *agility,* which can compensate for deficiencies in physical stature.

Individual Responsibilities

Fielding Ground Balls and Line Drives

The second baseman should field most grounders to the right-field side of the infield. The only exceptions are balls hit to the pitcher and balls hit within a step or two of the first baseman. If the first baseman ranges too wide, there may be confusion regarding base coverage. We recommend, therefore, that the second baseman field everything except slow rollers close to the first-base line and grounders on which the first baseman can make an unassisted putout.

Executing Double Plays

Having fielded a ground ball with a runner or runners on base, the second baseman should make a play on the lead runner, if possible. For example, with a runner on first, the second baseman has two options, depending upon the relative positions of the runner, the bag (second), and the second baseman:

1. Tag the runner, perhaps with the aid of a preliminary fake throw to second, and throw to first. If the tag is missed, the ball should be thrown to second. If the runner leaves the base path, he should be called out by the umpire. The ball should be thrown to first. If the runner stops or retreats toward first to avoid a tag, the second baseman must remember that the lead runner is the primary target. The baseman should force the lead runner to commit toward first, and then throw to first to force the batter–baserunner. Subsequent action is a rundown play on the lead runner, who is caught off base between first and second. If the throw to first will retire the batter–baserunner, but will probably allow the lead runner to reach second safely, the baseman should throw to second and at least make sure of one out.
2. Tag second base and throw to first. By personally handling the play at second, the baseman eliminates the exchange with the shortstop, reducing the chance of error on the play.
3. Throw to the shortstop covering second base. Throws to a covering baseman for the start of a double play should be shoulder high. If the receiver is moving into position, the ball should be thrown a step in front of him so that he can catch it on the run

and before touching or crossing the base. A quick, accurate throw is essential to the success of the play.

Having fielded a line drive or fly ball, the second baseman should be alert for a play on a runner who is well off base and has failed to tag up, or who has tagged up and is attempting to advance on the catch. Quick action by the baseman could produce a double play.

When the ball has been hit to the left-field side of second, the second baseman covers second and serves as the *pivot* player for double-play attempts. The majority of the time the second baseman receives the initial throw while running toward second base. The baseman extends both arms toward the thrower, with the glove chest high and the pocket facing the thrower. The baseman should also set mentally by anticipating a bad throw and by placing his mind and muscles on alert. The last few steps that the second baseman takes before reaching the base are usually shorter and slower so that he can balance and prepare to shift in any direction, depending upon the accuracy of the throw. An early arrival of the ball allows the second baseman to concentrate fully on the catch before having to locate and touch the base. Timing is critical, and an accurate throw is necessary. Receiving the ball, between waist and shoulder height, along the path of his approach to the base, allows the second baseman to make the catch with both hands, and to maintain both stride and balance while tagging the bag and taking the ball back to the right ear in preparation for a snap throw to first.

The second baseman may execute a variety of pivots (turning movements that put the player's body in proper position to tag second and throw to first for a double play), but the most appropriate one depends upon the accuracy of the initial throw to the second baseman, the direction of the runner's approach (the second baseman must use a pivot that will prevent the advancing runner from interfering with the throw), and the time available for the play. Consequently, the baseman should not commit himself too soon to any one particular technique. Some pivots frequently employed to effect the force-out at second and to prevent the advancing runner from interfering with the second baseman's throw to first are as follows:

1. STEP-BACK PIVOT

Step on the near edge of the base with the left foot, but keep the right foot and most of the body weight back. Catch the ball at shoulder height with both hands. Immediately take the ball back to the right ear in preparation for a snap throw. Step back off the base to clear the base path to the outfield side of the bag, and transfer body weight to the right foot. Push off the

Figure 6-7. Step-Back Pivot for Double Play

*right foot and throw with a step toward first on the left foot.
Follow through directly toward first base. (See Figure 6-7.)*

The step-back pivot is usually used when the baseman is a little late
getting to the bag or when the ball is caught to the near side of the base. It
is also used when the runner is close and approaching from the infield
side of the base line. It requires a strong arm.

2. STEP-ACROSS PIVOT

*Step on the center of the base with the left foot. Catch the ball
at shoulder height with both hands. Immediately take the ball
back to the right ear in preparation for a snap throw. Step
across the base to clear the base path to the infield side of the*

Figure 6-8. Step-Across Pivot for Double Play

bag, and transfer body weight to the right foot. Push off the right foot and throw with a step toward first on the left foot. Follow through directly toward first base. (See Figure 6–8.)

The step-across pivot is generally regarded as the most desirable. It is also one of the quickest and easiest for most basemen to learn. It is used when the baseman is a little early getting to the bag or when the baseman catches the ball to the far side of the base. It is also used when the runner is close and approaching from the outfield side of the base line.

3. STEP-AWAY PIVOT

Step on the left-field side of the base with the left foot. Reach for the ball and step toward it with the right foot. The right leg checks body momentum and supports most of the body weight. Make a snap throw off the braced right leg, pivoting to the left so that the toe of the lead (left) foot points almost directly toward first base. Take no additional step, but shift body weight to the left leg. The throwing arm follows through directly toward first base.

This pivot is used primarily when the throw is wide to the right.

4. RIGHT-FOOT DRAG PIVOT

Step over the base, or base path, with the left foot—in the direction of the approaching ball. Make the catch and drag the rear (right) foot across the bag to a position in front of the left foot. Snap throw to first base with or without a crow-hop. (See Figure 3–8.)

This pivot is most often used when the ball has been thrown wide to the baseman's left. It is a difficult play to make. If it is necessary to leave the base to make the catch, the baseman should either tag the approaching runner or throw to first base for an attempted force of the batter–baserunner.

5. BASE-LINE PIVOT

Await the throw from a set position behind the bag, to the right-field side. Step on the front, first-base side of the bag with the

Figure 6-9. Base-Line Pivot for Double Play

right foot while making the catch, and snap throw with a step toward first on the left foot. (See Figure 6–9.)

This is one of the fastest pivots. Because the baseman's body remains in the base path, however, the pivot is used when the advancing runner is some distance away and there is no immediate threat of contact.

The preceding list of pivots is not all-inclusive. There are other varieties. Most second basemen find that one or two methods are easier and more natural for them, however. As a rule, they master at least two pivots—one to the infield side of the base line and one to the outfield side. Consequently, the approaching runner will have difficulty guessing where to slide in an attempt to break up the double play. By repeatedly practicing double plays, basemen can perfect pivots and throws until they become automatic.

The second baseman's pivot throw to first should be quick and accurate. A snap throw, similar to that used by a catcher, is recommended (see Chapter 5). If no play is possible on the back runner, the ball should be held. A nonproductive or unnecessary throw should never be made.

Team Responsibilities

Covering

Unless committed elsewhere, the second baseman covers first whenever the first baseman is unable to cover the bag. Assistance in covering first base may be needed when a runner at first is a candidate for a pick-off attempt, but the first baseman is pulled in toward home plate in

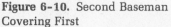

Figure 6-10. Second Baseman Covering First

anticipation of a bunt. Coverage assistance may also be needed when the first baseman has left his position, regardless of the position of baserunners, to field a bunted or batted ball. In the case of a bunt, the second baseman should break for first as soon as the batter's intent becomes evident. The baseman must be reasonably certain, however, that the bunt is not a slug. If the batter's actions indicate a potential slug, the baseman should remain in position until the direction of the bunt can be determined. If it is not within the second baseman's area of fielding responsibility, the baseman should move to first base as quickly as possible and set to receive a potential throw, as shown in Figure 6–10. The player places her left foot against the nearest side of the base, turns to face the thrower, extends a glove target, calls the ball in, makes the catch, and clears out of the immediate base area. The target is to the inside of the base line so that the path of the ball from the thrower to the receiver will not be bisected by the runner. If the throw is wide to the foul side of first, the covering second baseman shifts to the foul side of the bag or makes the catch while crossing the bag and clearing the base line to avoid contact with the batter–baserunner. When the first baseman calls for a fly ball, the second baseman may either call him off the ball and attempt the catch or cover first.

The second baseman covers second base when the ball is hit to the left-field side of second; when a play is made on a runner at third with back runners on first, second, or both; when the shortstop has called for a pop-up with runners on first, second, or both; and when a pitchout and pickoff have been called in response to a double-steal situation (runners on first and third). Some coaches have second basemen cover second on steals, some assign this responsibility to the shortstops, and others recommend that second basemen and shortstops share coverage responsibility—the second basemen take the bag when there is a right-handed batter, and the shortstops cover with a left-handed batter. We recommend that shortstops cover attempted steals of second because they are in better position to approach the bag, make the catch, and apply the tag to the runner. This arrangement also eliminates coverage confusion, particularly when the offense bunts, or fakes a bunt, with a runner on first. The second basemen know that they will cover first on all bunts, regardless of the position of baserunners. They also know that they are always the backup on straight and delayed steals.

A variety of ways to cover a base for a force- and tag-out were described in Chapter 4.

If no play is possible on a runner at second following the receipt of a throw-in from the outfield, the second baseman should be alert for a play elsewhere. For instance, a quick relay throw to first might catch the batter–baserunner off base if he has rounded too far or has turned his back to return nonchalantly to the bag.

Backing Up

The back-up responsibilities of the second baseman are extensive. They include the following:

1. Throws from the catcher to the pitcher. Backing up such throws is particularly important when runners are on base because an erratic throw, without alert back-up play, could allow a runner to advance. Usually, the second baseman shares this duty with the shortstop.
2. Throws to first base from the catcher or the pitcher or from the third baseman when he is close to home plate. Usually the second baseman covers the throwing angle to the inside of the diamond, while the right fielder covers the angle to the foul side of the first-base line.
3. Throws from the catcher or pitcher to the shortstop covering second.
4. Throws from the catcher to the shortstop, positioned between the pitcher's plate and second base, with runners on first and third and fewer than two outs.
5. Routine throw-ins from left and center field to the shortstop.
6. Relay throws from left and center field to the shortstop, if coverage of second base is unneccessary.
7. Hits to the pitcher and first baseman.

The technique for backing up is described, in detail, in Chapter 4.

Relay and Cutoff

When the ball has been hit to deep right field, the second baseman should move into position to serve as a relay, if necessary. (The technique for executing a relay play is described in detail in Chapter 11.)

When the ball has been hit to left or center field, the shortstop is the relay, and the second baseman either covers second base or backs up the outfielder's throw to the shortstop. Some coaches prefer to have their second baseman cover second because they believe that he creates confusion when he assumes double cut-off position in line with the throw. Three players (shortstop, second baseman, and cut-off player) would be positioned between the catcher and the outfielder making the initial throw. Other coaches recommend that the second baseman back up the shortstop. The outfielder's throw is to the first player out. If it is erratic, or mishandled, the second baseman is in position, potentially, to salvage the play. The second baseman can also instruct the shortstop, telling him where to throw and lining him up between the outfielder and the base to which the ball is to be thrown. The relay is free to keep his eyes on the ball and can concentrate fully on the catch. The double cut-off system is particularly recommended for use by teams whose outfielders lack the ability to throw with consistent accuracy to the primary relay. The second baseman must be alert to leave his back-up position and to cover second, however, when it becomes evident that the only play may be on the back runner. Failure to resume coverage of second allows the batter–baserunner a great deal of freedom to approach and to round second.

When the shortstop's arm is significantly stronger and more accurate than that of the second baseman, the shortstop may be assigned to make all relay throws. In that case, wherever the outfielder is when he makes the initial throw, the second baseman either covers second or backs up the shortstop.

Pickoff

A runner who takes a big lead on the pitch, or a runner who is not alert when returning to base after the pitch, is a candidate for a pick-off attempt. When the runner is on first base, the second baseman usually backs up the throw from the catcher to the covering first baseman. When the first baseman is pulled in toward the plate, in anticipation of a potential bunt, the second baseman may cover first, receive the throw, and attempt the tag-out. Usually a pitchout is called in that case so that the second baseman can break early to cover first and to cut the runner off.

When the runner is on second base, a pick-off throw from the catcher is rare. By breaking to cover the base, however, the second baseman may discourage the runner from taking a big lead and may even force him back to the bag. Occasionally, the pitcher may throw the ball to the covering second baseman, but it is usually a soft, conservative toss designed more as a warning than as a legitimate pick-off attempt.

Rundowns

The second baseman takes part in the play on a runner caught off base between first and second. The responsibility of the second baseman is to serve as the rundown player. This requires receiving the ball and running full speed toward the trapped runner, thereby forcing him to retreat toward first. Once the runner is committed to first, a soft toss to a receiver waiting at first base should result in a tag-out. If the runner fails to commit himself toward first, he may be tagged out by the second baseman.

The second baseman also takes part in the play on a runner caught off base between second and third. In this case, however, the responsibility of the second baseman is to receive the throw and to apply the tag to the runner. If a tag is not possible, the second baseman should immediately throw to third and clear out of the base line to avoid contact with the runner. The runner is again forced back toward second while the second baseman goes to the end of the back-up file at either second or third, depending on the procedure adopted by the team.

The technique for executing a rundown is described in detail in Chapter 11.

Tips for Second Basemen

1. As a rule, flow with the ball. When it is hit to the right, move right and cover second. When it is hit to the left, back up the first baseman or cover first.
2. Either back up or cover first base on all bunt attempts, regardless of the position of baserunners.
3. Talk to the shortstop regarding coverage of second when anticipating a steal of second or a bunt.
4. When possible, on a double-play attempt with a runner on first, tag second for the force-out and then throw to first without assistance.
5. Vary the double-play pivot you use so that the runner will have difficulty guessing where to slide to break up the double play. Consider the accuracy of the throw and the direction of the runner's approach.
6. Repeatedly practice double plays with the shortstop.

7. When making throws, keep the ball in view of the receiver at all times. Vary the speed of the throw, depending on distance to the receiver.
8. Occasionally break, or fake movement, toward second with a runner on second base in order to discourage the runner from taking a big lead.

SHORTSTOP

Area of Responsibility and Position

The shaded area in Figure 6–11 represents the shortstop's domain. The X indicates where the infielder is most frequently positioned, although situational adjustments will be made throughout the course of a game.

The shortstop, like the second baseman, should position as far from home plate as his arm and fielding ability permit. By playing deeper he will have more time to react to the ball, will have a better angle to cut off ground balls up the middle and in the hole to his right, and will be in better position to assist with pop flies. A shortstop who charges grounders well and has a strong throw can play deep when, for instance, a slow runner or a strong, right-handed power hitter is at bat.

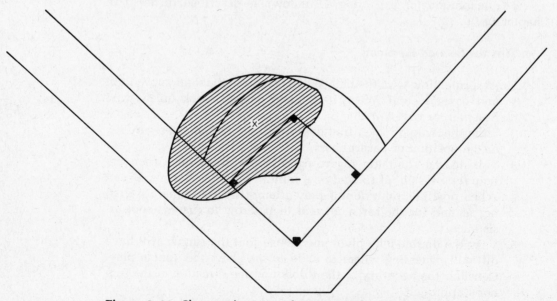

Figure 6-11. Shortstop's Area of Responsibility and Position

Generally, the shortstop moves *in* (toward home plate) under the following circumstances:

1. The infield is wet and soft.
2. A steal or bunt is anticipated, or a double play is possible.
3. A weak, but fast-running, hitter is at bat.
4. A runner is on third with fewer than two outs, particularly in the late innings of a close game (option of getting the runner at home).
5. The fielder is slow charging the ball or has a weak throw.

The shortstop usually moves *back* under these circumstances:

1. The infield is hard and fast.
2. A strong, right-handed power hitter is at bat.
3. A slow runner is at bat.
4. The fielder charges grounders and slow rollers well and has a strong throw.

In general, the distance the shortstop positions from second base may be influenced by variables such as the following:

1. *Power and history of the batter* (e.g., the shortstop moves right, toward third base, when a strong, right-handed pull hitter is at bat; the shortstop moves left, toward second base, when a strong left-handed pull hitter is at bat).
2. *Number and position of baserunners* (e.g., the shortstop moves slightly right in anticipation of a bunt or steal with a runner on first and second base and moves a shade left in anticipation of a bunt or steal with a runner on first base).
3. *Score and inning* (e.g., in the late innings of a close game, the shortstop moves right to cover the hole between short and third and to enable the third baseman to guard the line to a greater extent).
4. *Pitcher's speed and stuff* (e.g., the shortstop moves right when the pitcher is slow or tiring or throwing a change-up; the shortstop moves left when the pitcher is exceptionally fast and overpowering and when opposing right-handed hitters are swinging late).
5. *Personal strengths and weaknesses* (e.g., shortstops who don't have a good backhand catch shade right if they are right-handed throwers and shade left if they are left-handed throwers).

The location, toward and away from second base, is a compromise between two conflicting factors. First, the closer the shortstop is to second base, the easier he can cut off balls hit up the middle of the diamond, and the quicker he can reach second to cover for steals and bunts. On the other hand, the farther to his left he positions, the greater his vulnerability to a hit in the hole (between the shortstop and the third baseman), and the greater the necessity of a strong backhand catch and throw. Consequently, the distance from second is fixed, to a large extent, by the shortstop's quickness, lateral mobility, fielding ability, and handedness. Right-handed throwers usually position closer toward third than left-handers because the right-handers' backhand catch is in the hole. The backhand catch for left-handers is up the middle, so they usually shade a little more toward second. When a shortstop positions as far from second as possible, the third baseman can guard the line to a greater extent. This is significant when an extra-base hit would be particularly damaging.

Characteristics

Shortstops should possess many of the skills and attributes that characterize second basemen—*speed, quickness, agility, range,* and a *quick release.* Like a second baseman, a shortstop must get a good *jump on the ball* and be capable of throwing with appropriate speed and accuracy from a variety of body positions while moving to the right of, to the left of, away from, or toward, the target receiver.

Because shortstops frequently have to make long throws and, therefore, have less time with which to work than other infielders, they must have an exceptionally strong and accurate throw. Because of their great distance from first base in particular, it is unlikely that shortstops can mishandle a ball and still effect a force-out at first. Consequently, they must also be exceptional and *consistent fielders.* They have a lot of territory to cover, and they will handle many balls during the course of a game. Often, the shortstop is the team *leader*—anticipating plays, coordinating defensive effort, boosting morale, and promoting emotional stability.

Individual Responsibilities

Fielding Ground Balls and Line Drives

As a rule, the shortstop should try to field all balls hit between second and third base. However, if the third baseman can field a ball hit in the hole and throw with control, he should cut off the shortstop and make the play. The shortstop should back up.

Executing Double Plays

Having fielded a ground ball with a runner or runners on base, the shortstop should make a play on the lead runner, if possible. For example, with runners on first and second, the shortstop has three options, depending upon the relative positions of the runners, the bag (second), and the shortstop:

1. Tag the runner advancing to third and throw to first. If the tag is missed, the ball should be thrown to third. It will probably be too late to complete a double play from second to first. If the runner leaves the base path, the ball should be thrown to first. If the runner stops or retreats toward second to avoid a tag, the shortstop must remember that the lead runner is the primary target. The baseman should force him to commit toward second, and then throw to second to force the back runner. Subsequent action is a rundown play on the lead runner, who is caught off base between second and third. If the throw to second will retire the back runner, but will probably allow the lead runner to reach third safely, the shortstop should throw to third for the force-out.

2. Tag second base and throw to first. By personally handling the play at second, the shortstop eliminates the exchange with the second baseman, reducing the chance of error on the play.

3. Throw to the second baseman covering second base. Throws to a covering baseman for the start of a double play should be shoulder high. If the receiver is moving into position, the ball should be thrown a step in front of him so that he can catch it on the run and before touching or crossing the base. A quick, accurate throw is essential to the success of the play.

Having fielded a line drive or fly ball, the shortstop should be alert for a play on a runner who is well off base and has failed to tag up, or who has tagged up and is attempting to advance on the catch. Quick action by the shortstop could produce a double play.

When the ball has been hit to the right-field side of second, the shortstop covers second and serves as the pivot player for double-play attempts. The majority of the time the shortstop receives the initial throw while running toward second base. The last few steps that the shortstop takes before reaching the base are usually shorter and slower so that he can balance and prepare to shift in any direction, depending upon the accuracy of the throw. An early arrival of the ball allows the shortstop to concentrate fully on the catch before having to locate and touch the base. Timing is critical, and an accurate throw is necessary. Receiving the ball between waist and shoulder height, along the path of his approach to the base, allows the shortstop to make the catch with both hands and to maintain both stride and balance while tagging the bag and taking the ball back to the right ear in preparation for a snap throw to first. The momentum of the shortstop, unlike that of the second baseman, is frequently toward first base, thereby contributing to a more forceful throw. The pivot throw of a double-play attempt should be quick and accurate. A snap throw, similar to that used by a catcher, is recommended (see Chapter 5). If no play is possible on the back runner, the ball should be held. A nonproductive or unnecessary throw should never be made.

The shortstop may execute a variety of pivots (turning movements that put the player's body in proper position to tag second and throw to first for a double play), but most shortstops find that one or two methods are easiest and most natural for them. As a rule, the shortstop, like the second baseman, should master at least two pivots—one to the infield side of the base line and one to the outfield side—so that the approaching runner will have difficulty guessing where to slide in an attempt to break up the double play. The most appropriate pivot for a given situation depends upon the accuracy of the throw to the shortstop, the direction of the runner's approach (the shortstop must use a pivot that will prevent the advancing runner from interfering with the throw), and the time available for the play. Consequently, the shortstop should not commit himself too soon to any one particular technique. Following is a list of frequently used pivots.

Pivots to cross over base path to right-field side of second base.　It is recommended that the base path be cleared to the right-field side of second (1) when the runner is close and approaching from the infield side of the base line or (2) when the ball is received late and either over the bag or to the right-field side (to the shortstop's left). The specific pivot executed depends upon the preference of the shortstop and on his body and foot positions as the ball is caught. Usually, the right foot tags the bag.

RIGHT-FOOT DRAG

Plant the right foot just short of the bag. Step forward with the left foot, past and to the right-field side of the bag. Drag the right foot across the bag and snap throw to first with a crow-hop (Figure 3–8) or a drop shift (Figure 3–3).

RIGHT-FOOT HOP

Step onto the bag with the right foot. Hop off the bag to the right-field side of second, and simultaneously twist to the right until the tip of the nonthrowing (left) shoulder faces first. Land on the right foot and snap throw with a step toward first on the left foot.

RIGHT-FOOT STEP

Step onto the bag with the right foot. Step over the bag with the left foot, toward right field. Drop the right foot back behind the left, and twist to the right until the tip of the nonthrowing (left) shoulder faces the target. Push off the right foot and step forward onto the left foot in the direction of first base.

LEFT-FOOT STEP

Step onto the center of the base with the left foot. Swing the right foot behind the left and well to the right-field side of the body, while simultaneously pivoting to the right until the tip of the nonthrowing (left) shoulder points directly toward first base. Push off the right foot and step forward onto the left foot in the direction of first base.

Pivots to cross over base path to infield side of second base. Pivots to the infield side of second base are primarily used when the throw is wide to the infield side (to the shortstop's right). They are also used when the runner is close and approaching from the outfield side of the base line. Usually, the left foot tags the bag.

LEFT-FOOT DRAG

Plant the left foot just short of the bag. Hop to the infield side of second (toward home plate) onto the right foot, drag the left foot across the bag, and snap throw to first as the left foot continues forward in the direction of first base.

LEFT-FOOT STEP

Step with the left foot onto the bag. Push off the bag to the infield side of second (toward home plate). Land on the right foot, pivot until the left shoulder points to first, and snap throw to first with a step forward onto the left foot.

Base line. The right-foot drag and the right-foot step in the base line are the fastest pivots that the shortstop can execute. Because the body remains in the base path, however, they are primarily used when the advancing runner is some distance away and there is no immediate threat of contact. A left-foot-step pivot may also be used, but the shortstop is farther from first base when he releases the ball and, therefore, has a longer throw. This pivot requires a strong arm.

RIGHT-FOOT DRAG

Approach the base in direct line with the throw. Plant the right foot just short of the bag. Catch the ball, push off the right foot, and throw as the left foot strides forward (past the base and directly in line with first) and the right foot drags over the bag. Follow through directly toward first base.

RIGHT-FOOT STEP

Await the throw with the right foot on the center of the base. Make the catch and snap throw with a step toward first on the left foot. Follow through directly toward first base. Note: If it becomes necessary to evade a sliding runner, push off the left leg, jump into the air to the inside of the diamond, and swing the left leg back.

LEFT-FOOT STEP

Assume covering position as quickly as possible. Establish a balanced position for the catch and throw. Set about two to three feet from second, to the left-field side of the bag, in line with the approaching throw. Expect a bad throw and prepare to shift in any direction to make the catch. Extend both arms toward the thrower and provide a stationary target. Catch the ball with a hop to the right foot about a step behind the base (to the left-field side). Throw to first as the left leg strides forward and tags the base. Body weight stays behind the lead (left) leg and the bag, which serves as some protection from the approaching runner. The throwing arm follows through directly toward first base.

Team Responsibilities

Covering

The shortstop covers second base when the ball is hit to the right-field side of second, when the ball is bunted with no one on base or with a runner on first, and when the second baseman calls for a pop fly. Coverage of an attempted straight or delayed steal of second varies. The assignment may be given to the shortstop, the second baseman, or both. When coverage responsibility is shared, the shortstop covers when there is a left-handed batter, and the second baseman takes the bag when there is a right-handed batter. We recommend that the shortstop cover all attempted steals of second, because he is in better position to approach the bag, make the catch, and apply the tag to the runner. This arrangement also eliminates coverage confusion, particularly when the offense bunts, or fakes a bunt, with a runner on first. The shortstop also covers second when a play is made on a runner at first, and when the batter receives a walk, with no other runners on base.

The shortstop covers third whenever the third baseman is out of position, for whatever reason, and is unable to cover the bag himself—provided, of course, that the shortstop is not committed elsewhere. Assistance in covering third base may be needed when a runner at third is a candidate for a pick-off attempt, but the third baseman is pulled in toward home plate in anticipation of a bunt. The shortstop should also be prepared to cover third whenever there is a bunt, fake bunt, straight steal, or delayed steal with a runner on second, third, or both. Coverage assistance may also be needed when the third baseman has left his position to field a short pop-up, bunt, or hit, regardless of the position of baserunners. In these situations, if the third baseman is able to recover quickly enough to assume primary covering responsibility, the shortstop establishes a back-up position.

Techniques described in Chapter 4 are used for force-outs and tag-outs when covering either second or third base. Figure 6–12 shows the

Figure 6-12. Shortstop Covering Third Base

position of the shortstop when covering third and preparing to tag a runner who is approaching from second (straight steal).

Backing Up

The shortstop is responsible for backing up the following plays:

1. Throws from the catcher to the pitcher. Backing up such throws is particularly important when runners are on base, because an erratic throw, without alert back-up play, could allow a runner to advance. This back-up duty is usually shared with the second baseman.
2. Throws to the third baseman from the catcher or the pitcher or from the first baseman when he is near home plate. Usually, the shortstop covers the throwing angle to the inside of the diamond, while the left fielder covers the angle to the foul side of the third-base line.
3. Routine throw-ins to the second baseman from right field.
4. Relay throws to the second baseman from right field if coverage of second base is unnecessary.
5. Hits to the pitcher and third baseman.

The technique for backing up is described in detail in Chapter 4.

Relay and Cutoff

When the ball has been hit to deep left or center field, the shortstop should move into position to serve as a relay, if necessary. (The technique for executing a relay play is described in detail in Chapter 11.)

When the ball has been hit to right field, the second baseman is the relay, and the shortstop either covers second base or backs up the outfielder's throw to the second baseman. A double cutoff (shortstop backing up the outfielder's throw to the relay) is frequently used when outfielders can't throw with consistent accuracy to the primary relay and when no play on a back runner at second is likely. The major benefit of a double cutoff is that the shortstop is in position, potentially, to salvage the play if the outfielder's throw is erratic or mishandled. The shortstop can also tell the second baseman where to throw and can line him up between the outfielder and the base to which the ball is to be thrown. The major disadvantage of a double cutoff is that it might be confusing to the outfielder and the catcher to have so many players (second baseman, shortstop, and first baseman) in line with the throw. Another disadvantage is that second base is temporarily uncovered. If no play at home is possible—because of the speed or position of baserunners or because of the distance of the hit—the shortstop may be used to greater advantage covering second base in preparation for play on a back runner. He should adjust his position accordingly.

When the shortstop's arm is significantly stronger and more accurate than that of the second baseman, the shortstop may be assigned to make all relay throws.

Pickoff

A runner who takes a big lead on the pitch, or a runner who is not alert when returning to base after the pitch, is a candidate for a pick-off attempt. When the runner is on first base, the shortstop covers second. When the runner is on third, the shortstop usually backs up the throw from the catcher to the covering third baseman. If the third baseman is pulled in toward the plate, in anticipation of a potential bunt, the shortstop may cover third, receive the throw, and personally attempt the tag-out. Usually a pitchout is called in that case so that the shortstop can break early to cover third and to cut the runner off.

Caution is advised when considering a pick-off play at third, because an error will very likely enable the runner to score. When the shortstop covers, there is only one player (left fielder) in position to back up the play.

Rundowns

When a runner is caught off base between first and second, or between second and third, the shortstop cooperates with the second baseman for coverage of second. Usually, the player who gets to the bag first covers and the other player assumes a back-up position.

When covering second for the play on a runner caught off base between first and second, the shortstop should be the rundown player. This requires receiving the ball and running full speed toward the trapped runner, thereby forcing him to retreat toward first. Once the runner is committed to first, a soft toss to a receiver waiting at first base should result in a tag-out. If the runner fails to commit himself toward first, the shortstop may tag him out.

When covering second for the play on a runner caught off base between second and third, the shortstop is responsible for receiving the throw and tagging the runner. If the tag-out is not possible, the shortstop should immediately throw to third and clear out of the base line to avoid contact with the runner. The runner is again forced back toward second, while the shortstop goes to the end of the back-up file at either second or third, depending on the procedure adopted by the team.

When a runner is caught off base between third and home, the short-stop backs up the third baseman at third and participates in the rundown, if necessary.

The technique for executing a rundown is described in detail in Chapter 11.

Tips for Shortstops

1. As a rule, flow with the ball. When it is hit to the right, move right and field the ball, back up the third baseman, or cover third. When it is hit to the left, field the ball or cover second.
2. Charge the ball, set, and throw whenever possible. Otherwise, catch and throw in one continuous motion, quickly but accurately. Use as few steps as possible before throwing.
3. Keep the ball in view of the receiver at all times. Vary the speed of the throw, depending on the distance to the receiver.
4. Talk to the second and third basemen regarding coverage of their bases when anticipating a steal or bunt.
5. Cover second on a double-play throw from the pitcher or catcher.
6. When possible, on a double-play attempt with a runner on first, tag second for the force-out and then throw to first without assistance.
7. Don't try to throw around a runner—throw directly to the target receiver.
8. When possible, on a double-play attempt with runners on first and second, tag the runner advancing from second base, and then throw to second or first.
9. Vary the double-play pivot you use so that the runner will have difficulty guessing where to slide to break up the double play. Consider the accuracy of the throw and the direction of the runner's approach.
10. Be sure to tag an approaching runner at second to complete a double play that began with an out at first.
11. Repeatedly practice double plays with the second baseman.

THIRD BASEMAN

Area of Responsibility and Position

The shaded area in Figure 6–13 represents the third baseman's domain. The X indicates where the baseman is most frequently positioned, although situational adjustments will be made throughout the course of a

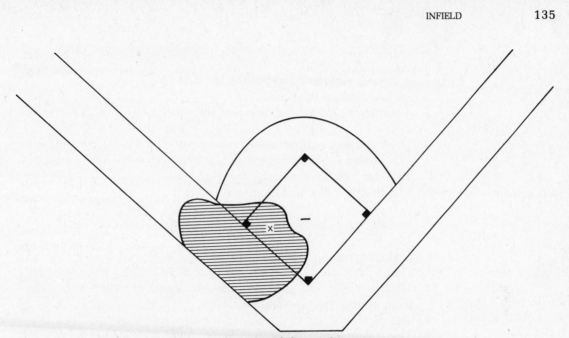

Figure 6-13. Third Baseman's Area of Responsibility and Position

game. The location, toward and away from home plate, is a compromise between two conflicting factors. First, the farther the baseman is from home plate, the longer it will take for a batted ball to reach him, and the more time he will have to react to it and to catch it. On the other hand, the farther back he is, the greater his vulnerability to a bunt or slow roller, and the greater the necessity of a strong arm. The distance from the foul line is fixed, to a large extent, by the baseman's quickness, lateral mobility, and ability to make a backhand catch. If he stands too close to the line, he is likely to be troubled by balls hit into the hole between him and the shortstop. If he positions too far away, he may experience difficulty in guarding the line. A ball that is hit past the baseman and down the line will frequently result in extra bases for the batter–baserunner.

Generally, the third baseman moves *in* (toward home plate) under the following circumstances:

1. The infield is wet and soft.
2. A weak, but fast-running, hitter is at bat.
3. A strong, left-handed pull hitter is at bat.
4. A bunt is anticipated.
5. A runner is on third with fewer than two outs, particularly in the late innings of a close game (option of getting runner at home).
6. The fielder is slow charging the ball or has a weak throw.

The baseman usually moves *back* under these circumstances:

1. A strong, right-handed pull hitter is at bat.
2. A slow runner is at bat.
3. A pitchout and pick-off attempt on a runner at third is forthcoming.
4. There are two strikes on the batter or two outs (a bunt is unlikely).
5. The fielder reads and responds quickly to bunts and slow rollers, but does not have a quick reaction time.
6. The fielder has a strong throw.

It is advisable to move *right* (toward the third-base line) when:

1. A strong, right-handed pull hitter is at bat.
2. The team is in the late innings of a close game (guard the line).
3. There are two outs and no runners on (prevent batter–baserunner from getting into scoring position).
4. The pitcher is slow, tiring, or throwing a change-up.
5. The fielder has a weak backhand catch.

A shift *left* (toward second base) is recommended when:

1. A left-handed hitter is at bat.
2. A right-handed, late-swinging hitter is at bat.
3. A right-handed, opposite-field hitter is at bat.
4. The shortstop has moved toward second in anticipation of a bunt or steal with a runner on first or in anticipation of a hit up the middle.
5. The fielder has a good backhand catch.

Characteristics

The proximity of the third baseman to home plate requires that the baseman be alert, ready, and exceptionally *quick*. Willingness to maintain position in front of hard-hit balls—and to *block* them *with* the *body*, if necessary—is an invaluable asset for any athlete who aspires to play the "hot corner."

Although third basemen must react and move quickly, running speed is not essential, as the area they cover is relatively small. They must be able to respond quickly, however, to bunts and slow rollers. Such response frequently requires charging, catching, and throwing in one continuous motion. To play their position well, third basemen must be capable of *throwing* with speed and accuracy from a wide variety of *set* and *off-balanced* positions and from the height at which the ball is fielded.

Sure hands and a *strong* throwing *arm* will allow third basemen to play deeper, thus gaining time to react to the ball and increasing their range. Height and size, though not too important, will provide a better target for outfield throws and a longer reach for line drives down the line.

Individual Responsibilities

Fielding Slow Rollers and High Bouncers down the Line or toward the Shortstop's Position

Whenever possible, third basemen should move toward the ball (charge) in order to reach it sooner, to select the best hop for the easiest catch, and to provide added time to throw out the runner. They should try to field the ball directly in front of their bodies, assuming throwing position as they pick up the ball. They can save more time by throwing from the height at which they field the ball.

Any ball that can be fielded by the third baseman with control and in position to throw should be played by the baseman, even if the catch must be made to the left, or in front of the shortstop. The third baseman will be moving toward first, so his approach angle will be better for the throw than that of the shortstop, who will be moving toward home. The throw is also shorter for the third baseman. If the ball cannot be fielded and thrown with control, it should be let through to the shortstop.

Fielding Bunts

Third basemen must learn to recognize bunt situations. For example:

1. Runner on first, no outs, weak hitter at bat, good hitter on deck.
2. Runner on first, no outs, late innings of a close game.
3. Runners on first and second, no outs, weak hitter at bat.
4. Runners on first and second, no outs, late innings of a close game.
5. Fast runner on third, good bunter at bat, close game.

The baseman should pay careful attention to mannerisms and actions of the batter that might indicate a bunt. Particular attention should be focused on the batter's hands and feet. Changes in customary grip (choke, split, or sliding of hands up the handle), stance (square-around), or bat position are noteworthy. When such cues are presented, the third baseman should move toward home plate, but must maintain body control. Charging wildly, and before the batter has committed to bunt, greatly increases the fielder's vulnerability to a slug or punch bunt.

All bunts down the third-base line are the responsibility of the third baseman. How far toward the left the baseman should range depends upon the fielding ability of the pitcher. As a rule, third basemen take what they can reach and play with control.

As the ball approaches, the third baseman should set in forward-stride position—right foot back. Weight is placed on the right foot as the ball is caught, and the throw is made with a step on the left foot in the direction of the receiver. When time is crucial, the ball should be fielded on the run and thrown overhand, or sidearm, in one continuous motion. An underhand throw is recommended only when the ball is to be thrown home.

Whenever possible, bunts should be fielded with two hands, as described in Chapter 2. If a bare-hand catch is necessary, the baseman should approach to the left of the ball and place the open right palm, with fingers extended at right angles to the ground, directly in line with the path of the oncoming ball. The ball is allowed to roll into the hand and is then squeezed tight. Because the ball is rather large for the hand size of most players, the one-handed fielding technique should be used only as a last resort and when the ball is almost motionless on the ground.

The catcher normally calls the direction in which the ball is to be thrown. If no play is possible at any base, and the ball is close to the foul line, it should be left to roll with hope that it will go foul. The wait cannot be too long with runners on base, however, as they may advance while the ball is rolling. If the bunt is clearly foul, it should be touched immediately as a precaution against its curving, hitting a stone or clump of dirt, and entering fair territory.

After fielding the bunt and throwing, the baseman must remain alert for possible reinvolvement in a continuation of the play. For example, when there is a runner on first and a bunt is fielded by the third baseman and thrown to first, the advancing baserunner may continue past second base and head for third. The third baseman must play the bunt and then retreat immediately to cover third base.

Team Responsibilities

Covering

The third baseman almost always covers third base. When out of position and unable to cover third, for whatever reason, the baseman may get help from the catcher, pitcher, shortstop, or left fielder, depending upon the situation. Assistance in covering third base may be needed in the following instances:

1. A bunt to third with a runner on first attempting to advance two bases
2. A fake bunt and steal with a runner on second attempting to advance
3. A tag or force play at third when the third baseman has left his position to field a fly or ground ball

In these situations, the third baseman may be able to recover quickly enough to assume primary covering responsibility. If not, the baseman should make every attempt to establish a back-up position.

The third baseman covers second base when the shortstop and second baseman both go for a fly ball and there are no runners on base, but this situation occurs very rarely.

A variety of ways to cover a base for a force- and tag-out were described in Chapter 4.

Backing Up

The third baseman must back up throws from first base to the pitcher. This backup is particularly important when runners are on base. An erratic throw, without alert back-up play, could allow a runner to advance. The third baseman also backs up the throw to second following a single to right field or right-center. The technique for backing up is described in Chapter 4.

Relay and Cutoff

Some coaches assign the third baseman to serve as the cut-off player on throws to home plate from left field when there is little chance of a play at third—for example, a single to left field with a runner on third base. This assignment frees the first baseman to cover first in case the batter–baserunner can be caught off base between first and second. Under all other circumstances, however, the first baseman serves as the cut-off player and the third baseman covers third.

Other coaches designate the first baseman as the cutoff for *all* plays. This eliminates potential communication gaps and coverage mix-ups between the first and third baseman, but it also allows a batter–baserunner to take a larger turn when rounding first.

Cut-off position and technique are described in Chapter 11.

Pickoff

A third-base runner who takes a big lead on the pitch, or who is not alert when returning to third after the pitch, is a candidate for a pick-off attempt. The third baseman steps back with the right foot, pivots toward the third-base line, executes a cross-over step with the left foot, and runs back toward third base. The eyes of the baseman remain focused on the ball in the catcher's hand. The baseman's glove is extended across his body to the backhand side, thereby providing a target for the catcher's throw to the inside of the base line. At no time does the baseman's back turn completely toward either the catcher or the runner. The ball is clearly visible to the baseman at all times. The tag itself is usually made at the earliest possible moment.

Rundowns

The third baseman takes part in the play on a runner caught off base between second and third. The responsibility of the third baseman is to serve as the rundown player. This requires receiving the ball and running full speed toward the trapped runner, thereby forcing him to retreat toward second. Once the runner is committed to second, a soft toss to a receiver waiting near second base should result in a tag-out. If the runner fails to commit himself toward second, he may be tagged out by the third baseman.

The third baseman also takes part in the play on a runner caught off base between third and home. In this case, however, the responsibility of the third baseman is to receive the throw from the catcher and to apply the tag to the runner. If a tag is not possible, the third baseman should immediately throw back to home and clear out of the base line to avoid contact with the runner. The runner is again forced back toward third, while the third baseman goes to the end of the back-up file at either third or home, depending on the procedure adopted by the team.

The technique for executing a rundown is described in detail in Chapter 11.

Tips for Third Basemen

1. Check the fence before each game to determine how a ball will rebound off it.
2. Touch your glove to the ground before each pitch. It is very important to stay low because of your proximity to home plate and because of the speed with which the ball often reaches third.
3. Block hard-hit balls and stay with them, because an out may still be made at first base on the batter-baserunner.
4. Whenever possible, get into good throwing position before releasing the ball. When time is not available, as when playing slow rollers, plant the right foot as you field the ball, and throw off that foot.

5. Talk to the shortstop regarding coverage of third when anticipating a steal of third or when anticipating a bunt down the third-base line with a runner on second base.
6. When a runner is on third, assist teammates by letting them know if and when a runner at third breaks for home.
7. Use an underhand toss after fielding a squeeze bunt.
8. On throws to third, the ball is your prime responsibility. A miss will very likely result in a run for the opposition. Go for the ball first, then the base or runner.

"AROUND THE HORN": TIPS FOR ALL INFIELDERS

1. Know the ground rules pertaining to play in foul territory and near fences, dugouts, and other obstacles.
2. Check your base frequently to know the relative position of the bag and to make sure it is properly aligned. Develop a mental picture of it.
3. When far ahead, or with two out, play deep and take the sure out. Guard the line, and try to prevent a big inning.
4. When the score is close and a runner is in scoring position with fewer than two outs, play in. With runners at first and third, play halfway (in the base line).
5. Wait until reasonably certain that the batter intends to bunt before fully committing to the bunt. A charging baseman is vulnerable to a slug or push bunt. When a double-play ball is fumbled, the best play is usually to first base for the force-out of the batter-baserunner.
6. Maintain a low ready position, and lean forward on every pitch. Be prepared to knock down hard-hit balls and to push off either foot, in any direction.
7. Keep the weight forward, and lean into hard-hit balls even if they have to be caught on a short hop.
8. Expend maximum effort to keep batted balls in the infield. By diving and knocking a ball down you may be out of position to throw and to effect a force-out at first base, but you can hold the batter-baserunner to a single, and you can limit the advance of other runners. You can afford to take greater chances when fielding batted balls, and are encouraged to do so, because you are backed up by outfielders.
9. When time is critical, field the grounder and throw from the height at which the ball is fielded.
10. Use an underhand or sidearm throw when time is critical or when you are near the intended receiver. Otherwise, throw overhand or use a modified (three-quarter) overhand.

11. A timely, accurate throw is the objective. Hold the ball rather than throw wild or late. When a ball is misplayed, rush to retrieve it, but control the throwing action.

12. Throws to second for the start of a double-play attempt should be approximately chest high, where the exchange from catch to throw can be made more quickly. If the receiver is moving into position, the ball should be thrown a step in front of him so that he can catch it on the run and before touching or crossing the base.

13. After fielding a ground ball with fewer than two outs and with a runner on second, runners on second and third, or a runner on third, be sure to check and hold the lead runner before throwing to first. A fake throw may be necessary to drive the runner back. If the runner can probably be picked off and there is adequate coverage and backup, make a play on the lead runner. If the lead runner is caught off and undecided about which direction to go, run directly at him and force the play.

14. With two out, play the ball to the easiest or nearest base at which a putout is possible.

15. Yield to an outfielder if he calls for a fly ball.

16. For force and tag plays (including potential double plays) move to a base as quickly as possible, set, and prepare for subsequent play.

17. When possible, approach a base in line with the throw. This places the covering baseman in the best position to throw or to otherwise participate in continuous play.

18. Clear the base path as soon as possible following force and tag plays.

19. When the throw to a base you are covering is wild or late, and there is no possibility of retiring a runner, rush to the ball, catch it on the fly, and be alert for a potential play elsewhere.

20. Call and wave off a relay throw from the outfield to the base you are covering when there is no chance of retiring the advancing baserunner. The relay player can then hold the ball and run it in to the diamond.

21. Watch runners rounding your base to be sure that they touch the bag. Also check a runner tagging up on a caught fly ball to be certain that he did not leave the base too soon. Appeal when appropriate.

7

Outfield

The outfield includes the left, center, and right fielders.

AREAS OF RESPONSIBILITY AND POSITIONS

The shaded areas in Figures 7–1, 7–2, and 7–3 represent the domains of the left, center, and right fielders, respectively.

The X in each figure indicates where the fielder is most frequently positioned, although situational adjustments will be made throughout the course of a game. Outfielder's positioning can be influenced by the following:

1. Hitter's tendencies
2. Pitcher's speed and pitch selection
3. Outfielders' individual and relative defensive (running, fielding, throwing) abilities
4. Game situation (number of outs, inning, score)
5. Environmental variables (wind, in particular)

Table 7–1 suggests how the left, center, and right fielders might adjust their positioning in accordance with some of these factors.

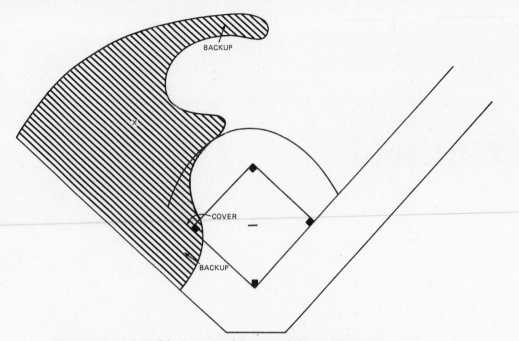

Figure 7-1. Left Fielder's Area of Responsibility and Position

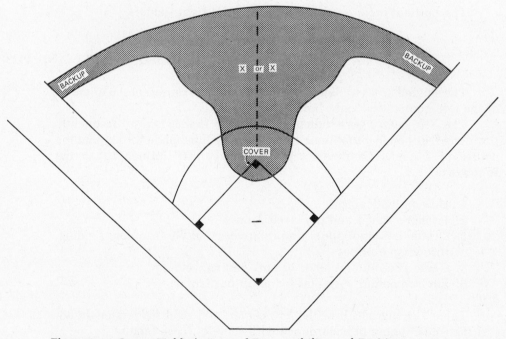

Figure 7-2. Center Fielder's Area of Responsibility and Position

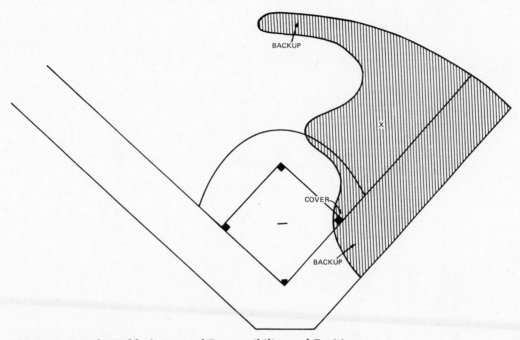

Figure 7-3. Right Fielder's Area of Responsibility and Position

Sometimes shifts are developed for specific hitters or teams. Usually, however, outfielders attempt to space themselves so that there are no outstanding gaps.

CHARACTERISTICS

Outfielders are the last line of defense. A misplayed ball in the outfield will very likely enable a runner to advance at least one base, and maybe more. Therefore, players chosen as outfielders must be good, *surehanded fielders*. They not only must be able to judge and catch fly balls, but also must have the courage to block ground balls, to field fly balls near a fence or other obstacle, and to stay in front of low line drives that may bounce before they can be caught. On occasion, a dive and roll may be necessary to make a catch or to stop a ball's progress.

Outfielders are responsible for a relatively large area of the playing field, and they must frequently run long distances to make catches. *Speed* is an invaluable asset, as it enables outfielders to cover more distance in a given period of time and to reach balls sooner. Speed can also help outfielders to compensate, to some extent, for faulty judgment.

The distance of outfielders from bases, and from home plate in particular, makes it imperative that they have *strong, accurate arms*. In some

Table 7-1. The Influence of Selected Factors on Outfielders' Positioning

General Adjustment	Left Fielder	Center Fielder	Right Fielder
In (Toward Home Plate)	Batter is weak hitter.	Same.	Same.
	Batter is left-handed hitter.	—	Batter is right-handed hitter.
	Pitcher throws low, or slow.	Same.	Same.
	Fielder is fast runner and good at going back for fly balls.	Same.	Same.
	Winning run is on third base with fewer than two outs.	Same.	Same.
	Pitchout and pick-off attempt on runner at third base is forthcoming.	—	Pitchout and pick-off attempt on runner at first base is forthcoming.
	Strong wind is blowing in toward plate.	Same.	Same.
Back	Batter is long-ball (strong, power) hitter.	Same.	Same.
	Batter is right-handed pull hitter.	Batter is pull hitter.	Batter is left-handed pull hitter.
	Pitcher throws consistently high, or fast.	Same.	Same.
	Fielder has strong arm, but is not able to go back well for fly balls.	Same.	Same.

Condition		
Shortstop has good range and handles deep pop-ups exceptionally well.	Shortstop and second baseman both handle deep pop-ups well.	Second baseman has good range and handles deep pop-ups exceptionally well.
It is early in game, and team is playing an unfamiliar opponent.	Same.	Same: however, must weigh these factors against advantage of remaining shallow for potential force play at first.
Team is protecting substantial lead in late innings of game; or game is close in late innings, when an extra-base hit would be particularly damaging.	Same.	Same.
Strong wind is blowing out away from plate.	Same.	Same.
Right (Toward Third-Base Line)		
Batter is strong, right-handed pull hitter.	Same.	Same.
Batter is left-handed, late swinger, or opposite-field hitter.	Same.	Same.
Pitcher is slow or tiring or is throwing change-up to right-handed batter.	Same.	Same.
Pitcher is particularly fast, and left-handed batter is not getting around on the pitch.	Same.	Same.
Center fielder is exceptionally fast and covers a lot of territory.	—	—

Table 7-1. The Influence of Selected Factors on Outfielders' Positioning (continued)

General Adjustment	Left Fielder	Center Fielder	Right Fielder
	Game is close in late innings, when an extra-base hit would be particularly damaging.	—	—
	Strong cross-wind is blowing toward third-base foul line.	Same.	Same.
Left (Toward First-Base Line)	Batter is strong, left-handed pull hitter.	Same.	Same.
	Batter is right-handed, late swinger, or opposite-field hitter.	Same.	Same.
	Pitcher is slow or tiring or is throwing change-up to left-handed batter.	Same.	Same.
	Pitcher is exceptionally fast (overpowering), and right-handed batter is not getting around on the pitch.	Same.	Same.
	—	Center fielder is particularly fast and covers a lot of territory.	Same.
	—	Game is close in late innings, when an extra-base hit would be particularly damaging.	Same.
	Strong cross-wind is blowing toward first-base foul line.	Same.	Same.

cases, however, outfielders can compensate for weaker arms by getting rid of the ball quickly. If they are fast and especially adept at going back for fly balls, they may even be able to position closer to the infield, thereby decreasing distance to target receivers and reducing the chance that their arms will be challenged. At the same time, they will be in better position to catch low line drives. Furthermore, they can field ground balls sooner, giving baserunners less time in which to advance. As a rule, outfielders play as close to the infield as their speed and fielding skills warrant.

Because their direct involvement in play is sporadic, outfielders must make a conscious effort to remain alert. Before each pitch, they should want balls to be hit to them. When balls are not hit their way, they should become indirectly involved by backing up or covering a base. When an unexpected throw is made or an error occurs, the alert outfielder is ready to respond to the situation immediately and appropriately.

Ideally, the best all-round outfielder (fastest runner; best fielder; quickest, strongest, most accurate thrower) should be in position to handle the greatest number of balls, to cover the largest amount of territory, and to make the most difficult catches. Before assigning this player to left, center, or right, however, the coach must consider a number of variables.

1. There is more area to be covered in center than in left or right field.
2. Balls that are hit to left or right field frequently curve toward the left or right foul line, respectively. Catching those balls is more difficult than catching those that are hit to center, which usually follow a more direct (straight-line) path. In some cases, the proximity of the fence to the foul lines also adds to the difficulty of left- and right-field catches.
3. One of the longest throws an outfielder may have to make is from right field to third base following a single to right with a runner on first base. A very strong and accurate throw is necessary to keep the runner from advancing more than one base on the hit.
4. A player who is particularly adept at fielding ground balls may be able to throw a batter–baserunner out at first base following an apparent single to right field. A strong arm and a quick release are essential, however, if this play is to be possible.
5. The majority of batters are right-handed hitters. As such, they are more likely to hit the ball to left or center field than to right field. Furthermore, hits to the opposite field (right for a right-handed batter) are generally shallower than those hit to left or center and don't require as strong a throwing arm to return them to the infield.

Some coaches consider the variables listed above and shift their outfielders accordingly. The advantage of this is that the best outfielder can be positioned where he is most likely to be needed, and the weakest outfielder can be placed where he is less apt to become directly involved in play. The major disadvantage is that left, center, and right field are unique in several ways. Differences between them are related to the following:

1. General field orientation
2. Angle the ball leaves the bat
3. Amount and direction fly balls curve
4. Relative position of target receivers for throws
5. Covering, backing up, and rundown responsibilities

Some players adjust quickly and easily to shifts from one field to another, but others experience problems. Usually, coaches who resort to shifting do so because there is great skill differential between outfielders or because injury or sickness makes change necessary. Traditionally, coaches place their speediest, quickest, and best-fielding outfielder in center; a very strong, accurate thrower, with a quick release, in right; and a better than average fielder, with a fairly strong arm, in left. Some coaches, however, prefer to place their stronger thrower in left field, rather than in right. The rationale for this is that the majority of batters are right-handed and hit farther to left field than to right. The right fielder, then, would be able to play shallower and wouldn't need the stronger arm.

INDIVIDUAL RESPONSIBILITIES

Positioning

The large area that must be covered by each outfielder makes it important that he position appropriately and get a good jump on the ball. As soon as the ball has been hit, the fielder should be off and running to the spot where he expects to catch the ball. In general, an outfielder is responsible for fly balls and for ground balls and line drives that get past the infield.

Because of the large area outfielders must cover, it is imperative that they learn to "play the hitter." This involves *shading* or moving toward the area where the batter is expected to hit the ball. For example, if a hitter seems weak, generally doesn't get around on the pitch, and doesn't often hit the ball very hard, the outfield may pull in (play shallow) and shade toward right field. If a batter squares around to bunt, each outfielder should move into position to either protect against a slug bunt or back up the play. An extremely powerful slug bunter, of course, will force the outfielders to hold their positions until the ball has been hit. Table 7–1 suggested how the left, center, and right fielders can adjust their positioning in order to increase the chance that they will be in the right spot at the right time to field a batted ball. A coach, throughout the course of a game, should constantly check outfielders to make sure they are in the best preliminary positions.

Fielding Fly Balls

Because there is a lot of outfield to be covered, each outfielder must start after every batted ball regardless of its direction. Special care must be taken to keep the ball in front of the body and to hustle after any ball hit overhead. When a fly ball is hit between an outfielder and an infielder, the outfielder always has the right-of-way because he is moving in to make the catch and has the ball and subsequent play in front of him. When a fly ball is hit between two outfielders, or past both of them, the fielder with the best arm (combination of strength and accuracy) plays the ball. If both outfielders have similar ability, the one moving in the direction of the throw should make the play. For example, if a ball is hit between center and right, and the ensuing throw is to third base, the right fielder should make the play, unless his arm is significantly weaker. Both players must continue toward the ball, however, until one calls for it. The other fielder then swings behind to back up his teammate and, if time permits, checks the infield to see where the play will be made.

With runners on base, outfielders must react quickly after catching fly balls. This is particularly important when the ball is tailing toward the foul line or when the fielder is running away from the infield. Runners often tag up and attempt to advance following such catches. When a long foul fly is hit with the winning or tying run on third base and with less than two outs late in the game, the ball should be allowed to drop if the runner is likely to score following the catch.

Throwing

Before each pitch, outfielders should anticipate what possible plays they might have to make. The fielders should check each baserunner and consider the speed of each when they project what the runners might do and where the ball might need to be thrown. By thinking ahead, outfielders will make the task following the catch easier.

If it is obvious that a runner does not intend to advance on the catch, the outfielder who fielded the ball should run the ball into the infield or throw carefully to a relay infielder who can then check the runner and run or throw the ball to the pitcher. Running the ball in forces the runner to commit himself, shortens throwing distance, and reduces the risk of error. Regardless of the situation, outfielders either *throw* the ball or *run* toward the infield with it as soon as they have made the catch and the ball is secure. Never should the ball be held when there are runners on base.

As a rule, outfielders should throw fly balls one base ahead, and ground balls two bases ahead, of the lead runner. They should make the play on the lead runner when possible; but if a putout is not probable, they should keep back runners from advancing.

If the play is a force, the outfielder should throw the ball so that the covering baseman can catch it between waist and chest height. If the baseman must tag the runner, the outfielder should throw low, attempting to *put the throw on the runner*. A low throw decreases the distance the ball must be lowered for the tag, saves time, and places the baseman in the best position to deal with a sliding baserunner. An outfielder's relay throw should be directed toward the receiver's nonthrowing shoulder.

TEAM RESPONSIBILITIES

On occasion, an outfielder may be called upon to cover a base. If so, techniques discussed in Chapter 4 will be employed. As a rule, the left fielder cooperates with infielders for the coverage of third base, the center fielder assists with coverage of second base, and the right fielder covers first base, when necessary.

As the last line of defense, outfielders are responsible for backing up all infield plays, including throws. They are also responsible for backing up their fellow outfielders. The technique for backing up is described in detail in Chapter 4. When not actively involved in making the play, the back-up outfielder can provide valuable assistance by calling out the base to which the ball should be thrown.

Outfielders also have responsibilities when a runner is caught off base, in a rundown. They either back up the play or actively participate in the rundown. (The technique for executing a rundown is detailed in Chapter 11.)

Table 7–2 summarizes the covering, backing up, and rundown responsibilities of the left, center, and right fielders.

TIPS FOR OUTFIELDERS

1. Be aware of the position of dugouts, fences, and other obstacles down the base lines, and know the ground rules governing foul-ball play.

Table 7-2. Team Responsibilities of Outfielders

Left Fielder	Center Fielder	Right Fielder
COVERING:		
Cooperates with infielders for coverage of *third* anytime the third baseman is out of position and the shortstop must cover second base. For instance, when a runner on first base attempts to advance from first to third on a bunt, the left fielder covers third if the baseman cannot recover in time to take third himself.	Cooperates with infielders for coverage of second anytime the second baseman and shortstop are committed elsewhere. For instance, on a bunt with a runner on second, the second baseman covers first; the shortstop covers third; and the center fielder must cover second. Covers second base on a surprise pick-off throw from the catcher (a rare play), with a runner on second.	Cooperates with infielders for coverage of first anytime the first baseman is out of position and the pitcher and second baseman are committed elsewhere. For instance, on a hit to left field with runners on first and second, the second baseman covers second; the pitcher backs up home; the first baseman is the cutoff; and the right fielder must cover first.
BACKING UP:		
Balls hit to shortstop and third baseman.	Ball hit near second base—to shortstop or second baseman.	Balls hit to first and second basemen.
Balls hit to center field.		Balls hit to center field.
Throws to third base.	Balls hit to left or right field.	Throws to first base.
Throws to second base from the right side of the field.	Throws to, or toward, second base from the pitcher, catcher, first baseman, or third baseman.	Throws to second base from the left side of the field.
Pick-off throw to center fielder at second base.	The catcher's throw to the pitcher.	
RUNDOWNS:		
When a runner is caught off base between second and third or between third and home, the left fielder takes a position behind the third baseman and either backs up the play or participates in the rundown.	When a runner is caught off base between first and second, or between second and third, the center fielder takes a position behind the second baseman and either backs up the play or participates in the rundown.	When a runner is caught off base between first and second, the right fielder takes a position behind the first baseman and either backs up the play or participates in the rundown.

2. Observe wind direction and velocity before taking the field, note wind changes, and plan accordingly when fielding fly balls or throwing. Before the start of each game, if possible, field some balls in outfield position and throw to bases.

3. Check the sun, background of balls in flight, and field conditions (effect of grass on the ball's speed, hard and soft spots, dips and rises) before each game.

4. Check the fence before each game to determine how a ball will rebound off it and how far the fence is from normal fielding position.

5. Run out to, and in from, fielding position between innings.

6. To warm up between innings, take a ball to the outfield and throw with other fielders.

7. The center fielder usually takes charge on most plays in the outfield. The degree of priority depends upon the difference between his skill and that of the other fielders.

8. With runners on base, charge ground balls.

9. The right fielder should be alert for an opportunity to field a ground ball and throw to first base for the force-out of the batter.

10. Block hard-hit ground balls and low, sinking line drives, particularly when no subsequent throw is imminent.

11. Keep in mind that fly balls hit to right or left field tend to curve toward the right- or left-field foul lines, respectively.

12. Do not backpedal to field a fly ball.

13. Get into set position to field a fly ball as quickly as possible. Do *not* drift under the ball.

14. Consider the score, inning, number of outs, and baserunners (number and position) when deciding whether to attempt to field a ball in the air.

15. With a lead in late innings, play deeper to reduce the probability of an extra-base hit. Play sinking line drives cautiously.

16. Attempt to catch balls in throwing position, on the move in the direction of the target, when a quick throw is necessary. Be sure the ball is secure, however, before attempting to throw.

17. Never challenge a runner. Return a fly ball to the infield as quickly as possible.

18. Run a ball into the infield whenever possible.

19. When fielding an extra-base hit, listen to the relay and to the back-up fielder for instruction as to where the ball should be thrown.

20. Throw low to home plate so that the ball can be cut off, if necessary.

21. Make the longest throw of the relay.

22. Back up throws to, and among, infielders. Be alert for a pick-off signal with a runner or runners on base.

23. Unless a pitchout and a pickoff are called, do not leave your position to back up a play until the ball has passed the batter.

THREE

Individual Offensive Fundamentals

8

Hitting

At the beginning of a game, each player is assigned a position in the batting order. Regardless of this position, however, each player will share equal responsibility for contributing to the offense necessary for a victory. Hitting is, after all, an individual skill. Once the pitch is released, the hitter is the only person in control of the situation. It is the hitter versus the ball.

ANALYZING THE SITUATION

While awaiting a turn at bat it is essential that the potential hitter analyze the situation. Consideration should be given to the following:

1. Inning and score
2. Number of outs
3. Absence, or presence and position, of baserunners
4. Defensive alignment
5. Pitcher's past performances (speed, stuff, control, best pitch)
6. Pitcher's performance at the present stage of the game (speed, stuff, control, best pitch, trouble pitch, operating methods, general placement, mix of pitches—is there a consistent pattern?)
7. How the pitcher threw to the batter in the past and which, if any, personal weaknesses were exploited
8. Selection of a bat to meet situational demands and objectives

SELECTING A BAT

Problems in batting are sometimes due as much to a poorly selected bat as to faulty technique. A properly selected bat should meet the following criteria:

1. *Length.* As a rule, the bat should be as long as possible without sacrificing control. It should also be of such length, considering the stance and grip of the batter, that the hitting surface of the bat covers all areas within and near the strike zone.
2. *Weight.* Greater momentum (weight of the bat times its speed) is possible with a heavier bat and a faster swing. The critical point is that the hitter must be able to handle the weight of the bat and control it to produce an effective, efficient swing.
3. *Shape.* The bat should have a fairly wide barrel, as that will be the primary hitting surface. The handle should allow the hitter to grip the bat comfortably and with control.
4. *Balance.* The length, weight, and shape of the bat will affect its balance, or distribution of weight. The position of the hitter's hands on the bat can also affect its balance. If the hands are moved closer to the balance point, or *choked up*, the distribution of weight will feel more even and control will be increased. Some hitters prefer to choke up on a long or heavier bat, while others choose to grip a shorter or lighter bat at the end. This is largely a matter of personal preference.
5. *Appropriateness.* The bat should fit the hitter's objective. If a long ball is called for, a large bat with a narrower handle may be selected for maximum leverage, force, and whip action. Some hitters will consider the pitcher's speed and will switch to a lighter bat for a faster pitch. Other reasons for switching to a lighter bat include weakness due to unusually hot or muggy weather; fatigue from several games over a one- or two-day period; and sub-par physical condition.
6. *Feel.* Regardless of the type of bat selected by a hitter, it must *feel* good. It must be comfortable to hold and swing, and it should give the hitter a feeling of control.

PREPARING ON DECK

While in the on-deck circle, the batter should become familiar with the timing of the pitcher's delivery and the speed of his pitches. The batter may accomplish this task by executing imaginary (dry) swings as the ball moves toward home plate. It might be helpful to time the pitch by counting to oneself, "one, two, three . . . swing." The count may begin with the start of the delivery or the release, but should finish in time for a swing that meets the ball in front of the plate.

Some players like to take a few dry swings with a weighted bat during this waiting period. Such a practice makes the bat to be used seem lighter, warms up the muscles, and may help the batter to relax. Aside from the obvious conditioning benefits of swinging a weighted bat, however, its contribution to the hitting act itself appears to be more mental than physical.

Batters' rosin should be available for use by those hitters who have problems maintaining a firm grip on the bat. Without friction between the bat and the hands, bat control will be difficult. Many hitters today choose to wear a batting glove on the lower hand or on both hands. The glove serves several purposes. It reduces the slippage problem of a player who sweats profusely and, subsequently, has a tendency to lose his grip on the bat while swinging. It also prevents blisters and calluses. In addition, it protects the hand by absorbing some of the bat-ball impact force, thereby alleviating the occasional, painful sting of the bat.

TAKING A POSITION IN THE BATTER'S BOX

Before stepping into the batter's box to receive *any* pitch, the batter should have a specific objective in mind—to hit, sacrifice bunt, protect a runner by swinging and missing, take the pitch (let the ball pass by), or one of a number of other options. Sometimes, the batter's objective and response to a pitch will be affected by the immediate objective of a baserunner. The batter should not attempt to hit the ball, for instance, if the baserunner is trying to steal on the pitch. Signals should be used to coordinate the individual actions of players.

Between pitches, the batter should step out of the box. This will provide an opportunity to reevaluate the situation and perhaps establish a new objective for the impending pitch.

The position the batter assumes at the plate is limited by the boundaries of the batter's box. Any batter who has his entire foot touching the ground completely outside a line of the box, or touching home plate, when the ball is hit, is immediately out. It is important, therefore, that the batter confine himself to the box. Within this area the athlete may move toward or away from the pitcher and toward or away from the plate.

Before deciding where to place the feet within the batter's box, the serious hitter will consider several factors. Probably the most important is timing. If the pitch is faster than what the batter is accustomed to, but the ball does not appear to move (curve, etc.), the hitter may wish to position toward the rear of the box to have a little more time to react to the pitch.

If the pitch is unusually slow, the hitter may wish to move up in the box to reduce the amount of time to wait before swinging. A second factor to consider is the pitcher's stuff. If the ball rises, drops, or curves, the hitter may move to the front of the box, hoping to establish contact with the ball before it has full opportunity to break. If the pitcher throws with speed *and* stuff, the batter must decide which of the two factors is creating the greater difficulty. If the speed of a riser, for instance, is such that the batter is completely off balance and unable to produce an effective swing before the ball has passed by, the fact that the ball rises is of little consequence. This particular batter might as well move to the rear of the box, take his chances with the rise, and try to increase his reaction time and movement speed so his timing is more appropriate for the speed of the pitch. If the hitter's timing appears to be good and the bat is in position to meet the ball, but no contact takes place, he should move up in the box. In other words, adjust to the speed of the pitch first, and then to its movement.

Another factor to consider in deciding where to position in the box is the pitcher's control and consistency. When facing a pitcher who frequently throws to the inside corner, some hitters choose to move away from the plate. Accordingly, against a pitcher who consistently throws to the outside corner, they will move closer to the plate so that the bat can better reach that pitch. The validity of these adjustments is dependent upon the pitcher's habits and ability to repeatedly throw to a given area of the strike zone.

Some hitters will adjust their position to cover a weakness or to exploit a strength. For example, two different hitters may crowd the plate—one because he has difficulty with pitches on the outside corner and the other because he believes the modification will permit more pitches to be pulled with power. These adjustments are not recommended. Frequently they create problems, and they may give the defense information that it may use to the batter's detriment.

In summary, position adjustments to counter actions of the pitcher may be effective if the pitcher is consistent and predictable. But if the pitcher has a variety of pitches or lacks control, such adaptations are of questionable value. Under those circumstances, it would be more advantageous to assume a constant position in the batter's box. The hitter can then learn to react to each pitch as it fits into a consistent visual image of the strike zone.

Most hitters choose to place their front (left) foot approximately even with the front, flat edge of home plate. They gauge their distance from the plate by gripping the bat with both hands and reaching over to touch the outside corner of the plate. From this position, a hitter can use a natural and controlled swing to make the fat part of the bat contact all pitches thrown over any part of the plate.

DIGGING IN

Most hitters will take a preparatory position facing toward home plate, with feet comfortably spread—a little more than shoulder distance apart. By adopting a fairly wide stance they will have a firm base of support and good balance. The rear (right) foot usually points directly toward the inside line of the batter's box, at a right angle to the pitcher. This position provides a solid base from which to push off and stride into the ball, and it also permits the right hip to rotate freely. The front (left) foot is often turned slightly toward the pitcher so that pelvic (hip) rotation will not be restricted during the swing phase.

A number of hitters place their right and left feet approximately equal distances from the inside line of the batter's box, on an imaginary line drawn perpendicular to the pitcher. This is frequently referred to as a *normal, square,* or *parallel* position. The front (left) shoulder and hip face the pitcher.

In a *closed* position, the hitter's front (left) foot is closer to the inside line of the batter's box, and the back is turned slightly toward the pitcher. A line drawn from the toe of the rear foot to that of the front foot, when extended, would reach toward right field.

In an *open* position, the hitter's rear (right) foot is closer to the inside line of the batter's box, and the hips are turned, somewhat, toward the pitcher. A line drawn from the toe of the rear foot to that of the front foot, when extended, would reach toward left field.

Hitters who swing late and have difficulty with fastballs or inside pitches might find that an open stance allows them to get their bat behind the ball more quickly and effectively. Hitters who tend to pull the ball foul may find a closed position beneficial. Generally, however, the position adopted by a batter is a matter of personal preference. Each batter assumes the stance that feels most natural and comfortable. Actually, when considering all aspects of hitting, how the batter digs in is not as critical a factor as the direction, length, and timing of the stride.

GRIPPING THE BAT

The hitter will be unable to produce force, and effectively apply it to the ball, without a comfortable grip that permits freedom of movement in the wrist joint. In addition, the grip must be firm, but not so tight that the muscles become overly tense.

One way to check for functional placement of the hands on the bat is to look at knuckle alignment (see Figure 8–1). With the fingers wrapped around the handle of the bat, the middle knuckles of the top (right) hand should be in a straight line with either the middle knuckles of the bottom

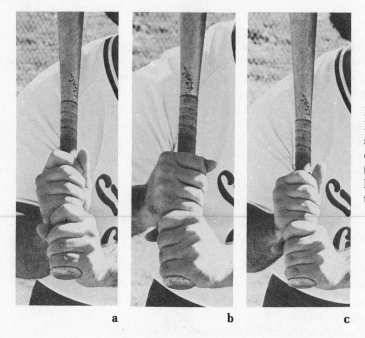

a   b   c

Figure 8-1. Knuckle Alignment: Middle knuckles of top (right) hand should be aligned with (*a*) the middle knuckles of the bottom hand, (*b*) the base knuckles of the bottom hand, or (*c*) somewhere in between those positions.

(left) hand (Figure 8–1a), the base knuckles of the bottom (left) hand (Figure 8–1b), or somewhere in between those positions (Figure 8–1c).

The bat should be gripped, primarily, by the thumb and the last three fingers of each hand. The index finger of the lower (left) hand may even be slightly open. The key point is that the pressure for the grip should be exerted by the fingers, and not the palms.

Where, along the handle, the hitter chooses to grip the bat will vary with the strength of the hitter, the weight of the bat, and the hitter's objective. A hitter with sufficient strength and the desire for greater long-ball (power) potential will choose to grip the bat as far toward the knob as possible. This *end* grip permits the hitter to swing the arms through a wider arc with a longer lever.

It is possible to compensate, to an extent, for weakness in the arms and wrists by gripping the bat about three to five inches from the knob end. This *choke* grip shortens the lever and places the hands closer to both the balance point of the bat and the anticipated point of ball contact. Power is sacrificed for control, and the strength requirement for an effective swing is reduced.

The *semi-choke*, or *modified choke*, is a compromise grip, with the lower (left) hand situated one or two inches from the knob end of the bat. The bat will be easier to control than with the end grip and will provide greater leverage, for more power, than the choke grip.

A few hitters use a *split* grip. They spread their hands slightly in the belief that this will further increase control and the possibility of a more level swing. This grip, like the choke, requires less strength for an effective swing. Most batters, however, place their hands so that they touch each other. When the hands are together they act as a single unit.

At first it may be necessary, especially for beginners, to concentrate and consciously work at placing the hands in a functional position on the bat. With practice and experience, the grip will become automatic. The position of the grip along the handle of the bat, however, will very likely be changed frequently to fit the batter's situational objective.

ASSUMING A BATTING STANCE AND PHYSICALLY PREPARING FOR THE PITCH

Having analyzed the situation, selected a bat, taken a position in the box, dug in, gripped the bat appropriately, and, perhaps, taken a few last moment half swings, the hitter is ready to complete preparation for the swing. The particular stance that the hitter will assume is dependent upon the athlete's size, strength, style, bat, objective, and personal preferences. Although no ideal stance can be prescribed for *all* batters, some fundamentals and common practices can be ascertained. These techniques are the same for right-handed and left-handed batters, but they will be analyzed for right-handed hitting only, in the interest of brevity.

As a rule, and particularly for beginners, the weight should be evenly distributed over both feet. By flexing the knees and hips and inclining the trunk forward slightly so that the shoulders are over the knees, the players center their weight on the balls of the feet rather than on the heels. Correspondent knee and hip flexion helps to maintain body balance over the center of gravity. From this position a batter can react quickly and is prepared to move in any direction to meet the ball.

The chances of a level swing will be improved by keeping the hips and shoulders level. The arms should be held fairly close to the body in order to shorten the radius of rotation of the bat, thereby permitting a more rapid, forceful swing. The arc of the swing will be decreased, but the bat will be easier to control. The arms should be far enough from the body to move freely.

The hands, as pictured in Figure 8–2, are usually held somewhere between shoulder and chest height, toward the rear of the center line of the body, and in toward the rear (right) shoulder. How far back will depend upon the batter's personal preference. Some athletes will hold their hands above the toes of their rear (right) foot, while others choose to gauge their placement as a little in front of, behind, or even with, the rear (right) shoulder. Regardless of the exact placement, both arms are flexed

Figure 8-2. Stance

but firm, and the wrists are cocked. The front (left) arm will necessarily be more extended than the back arm, and the forearm will deviate only slightly from a horizontal position. The elbow is lined up below the head. The rear (right) elbow and upper arm angle down toward the ground, but are still cocked away from the body.

Although the line of the bat may be anywhere from horizontal to vertical, the bat is usually tilted back over the shoulder about 45 degrees to the line of swing. It is held off the shoulder in readiness. The batter's head is turned to face the pitcher, the chin is tucked close to the front shoulder, and the eyes are level. Although there may have been some fidgeting or earlier bat movement, all is still as the ball nears the release point in the pitcher's delivery. The batter's hands, wrists, and forearms are firm and comfortable, but not tense.

In general, the batter's stance should be assumed as the pitcher steps on the pitcher's plate and presents the ball. Some adjustment may be necessary, depending upon how quickly the pitcher works. Batters must be set as the ball is released, but should not maintain their stance so long that they become tense or fatigued. A batter who begins to feel uncomfortable should immediately call time and step back out of the box before the pitcher removes his throwing hand from his glove. Some pitchers will intentionally delay the release of the ball in an attempt to gain an advantage—psychological, physiological, or both—over the hitter.

The batter's stance provides the foundation upon which a stride and swing will be built. Deviations from functional form at this point lead to compounded problems at later stages of the swing. The action the batter takes from the stance is critical.

ANTICIPATING THE PITCH

Sometimes a batter will attempt to anticipate the type of pitch to be thrown. Actually, most thinking hitters probably guess to one extent or another on more pitches than they might like to admit. Naturally, there would be no need to guess if a pitcher had only one pitch. As a pitcher develops variety, however, the batter's difficulties escalate. Timing becomes a problem. Most good pitchers today have at least a fastball, an off-speed pitch (knuckleball, slow curve), and a fast breaking pitch (riser, drop, slider). An educated guess, and a semicommitment based on that supposition, may be helpful to the batter in making necessary adjustments in timing and action. The batter must consider the situation, attempt to limit the various pitches that might be expected, and guess from there. Some examples of elements to be considered by the batter when using logic to anticipate a pitch are as follows:

1. A bunt situation (runner on first, nobody out). Be particularly prepared for a high pitch—the hardest ball to bunt—and keep the bat high. It is easier and safer to lower the bat for a low pitch than to raise it for a high one. Chances of bunting in the air are reduced.

2. Runners in scoring position (third, second & third, or first, second & third) and fewer than two outs, or a double-play situation. Be particularly prepared for a low ball, as the chance is greatest that it will be hit on the ground. The pitcher will most likely try to avoid a high pitch that may yield a sacrifice fly or an extra-base hit.

3. 3–2 count, or pitcher in trouble. Expect the pitcher's best pitch—the one he has the most confidence in.

4. 2–0 count. Again, expect a fastball or another pitch that the pitcher has confidence in. This is a good position for the hitter to be in because the pitcher will try to avoid, if possible, a 3–0 count, while the hitter can be selective.

5. 0–2 or 1–2 count. This is a difficult situation for the hitter. The pitcher can take chances and may waste a pitch hoping that the batter will go for it. The hitter can't afford to take a close pitch; on the other hand, the hitter must be careful not to go after a ball completely out of the strike zone. In general, the batter should

enlarge the strike zone and be prepared to swing at a borderline pitch.

In addition to situational considerations, the batter should pay close attention to the pitcher's habits and abilities. A pitcher who is having trouble controlling a particular pitch, for instance, can be expected to rely more heavily on other pitches within his repertoire. Some pitchers will move the ball around the plate in a fixed sequence. They may work high-low or inside-outside. They may even use one pitch exclusively to set up another. A change-up, for example, may always be followed by a high fastball. A studious batter may identify pitchers who are hesitant to throw a change-up or off-speed pitch with a runner on first and fewer than two outs for fear that the runner may attempt to steal. Others will never throw more than one change-up to a given batter. Some rarely, if ever, throw a change-up to the seventh, eighth, or ninth batter. Although most pitchers don't like to get behind in the count, some want to be ahead of the hitter from the start. The batter can anticipate a good first ball from this type of pitcher. In general, the more batters know about a pitcher's habits and abilities, the more apt they will be to anticipate pitches correctly, and the more successful they are likely to be as hitters.

Batters can also benefit from analyzing their own habits and abilities. For example, a batter who has trouble with a high fastball or a change-up can probably expect to see more of the trouble pitch. Similarly, a batter who tends to swing at bad pitches can expect to receive more borderline or bad balls. A batter who attempts to pull every pitch should prepare for a greater than average number of outside pitches. A batter who struck out on a particular pitch one inning might look for that pitch the next time at bat.

In summary, the ability to anticipate the type of pitch to be thrown can provide the edge needed to hit a particularly troublesome pitcher. Guessing right, however, is not easy. To be successful anticipators batters must develop and practice observational skills. They must study their opponents and the game so that they have a sound frame of reference from which to make educated guesses.

PREPARING MENTALLY FOR THE PITCH AND WATCHING THE BALL

The batter must react, both mentally and physically, within a very short time following the release of the ball from the pitcher's hand. Consequently, while in a stance and preparing for the pitch, the batter should attend acutely to those cues that he perceives to be relevant in enhancing his performance and should block out everything else. Cues may include the following:

1. *Position of the pitcher on the pitcher's plate.* Some pitchers change positions to create slants or to provide room for curves. They may also vary their foot position for different types of pitches.
2. *Presentation of the ball.* This alerts the batter that the pitcher is ready to deliver the ball and that the batter must concentrate fully on the task at hand. Attendance to this cue reduces susceptibility to *quick return* pitches. At the same time, however, when facing pitchers who present the ball for the full time allowed, the batter must guard against becoming too tense too soon.
3. *Pitcher's delivery.* Some pitchers have a variety of deliveries but can only throw certain types of pitches off a specific type of windup. Some pitchers vary the speed of the windup with various types of pitches (e.g., the windup for a change-up or off-speed pitch may be slower than for a fastball or rise). Many pitchers try to hide the ball as long as possible, and some may have distracting, elaborate windups that make following the ball difficult.
4. *Pitcher's grip on the ball, plus time spent assuming the grip.* At times, the batter may be able to detect different finger positions on the ball, or a different ball position in the hand. Knuckle and palmballs may be picked up in this manner. In addition, a pitcher may telegraph a particular pitch by taking more time to establish the grip. This happens most frequently with beginners and those who are just learning or experimenting with a new pitch.
5. *Pitcher's wrist action upon release.* Wrist action varies, depending on the type of pitch:
   a. Limited wrist action, a lot of white showing—change-up or knuckleball
   b. Inward or outward rotation, fingers on one side of the ball—curves
   c. Knuckles toward batter, little white showing—rise
   d. Palm facing batter, fingers behind and beneath the ball, upward action—drop
6. *Release point angle.*
7. *Ball's spin, speed, and path.*
8. *Catcher's body position, relative to the plate, and glove target (if they can be detected).*

On the basis of these cues, an experienced, perceptive batter may be able to determine early the type of pitch to be delivered, its speed, trajectory, and spin. This information is critical. The sooner it is obtained and processed, the earlier a decision can be made regarding the swing.

Beginners frequently attend to unnecessary cues or are unable to handle a number of relevant cues at the same time. Consequently, they may perceive the ball's speed, but neglect its flight path. In addition, it takes longer for them to interpret information, and their response is not automatic. For these reasons, beginners are often late swinging, and their movement speed is slow. The more speed the pitcher has, the more important it is to process information quickly, and the less time the batter has in which to decide to swing or to let the ball pass by. The ball is frequently almost at home plate before beginners are able to determine whether it will be close enough to the strike zone to hit. By the time they have sensed and perceived the speed, accuracy, and flight of the ball, and have responded accordingly, it is often too late. Some beginners occasionally give up attempting to interpret input and just swing where they think the ball might be, particularly if they sense that it is moving too quickly for them to handle. As a result, they will often swing at bad pitches, and their timing may be way off. Others may not swing at all.

Coaches can help beginners by initially exposing them to slow, straight balls and gradually increasing the speed. A light bat is also recommended because it can be swung faster. Those hitters who still have problems should stand at the plate, without a bat, and call out the placement of the ball (high, inside ball; low, outside strike) as it crosses the plate, or earlier if possible. The catcher can corroborate correctness of calls. The batter in this exercise is free to attend specifically to the ball's flight without responding to it. Later, when the hitter does swing, the coach can check the response by asking such questions as these:

1. Did the ball pass above or below the bat?
2. Where was the bat when it would have contacted the ball?
3. Was your swing early, late, or timed properly?
4. Did you see the ball move at all? What did it do?

Beginners can help themselves off the field by mental practice. Specifically, they can visualize themselves swinging at, and hitting, various pitches.

Another common problem of beginners is that they frequently start concentrating on the ball too soon. If the pitcher has a particularly extensive windup, they end up looking all over and moving their heads or blinking. A helpful coach might suggest that batters focus on the pitcher's belt during the initial windup and then shift their eyes quickly to the release zone as the pitcher's hips open up. By waiting until the pitcher has finished his excess motion and then picking up the ball at the release point—the small rectangular area shown in Figure 8–3—batters can prevent prolonged staring and blinking at an inopportune time; and they may also alleviate problems resulting from attendance to too many distracting cues.

Figure 8-3. Release Focal Point

While the batter is awaiting the pitch, his head should be turned to face the pitcher, chin tucked close to the front shoulder. Subtle changes in head position will take place to allow tracking of the ball from more advantageous angles. Basically, however, the head will remain stationary. The eyes are level and follow the ball as long and intently as possible. It may not be reasonable to expect the batter to see the ball hit the bat, but there is no harm in attempting to reach this objective. Batters who take their eyes off the pitch as they stride and swing will fail to see changes in the path of the ball as it nears the plate. These changes, of course, are critical. It will help batters to watch the ball longer, and to learn the strike zone, if they will follow *taken* pitches all the way into the catcher's mitt.

KNOWING THE STRIKE ZONE

Batters should not just watch the ball. They must interpret and evaluate the ball's position relative to the strike zone. Almost all good hitters know the strike zone and have a well-refined mental image of it. They increase their chances of getting hits by swinging at pitches that fall in the strike zone. They also know their own strengths and weaknesses. Many of these batters, for instance, recognize that they are better highball hitters than low or that they prefer inside pitches to those on the outside corners of the plate.

Smart hitters will be very selective with an 0–0 count. They will swing at the first pitch only if it is in their pet spot. If it is not, they will take the pitch. Once batters have one called strike or have swung at the pitch, they enlarge the pet spot and determine to hit the next pitch that enters the strike zone. If they fail to hit it, they have two strikes and must become defensive. Consequently, they expand the strike zone to include balls that are near enough to the boundaries of the strike zone to be called balls or strikes, at the umpire's discretion. This tactic is called *guarding the plate or strike zone.* It should be noted here that batters should try to learn the umpire's strike zone and use it as a frame of reference.

It takes practice and experience to develop a good "eye" at the plate; however, it will be very difficult to become a good, consistent hitter without knowing the strike zone and swinging at strike pitches. Weak batters who have a good eye for the strike zone are usually well advised to be picky. An exception is when the opposing pitcher has good control and can place the ball with consistent accuracy. The batter is advised, under those circumstances, to hit the first good pitch. Taking pitches can leave the batter in a hole. Once the batter is behind in the count, the control pitcher can waste pitches or force the batter to guard the plate and to go for borderline strikes.

If the opposing pitcher has questionable control (e.g., has just thrown a series of balls or has hit a batter); is in a tough pressure situation (e.g., bases loaded and fewer than two outs, or in a relief appearance and facing the first batter); or appears to be tiring, tightening up, aiming, or forcing pitches, the batter should certainly not help him out by swinging at bad, or even borderline, pitches. Some coaches will advise batters under these circumstances to take pitches until a strike is called. This may be good strategy if the batter is a weak hitter who has a better chance of walking than of hitting or reaching on an error, but more skilled batters might be better advised to simply be more selective. If the ball is not thrown to the batter's pet spot within the strike zone, it should be taken. If it is in the pet spot, however, a good hitter should be allowed to go for it. It may be the best pitch the hitter will get. In addition, the prospect of hitting will help the batter to maintain essential aggressiveness at the plate.

STRIDING

The purpose of the stride is to permit the transfer of body weight from the rear to the front foot in such a way that the momentum of the body, and the resultant force of the hit, may be increased. At the same time, body balance and steady vision must be maintained. Proper technique and timing of the stride are important if these objectives are to be realized.

As the pitcher releases the ball, the weight of the batter's body is distributed evenly on the balls of the feet. It is at this point that the stride begins. The front (left) knee, hip, and shoulder stay level but rotate in slightly, in a cocking action, as the weight shifts to the inside of the rear (right) foot. This cocking action produces more force by stretching the shoulder and hip muscles, increasing the arc of the swing, and starting the bat in motion. The placement of weight on the rear (right) foot insures, for the time being at least, that the body weight is behind the swing. (If the pitcher has a good fastball, or the batter has a slow swing, it may be necessary for the batter to initiate the cocking action during the late stage of the windup, rather than at the release of the ball from the pitcher's hand.)

The stride itself is nothing more than a low, gliding, slide step that is comfortable, *controlled*, and in the direction of the ball. The length of the stride and the placement of the front (left) foot should be consistent from one pitch to another. It is recommended that the hitter start with a fairly wide stance (at least shoulder width) and take a rather short stride. This technique will make it easier to control the forward motion of the body and to adjust the timing of the swing. It will also assist in controlling a tendency to lunge at the ball, and it will prevent an overstride that can lock the hips. Like the stride in throwing, this stride should be slightly to the left of the center line of the body to permit the hips to rotate freely through an optimum arc. (Many hitters, however, close the front foot slightly.) The front (left) leg, flexed but firm, acts to stabilize the trunk for final rotary movements in the last phase of the swing, thereby countering the force of the swing and keeping the weight behind it. Although the feet have been committed, the weight is evenly distributed and the hands remain back with the bat cocked.

SWINGING

The amount of force that can be applied to the ball at the moment of impact is determined by the velocity and momentum of the bat. Consequently, during the swing phase, the batter attempts to generate as much bat speed as possible without loss of control. A short, hand-wrist-forearm-dominated swing is essential in softball because of the short pitching distance and significantly short decision-making time. This is in contrast to the large, shoulder, left-arm-led baseball swing.

The softball swing begins (see Figure 8–4) with a strong inward pivot and push forward off the inside of the rear (right) foot, which turns the rear knee inward and forces the front (left) hip to open. The front leg, though perhaps flexed, is braced to withstand the force of weight thrust against it. The rear (right) hip pulls the weight into the swing as it thrusts

Figure 8-4. Start of the Swing

forward and moves through what will eventually be a ninety-degree turn. It also pulls the rear (right) shoulder through and produces a very powerful rotary action. (Note: The movement of the hips is critical, as they must lead the power thrust of the swing. Failure to use hip action in proper sequence, with proper timing, will severely limit the effectiveness of the swing and reduce the power input to what can be generated by the arms and wrists alone.) The hips and shoulders are still relatively level, and the lead shoulder remains in toward the midline of the body. The arms have stayed back as long as possible, although the bat has begun to level off, and the rear (right) elbow has moved down and forward, close to the body, to shorten the arc of the swing.

Suddenly, the front (left) arm extends from the shoulder, producing a longer lever for greater bat velocity, and pulls the end of the bat around sharply. The forearm remains *straight* and the rear (right) elbow continues to extend forward as the bat moves into a horizontal plane behind the path of the ball. (This sequence is important if the batter is to generate maximum force and to prevent the *handcuffing* effect that results from holding the elbow in close to the side of the body throughout the swing.) The hands have stayed back as long as possible, wrists are still cocked, and the bat lags behind the hands.

Both arms reach forward as the rear (right) foot completes its pivot. The shoulders, trunk, hips, and knee of the rear leg face the pitcher squarely. The upper segment of the rear leg is almost perpendicular, and the lower segment approximately parallel, to the ground. The batter will necessarily be up on the right toe in order to have freed the hips for maximum rotation.

Figure 8-5. Bat-Ball Contact

At the point of bat-ball contact (see Figure 8–5), the weight is taken off the rear foot as the center of gravity of the body shifts forward in the direction of the ball. The back leg may even leave the ground. The braced front leg helps to keep the weight behind the swing. The arms and wrists are fully extended, and the bat has whipped around to contact the ball in front of the body and the plate—ideally, at a right angle to the flight of the ball, with the swing in the plane of the ball. At contact, the hands and wrists are firm. This allows maximum force to be transmitted from the body to the bat and minimizes recoil effect. It also counters the pull of gravity and helps to prevent the head of the bat from dropping. It is the wrists that control the level of the bat, and at contact, the hands and the head of the bat should be on a line, with the top hand even with, or above, the level of the bottom hand. The line of extension of the forearm through the wrist and V of the thumb and forefinger is directly behind the bat in relation to the ball.

It is interesting to note that the wrists have not, as yet, rolled over. The roll takes place as part of the follow-through. Breaking the wrists too soon (before contact) decreases the strength of the impact position. The head has also moved very little since the batting stance was assumed. The head still faces the pitcher, with eyes level and chin tucked close to the front (left) shoulder. The head adjusts slightly to provide a better look at the flight of the ball, but, basically, the eyes do the tracking and the head remains relatively stationary. Turning or pulling the head out affects other parts of the body and alters the path of the bat, reducing the chance of bat-ball contact.

Ideally, all parts of the body that contribute to hitting will be brought into play in correct sequence, with correct timing. As a result, the speed of each succeeding part will increase until the velocity of the bat represents the sum of the velocities of all contributing body parts. The speed of the swing remains relatively constant, but the start of the stride and swing may be delayed, depending upon the speed of the pitch.

FOLLOWING THROUGH

Shortly *after* bat-ball contact, the top hand naturally rolls over the bottom hand as the bat continues its movement through the arc of the swing (see Figure 8–6). Both hands usually stay on the bat as it swings around and below the level of the opposite shoulder, to the rear of the body. Momentum will help to carry the rear hip and shoulder through. It will also help to carry the upper trunk of the batter forward, in the direction of the ball's flight, and onto or against the lead (left) foot. The head is still down, with chin tucked close to the front shoulder and with eyes fixed on the contact area. The amount of body turn will vary depending upon where and how the ball is hit.

The follow-through is an extension of the swing and prevents interference with it. When the bat strikes the ball, the total length of the body becomes a lever. Transferring the weight into the pitch and following through contribute to the use of the maximum length of lever. A vigorous follow-through is essential to reduce the diminished force possibility. The follow-through also provides distance over which to reduce the momentum generated by the swing, without counteracting its force and reducing its speed.

Figure 8-6. Follow-Through

PLACE HITTING

Batting techniques emphasized to this point have stressed actions necessary for the production of maximum force and speed. Whether or not maximum force is desirable, however, depends on the situation and the purpose of the hit. At times, it may be advisable to *place* the ball, rather than attempting to hit it over, or power it through, the defense.

The placement of the hit will be primarily determined by the direction of the bat at the moment of impact. Generally, the ball will rebound from the bat at an angle (*angle of rebound*) equal to that at which it contacts the bat (*angle of incidence*). Figure 8–7 shows how the timing of the swing affects the direction of the ball as it leaves the bat. Earlier swings produce hits to left; later ones produce hits to right.

Assuming that the ball is thrown at a ninety-degree angle to the front edge of the plate, with no spin, it is apparent that contact point *1* in Figure 8–7 will result in a hit to right field (an opposite-field hit); contact point *2* will produce a hit through the middle of the diamond (a hit straightaway); and contact point *3* will result in a hit to left field (a pull hit). Some deviation in rebound angle can occur because of the effects of spin and flattening as the ball and bat meet, but the effects are not of great consequence.

It is possible to place hit by altering the stance and stride. This is not recommended, however, as it blatantly signals intent to the defense, who can then make appropriate, timely adjustments.

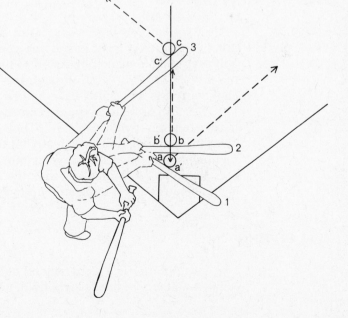

Figure 8-7. Bat Angles (*1, 2,* and *3*) for Place Hitting. Generally, the angles of incidence (*a, b,* and *c*) equal the angles of rebound (*a′, b′,* and *c′*).

OPPOSITE-FIELD HITTING

An opposite-field hitter is a right-handed batter who hits to right field or a left-handed batter who hits to left field. This type of hitter waits longer before starting the swing and, as a result, gets a better look at the pitch before committing to a swing. As Figure 8–7, swing 1 illustrates, the ball is contacted over the plate and even with the body, as opposed to in front. The right elbow remains close to the body, and the hands stay ahead of the bat. Wrist action is limited, and there is no roll. Some opposite-field hitters move their rear (right) foot away from the plate as the pitcher releases the ball and then stride toward right field with the front (left) foot.

Opposite-field hitters rarely obtain a lot of power because their arms are not fully extended, their wrists do not extend, and their follow-through is shortened. The arms are often brought into the body, which creates an inside-out swing. The shorter length of stroke and slower bat speed result in diminished impact force.

Perhaps because of the restricted arm action and the arc of the swing, opposite-field hitters are sometimes referred to as *push, punch, slap,* or *slice* hitters. They frequently use a closed stance and, more often than not, select a smaller bat with a thicker handle. A choke grip is common, but some batters use a split grip, pushing toward right field with the top hand.

STRAIGHTAWAY HITTING

A straightaway, or *spray,* hitter does not try to overpower the ball, but, instead, takes what comes and goes with it. Inside pitches will probably be pulled, outside pitches hit to the opposite field, and pitches down the middle hit right back through the middle. A medium bat and semi-choke grip are frequently used by this type of hitter.

Because of their flexibility and adaptability, straightaway hitters are harder to pitch to and strike out. They make the most of what the pitcher gives them and do not consistently hit to the same area. The defense must remain spread out, which creates more space in which to hit. For these reasons it is recommended that the majority of athletes direct their energies toward becoming straightaway hitters.

PULL HITTING

A pull hitter is a right-handed batter who hits to left field, or a left-handed batter who hits to right field, with power and often down the line.

As swing *3* in Figure 8–7 demonstrates, to pull a hit the batter *must* meet the ball well out in front of the body and the plate. This is absolutely essential. Otherwise, the arms will not be extended and power will be lost. The front hip opens quickly as the wrists and arms whip around early. Strong wrist action and a long, complete follow-through are essential.

Inside pitches are easier to pull than those that cross the outside corners of the plate, because the bat can get around on them better. For this reason some pull hitters will crowd the plate. Crowding is not recommended, however, as the hands may extend over the plate, necessitating an even earlier commitment to swing. Pull hitters will frequently employ an open stance to compensate for the longer arc of the swing. They also, more often than not, select a long, thin-handled bat and use an end grip for maximum leverage.

Pull hitting can be quite effective, particularly considering the shorter distances down the foul lines to the fence. It is not wise, however, to try to pull all pitches. Not only would that tactic be extremely difficult, but it would also help the pitcher plan an opposing strategy, since it would be a consistent, predictable, offensive approach. It would make defensive adjustments easier, too.

GETTING OUT OF THE WAY OF A PITCH

Assuming that the batter must take some action to avoid being hit by the ball, a general rule to follow is to roll with, but away from, the pitch. This movement will help to absorb some of the impact and will place the back of the shoulder, trunk, and hip in line with the ball should contact be unavoidable. The head should be bent down to the rear. The bat should be dropped to eliminate the off chance that the ball might hit it.

A HITTING SLUMP

A *hitting slump* is a relative term that can be defined as a marked or sustained decline in the expected level of performance. Failure to meet expectations frequently leads to frustration, but for a hitter a slump is difficult to avoid from time to time. Coaches should be aware that any slump, whether perceived as such by the coach or by the athlete, can lead to anxiety. The amount of anxiety associated with the slump will depend on its significance to the individual. It will also depend, to a great extent, on the way in which the situation is handled. For example, a hitter may use good technique and hit the ball extremely well, but still go 0 for 4. Such a hitter may become anxious. In dealing with this case the coach must not only pay attention to the player's technique, but also be aware of his attitude. The athlete may simply need a little encouragement and positive reinforcement. It would be premature, at this time, for the coach to place pressure on the athlete and reinforce his doubts and waning confidence by changing his position in the line-up or by benching him. If the decline continues, the coach should reanalyze the batter's technique to be sure there is nothing mechanically wrong. The coach may note that quite frequently the batter's swing is sound, but he isn't watching the ball closely enough. If that is the case, the batter might well benefit from emphasizing good bat-ball contact. Some extra bunting practice might also help.

Comments to a slumping athlete should always be constructive and useful. Such common statements as "Just keep trying," "They just didn't fall right," "Slumps don't last long, you'll get some breaks soon," "Keep swinging," "It'll come back," "You're due for a hit," are sympathetic, but provide no direction for the athlete. A more productive statement might take the following form: "You're not getting your bat out in front of the plate. Attack the ball! Start forward as the pitcher releases the ball. You're keeping your chin tucked nicely. Keep it there. Good!" Such a statement identifies a fault, provides a correction, and ends with approval for a positive response. It reminds the athlete that he is doing some things right.

If there is nothing basically wrong with a slumping batter's technique, it may still be helpful for the coach to suggest a slight change—for example, using a different bat. The athlete then knows that at least something is being done to help. If there are some technique breaks, the coach should determine the most significant fault and key on its correction. The coach should not attempt, or permit the player to attempt, wholesale changes in style and technique. Too many suggestions and alterations can lead to "paralysis by analysis."

If a slump becomes severe and the player is frustrated and confused, it might help to give him some time off or to place emphasis on some aspect of the player's game other than hitting. If it becomes necessary to remove him from the line-up, the coach should emphasize that the action is not a punishment but a temporary tactic designed to give the athlete a chance to rest, to engage in some mental practice, and to forget some of the details that may be interfering with a "feel" for the skill.

Patience, time, and directed practice are usually the keys in helping an athlete overcome a slump. Expressions of confidence and faith in the player's ability are also extremely important. The coach should encourage the athlete to remember his good hitting days—the positive moments when everything seemed right—and to strive to reproduce the techniques that contributed to past successes. Positive thinking is proper thinking when in a slump.

9

Bunting

Bunts are used to advance or protect runners, to influence the defense, or to get on base. A properly executed bunt is a useful and sometimes devastating offensive weapon.

Although the devastating effects of bunts are most visible at elementary levels of play, various types can be used to keep even the more advanced defensive players off balance. The name of each bunt describes its salient feature or specifies its function. There are seven types: sacrifice, surprise, push, slug (also called swinging, slash, slap, or punch), drag, knob, and fake.

SACRIFICE

A sacrifice bunt (Figure 9–1) is used to advance a runner or runners from one base to another at the anticipated expense of the batter. It is customarily employed when there are no outs and a weak batter is at the plate, when the score is close, or when a successful bunt will put a runner or runners in scoring position. It is, of course, not the only technique used to advance runners, but it is a relatively safe way to avoid a force-out at the advance base or a double play. All fast-pitch softball players should be able to *lay down* a sacrifice bunt.

a   b   c

Figure 9–1. Sacrifice Bunt

Assuming Bunting Position

Figure 9–1c illustrates the *squared-around* sacrifice bunt technique. The feet of the sacrifice bunter are in side-stride position. The toes may be turned slightly outward for increased lateral mobility, but they are in line with each other and at least shoulder width apart for good balance and stability. The knees flex, and the trunk inclines forward, toward the pitcher, placing the weight slightly forward, on the balls of both feet. The feet are clearly within the lines of the batter's box and remain stationary. They should be well in front of the plate to lessen the chance of a foul ball and to decrease running distance to first base. There will be no stride or transfer of weight forward.

The left and right hands of the bunter are separated from each other, thus shortening the lever, decreasing force, and increasing bat control. The left hand is in its normal ready-to-hit position on the bat, except that the back of the hand is on top of the bat and the palm faces directly toward the ground. The right hand has slid up the handle until it is about fifteen inches from the knob, close to the trademark. The thumb is on top; the fingers are underneath so that a V is formed between the thumb and

Figure 9-2. Standard Grip

the index finger; and the fleshy part of the palm is behind the bat, in line with the ball's approach. As shown in Figure 9–2, the fingers are *not* exposed to the approaching ball. The thumb and last two fingers of the left, or control, hand grip the bat rather firmly while the thumb and first two fingers of the right hand hold the bat loosely. It is very important that the grip of the top (right) hand be relaxed in order to maximize the recoil effect at impact and to absorb as much of the ball's force as possible.

Some bunters prefer an alternate grip with the right hand. It is the thumb-up grip shown in Figure 9–3, with the bat resting on the platform set by the clenched fingers. The bat is held in place by pressure from the

Figure 9-3. Thumb-Up Grip

thumb on top of the bat. This grip provides more surface area for bat-ball contact and protects the fingers to a greater extent than the more traditional grip. The force of impact will be withstood primarily by the thumb, however, rather than the fleshy part of the palm.

The elbows are partially flexed, but extended enough to hold the bat well out in front of the body and home plate. The bat itself is held level, at shoulder height, to protect against high pitches. (A bunter who holds the bat low will have to move it upward for a high pitch and will be more apt to pop up. It is easier, quicker, and safer to bend the knees and drop the bat down from the top of the strike zone into the path of the ball, as necessary.)

The bunter's head faces the pitcher, and the eyes are level. The ball is first sighted along the top edge of the bat, and it is tracked closely and intently from the point of release to contact. No ball above the level of the bat should be bunted, as it will be a ball.

The stance for the bunt is assumed when the batter enters the box or as the pitcher presents the ball. It is basically a pre-set position, with no backswing. The head remains still. This stance assures that the batter will be ready, balanced, and able to devote full attention to the speed and flight of the ball as it approaches. The batter need only determine the accuracy of the pitch so that appropriate body adjustments can be made for bat-ball contact—for example, bending the knees to lower the body and bat into the path of the approaching ball, should it be thrown below shoulder height.

The squared-around stance is a comfortable, set position with good coverage of the plate. It does not, however, enable the bunter to get out of the batter's box quickly. It is also a completely overt sacrifice bunt technique that clearly reveals to the defense the objective and intent of the batter. Most teams know anyway, however, when a sacrifice bunt is in order, and they prepare accordingly. A well-executed bunt will still place pressure on the defense and make the play to the advance base difficult. The bunter hopes to place the ball on the ground in fair territory so that the throw must be made to first.

Once the squared-around, or pre-set, sacrifice bunt technique has been mastered, the batter may maintain the ready-to-hit position longer, shifting into the bunting stance with the release of the ball from the pitcher's hand. By waiting until the last possible moment before assuming a sacrifice-bunt stance, the batter may prevent the defense from charging as early and freely as they might with the squared-around stance. The opposition may still expect a bunt, but the fractions of a second gained can be extremely valuable and may make the difference between a force-out at second and the anticipated sacrifice-out at first, particularly with a slower runner on base. Among the techniques for shifting into the bunting stance are the following:

1. *Drop step.* This technique basically involves a step back away from the plate with the rear (right) foot. At the same time the knees bend slightly; the right hand slides up the barrel of the bat and pushes forward slightly; and the left hand lifts the knob of the bat up and in toward the armpit so that the head of the bat points toward first.

2. *Pivot-in-tracks,* or *semi-square-around.* This shifting technique basically involves squaring the upper body, but leaving the feet in place. At the last possible moment the batter pivots on the ball of the rear (right) foot and the heel of the front (left) foot so that the head, shoulders, and hips directly face the pitcher. It is possible to raise the heels and pivot on the balls of both feet simultaneously, but this technique provides a less stable base and is not recommended.

Determining Bat Angle

Regardless of how the batter gets into bunting position, just before contact the angle of the bat must be set to give the desired direction to the ball. Theoretically, the ball will rebound from the bat at an angle equal to that at which it contacts the bat. If the batter holds the bat square to the pitcher, the ball will rebound directly back toward the pitcher. This is not usually a desirable tactic, however, unless the pitcher is a very poor fielder, has an injury that severely limits mobility, or has a consistently erratic throw to the bases. More often, the bunter will choose to direct the ball down the foul lines or midway between the lines and the pitcher. By

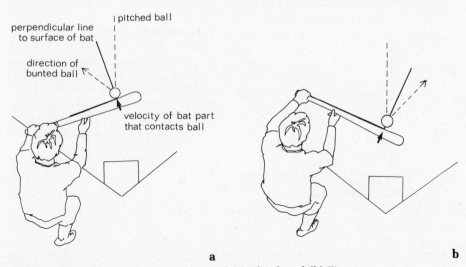

Figure 9-4. Bat Angles to Bunt toward (*a*) Third and (*b*) First

keeping the top (right) arm extended and pulling toward the body with the bottom (left) hand so that the left elbow is nearer the body, the batter will keep the fat end of the bat closer to the pitcher, and the ball will rebound toward third. Reversing this position, so that the bottom (left) hand pushes forward, will place the knob closer to the pitcher than the fat end of the bat, and the ball will rebound toward first. In both cases the bottom (left) hand is the control, while the top (right) hand maintains its position and keeps the bat level. These two positions are illustrated in Figure 9–4.

The mistake that many players make is to face the hitting surface of the bat in the direction they want the ball to go. For instance, when attempting to bunt down the third-base line, such players hold the bat at an angle approaching ninety degrees to the base line. Such a practice results in a foul ball.

The angle necessary to bunt down third is really much less than many realize. According to Bunn, "To bat the ball in a given direction, the bat should be held so that, when it meets the ball, it makes an angle with the front edge of the plate which is equal to one-half the angle formed by the line made by the thrown ball with the line of the intended direction of flight."[*] Assuming that the ball is thrown at a right angle to the front edge of the plate (Figure 9–5), a 22½-degree angle is sufficient to lay the ball down the base line. In actual practice, the angle is less in order to allow for the movement of the bat and the spin of the ball. The angle is further

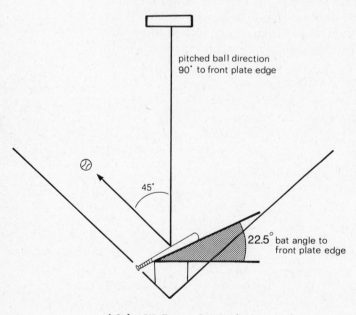

pitched ball direction
90° to front plate edge

45°

22.5° bat angle to
front plate edge

Figure 9-5. Angle to Hold Bat to Bunt Down Third-Base Line when Ball Is Delivered at Right Angles to Front Edge of Plate (John W. Bunn, *Scientific Principles of Coaching*, 2nd edition, © 1972, p. 176. Adapted by permission of Prentice-Hall, Inc., Englewood Cliffs, New Jersey.)

* John W. Bunn, *Scientific Principles of Coaching*, 2nd ed. (Englewood Cliffs, N. J.: Prentice-Hall, 1972), p. 177.

decreased if the batter chooses to place the ball between the pitcher and the base line.

Making Contact

At contact, the force of the ball is absorbed by *giving* or flexing the elbows, and allowing the bat to recoil closer to the body. In a sense, the bat is used to catch the ball. By regulating the amount of give, the player controls the distance the ball will rebound. Against a faster pitcher, more force has to be absorbed. Under some conditions—an extremely wet and sticky field, for instance—the bat may be allowed to meet the ball with no give at all.

Another technique that may be used to absorb bat-ball impact force is to grip the bat loosely with the fingertips of the right hand and to allow the force of the ball to drive the bat back into the fleshy part of the palm. The advantage of this method is that the bat is held stationary in the path of the approaching ball, well out in front of the body. The possibility that the bat may be raised or lowered during the give is minimized, as is the need to time the give. The force is absorbed over a shorter distance, however, and is more difficult to control. In general, the firmer the grip, the sharper the rebound.

Figure 9-6. Surprise Bunt

SURPRISE

The surprise bunt (Figure 9–6) is similar to a sacrifice except that the batter waits until the last possible moment to bring the bat out in front. One of the pivot shifts is usually employed in order to hide the bunt as long as possible. The pivot-in-tracks is recommended because of its speed, deceptiveness, and more advantageous positioning for running toward first base. This bunt is used primarily by right-handed hitters, to obtain a base hit.

PUSH

The stance and shifts for a push bunt are the same as those for a sacrifice bunt. The significant difference between the two is that when executing a push, instead of giving with the ball, the batter uses the bat to push it.

To execute a push bunt (Figure 9–7) the batter holds her arms and hands close to her body and shifts her feet into a comfortable, balanced position. Her hands assume her preferred grip on the bat. The lower hand controls the angle of the bat and, along with the upper hand, keeps the bat level—parallel to the ground and directly in line with the path of the ball. As the ball nears the plate, the batter may, or may not, choose to take a

Figure 9-7. Push Bunt

short step with her rear or front foot in the direction of the bunt. The grip of the hands on the bat is firm. Immediately before bat-ball contact the batter extends her elbows, thereby thrusting her hands and the bat toward the ball. Contact takes place well out in front of the plate.

A push bunt is particularly effective when fielders are playing shallow or charging prematurely in anticipation of a bunt. The ball may be pushed between the oncoming fielders or powered through a fielder. Usually, a right-handed batter will direct the ball between first and second base, while a left-hander will push toward short.

SLUG

To perform a slug bunt (Figure 9–8), the batter takes a stance like the one for a sacrifice bunt, with a split grip. The initial objective is to fake a sacrifice and fool the fielders into thinking that such a bunt is forthcoming. The fake must be convincing if fielders are to be pulled out of posi-

Figure 9-8. Slug Bunt

tion. This can best be accomplished if the sacrifice stance is maintained until the last possible moment.

As the ball approaches the plate, the batter slides her lower hand up the handle so that both hands are together in an extreme choke grip. At the same time, the hips and shoulders rotate toward the catcher until the chin is tucked close to the front shoulder. The head remains as still as possible, facing the pitcher, with eyes level and continuously focused on the ball. Both arms are flexed, but firm, and the wrists are cocked. The stance is tight and compact, with the bat a little forward from normal hitting position.

As the ball nears the plate, the bat is brought forward to slug or slap the ball. The slug requires, not a full swing, but a short, sharp chop.

The slug bunt is particularly effective when the sacrifice is in order or when the first and third basemen key on early movement of the batter and charge indiscriminately. It may also be used by a batter who is having difficulty timing the pitch, as the ball must be watched very closely and the swing is more compact than that required for a normal hit.

DRAG

A drag bunt is executed by starting the body forward and leaving the bat behind to drag the ball along with the body. It is used, primarily, by relatively fast left-handed batters, to obtain a base hit. It is an advanced skill that is not mastered easily, but it can be extremely effective.

Advantages

The major advantages of the drag are essentially the same for both right- and left-handers. Without the need to move the bat in front of the body, the batter can wait longer before assuming the bunting position, thus not revealing the bunt to the fielders until the last second. Because fielders can't detect a good drag bunt, they are prevented from charging early, giving the batter-baserunner more time to reach first base. In addition, because some movement of the body takes place before the ball is contacted, the drag bunter builds momentum. He literally gets a running start. The left-hander may gain a step or two before the ball is contacted. Obviously, right-handers cannot gain as much distance as left-handers because they must stay out of the path of the ball. Using the elements of surprise and precise placement, however, right-handers, too, can drag one down the line and beat it out. The right-handed drag bunt is particularly effective when used for a suicide squeeze play. Its use is advantageous because the batter's body blocks the catcher's view of the runner on third, as well as the third baseman's view of the ball. However, because it is im-

Figure 9-9. Drag Bunt (Left-Handed)

perative to execute a suicide squeeze properly and because the drag bunt is one of the most difficult to lay down, the bunt should be used for a suicide squeeze only by the most advanced, proficient bunters.

Left-Handed

To execute a drag bunt down the first-base line (see Figure 9–9) the batter assumes a normal hitting stance while waiting for the pitch. As soon as he determines that the pitch is good—and *not before*—he begins to move his feet and hands. Although either foot may be used as a pivot, it is recommended that the batter use his front (right) foot—stepping toward first base while levelling off the bat. Starting with the front (right) foot facilitates the body's turn and makes it easier to keep the arms and bat back. The hands are moved to the batter's preferred grip, and the bat is held parallel to the ground, just below the level of the shoulders, with the forearm of the front (right) arm almost parallel to the ground and in direct line with the longitudinal axis of the bat. The grip is firm. The angle of the bat is set so that the barrel is approximately perpendicular to the body. The hips and shoulders pull away from the plate as the body turns, and the rear (left) leg swings around toward first. By extending his arms, the batter ensures that the hands remain stationary and the bat stays out in front of the plate until the ball is contacted. At the moment of contact the weight is centered on the front (right) foot, with the rear (left) leg crossing over. The head has turned to the left to follow the flight of the ball, and the eyes remain focused on the ball. Once contact has been made, the bat is dropped; the left leg completes its cross-over step; and the batter-baserunner continues to first base in one fluid motion.

Most drag bunts by left-handers should be laid down the first-base line. However, by angling the bat slightly toward third, extending both arms, and bending at the waist, back toward the ball, batters can dump low-outside pitches down the third-base line.

To drag bunt successfully, the batter should concentrate on watching the ball hit the bat. He must also have strong hands, wrists, and forearms if he is to be able to control the bat while it's behind his body and subject to the pull of gravity. For this reason, most drag bunters keep both hands on the bat through contact with the ball. It is true, however, that a longer backward reach is possible when the bat is held solely with the back (left) arm. The one-handed technique can be very effective and exciting, but proper execution requires advanced skill and a lot of practice. Holding the knob against the elbow may help to steady the bat.

Right-Handed

To execute a right-handed drag bunt (see Figure 9–10) the batter maintains hitting position until the ball nears the plate. At the last possible moment, the rear (right) foot steps back away from the plate as the rear (right) hand slides up toward the barrel end of the bat. Body weight necessarily shifts to the front (left) foot.

The knob end of the bat is pulled in toward the right side, just above the hip, and the end of the bat is pointed toward first base. The bat is held parallel to the ground, with its longitudinal axis approximately perpendicular to the body. The head remains still, the chin is tucked, and the eyes remain focused on the ball. The body leans forward slightly so that the bat extends over the plate. The batter pushes off from her rear (right)

a   b   c

Figure 9–10. Drag Bunt (Right-Handed)

foot so that her body is in motion as the ball is contacted out in front of the plate. At the contact point, weight is over the front (left) foot, with the rear (right) leg about to cross over. Once contact has been made, the left hand leaves the bat, and the barrel end descends toward the ground. The bat drops from the right hand to the side and rear of the body as the right leg completes its cross-over step and the batter-baserunner continues to first base in one fluid motion. The ball has been directed toward third base.

This bunt may also be executed by dropping the front (left) foot back. In this case the first step would be a cross-over with the rear (left) leg.

KNOB

To execute a knob bunt (Figure 9–11), the batter assumes her regular hitting stance, with a choke grip on the bat. Once she has decided to bunt the pitch, the batter merely extends her arms so that the ball hits the knob end of the bat.

Although probably the most deceiving bunt, the knob is also one of the most difficult and dangerous bunts to perform. The difficulty stems from the small surface area of the knob. The danger results from the fact that the batter's hands, wrists, and forearms are almost directly in line with the pitch. A slight miscalculation or an unexpected curve may result in a pitch that hits the batter. Consequently, only highly skilled batters who have good eye-hand coordination, and who are not afraid of the ball, should attempt to master this bunt. Beginners, especially, should be discouraged from attempting it.

Figure 9-11. Knob Bunt

FAKE

The fake bunt, as the name implies, is executed by going through the motions of bunting without touching the ball. There are several occasions when such a technique may be useful. For example, when a runner is attempting to steal second base, the batter often assumes a sacrifice-bunt position. The bat is held behind the ball as long as possible to make it more difficult for the catcher to track. When the ball nears the plate, the batter uses as full a backward swing as possible to return the bat to his shoulder, taking the pitch all the way. This procedure makes it more difficult for the catcher to catch the ball and prevents him from jumping out in front of the plate for a quick, snap throw.

A fake bunt may also be useful when a runner is attempting to steal third. By faking a slug bunt, in particular, the batter prevents the third baseman and shortstop from breaking early to cover the bag at third. By holding his ground, the right-handed batter also helps the runner by making it more difficult for the catcher to throw.

A fake sacrifice bunt is often used to cover a slug or push bunt. If the defense doesn't respond to the initial fake, however, and holds its ground despite the batter's moving into slug position, the batter may bring his bat forward at the last moment and execute a surprise bunt. This play involves a double fake. The timing is as follows:

1. As the pitcher completes his windup, but before the ball is released, the batter uses the pivot-in-tracks shift to sacrifice-bunt position.
2. As the pitcher releases the ball, the batter draws his bat into position for a slug bunt.
3. As the ball nears the plate, the batter swings his bat forward a second time and positions to execute a surprise bunt.

10

Baserunning

Baserunning is an essential offensive skill. Sound, aggressive baserunning can lead to the production of more base hits, more extra-base hits, fewer double plays, and fewer injuries. In addition, good baserunning often forces the defense to rush throws and to make mistakes. Despite these advantages, however, coaches, with too few exceptions, allocate very little practice time to baserunning skills. Some, in fact, either leave them up to the individual or ignore them totally. Consequently, baserunning is probably the most neglected of all softball skills.

RUNNING

Getting Out of the Batter's Box

Although the specific technique used by batters to leave the box has not been the subject of much research, the vast majority of coaches contend that the first step is taken with the rear foot. The underlying rationale is that when the hitter shifts his weight to the front foot at the point of bat-ball contact, and follows through completely (see Chapter 8), the rear foot will pivot and may even lift. Thus, the weight is off the rear foot, and it is free to take the first step.

Research conducted by Kirby confirmed that hitters initially leave the batter's box with the rear foot.* The majority of the hitters in the study, however, shifted their weight back to the rear foot at the conclusion of the stride; lifted the front foot and replanted it toward the dugout side of the batter's box; and then took a step toward first base with the rear foot.

The technique used by a given batter to get out of the box as quickly as possible probably varies, to some extent, according to changes in body position and balance at the conclusion of the swing and follow-through. Coaches can assist players having problems by emphasizing and encouraging a controlled swing.

Running to First Base

The batter-baserunner runs hard from the moment the ball is hit. During the initial steps, the eyes focus on a spot a few feet past first base, and the batter-baserunner runs to that point. It is important that the runner *not* watch the path of the ball, as doing that will invariably decrease running speed. Players should not let up even if it appears that they will be put out.

Batter-baserunners should run to first base in as straight a line as possible. They must keep in mind, however, that a three-foot line is drawn parallel to, and three feet from, the base line, starting at a point halfway between home plate and first base. Batter-baserunners are out if they run inside the three-foot line and, in the opinion of the umpire, interfere with the fielder taking the throw at first base. The rule primarily applies when the ball is fielded near home plate, or down the first-base line, and the throw is made from behind the batter-baserunner; nevertheless, it would be wise for all batter-baserunners to develop the habit of running close to, and on the right side of (foulside of), the first-base line.

If it is anticipated that the play will be made at first, the batter-baserunner should maintain a consistent stride and speed and run directly across the bag, being sure to touch it before starting to slow down. Running to a spot past the base will alleviate the tendency to slow down prematurely and to jump at, leap at, or stomp on, the bag. Those movements are more time-consuming and increase the chance of injury. A slide should be used only to avoid a tag or a collision.

If the play is made at first base, as anticipated, the runner begins to slow down immediately after passing the bag. As a rule, the runner turns to the right (toward foul territory) and returns directly to the base. An ap-

* Ronald S. Kirby, "Baserunning—From the Batter's Box to Home," in *NAGWS Softball Guide January 1977–January 1979* (Washington, D.C.: American Alliance for Health, Physical Education, and Recreation, 1977), pp. 149–156.

peal play may result from a left turn (toward fair territory). If, in the judgment of the umpire, the baserunner was attempting to run to second base before returning to first, and was legally touched while off base, the baserunner is out. By turning to the right, away from second base, the runner makes his intent to return to first obvious, and the danger of appeal is removed. The runner must always be alert, however, to turn quickly and head for second base if an overthrow occurs.

Running to Second or Third Base

Unlike first base and home plate, second and third bases cannot be overrun without liability to be put out. Consequently, when a play is expected at second or third, the runner must sacrifice some running speed in order to control the forward momentum of the body and to retain initial base contact. Sliding accomplishes these purposes best, without undue loss of speed and without discontinuity of motion. When a close play is anticipated, a slide to the corner of the bag farthest from the throw, and away from the tag, is the only feasible technique to use. When time is not so critical, a stand-up stop at second or third base may suffice. The specific mechanics of the stop will vary somewhat, however, depending upon the direction from which the ball is thrown. The fundamental principle is to stay as far away from the throw as possible, while presenting the baseman with as small a tag area as possible.

The stand-up stop is recommended only when the play at second or third is not going to be close. It may also be used, however, when the base paths are rough and uneven, and when the athletes lack sliding skills so that the potential for injury is much greater with a slide than without one. If these circumstances prevail, the coach must take action to improve the condition of the field and to teach sliding techniques to the athletes. No baserunner is adequately prepared for softball competition without sliding skills. They are basic and essential.

Running Home

Many of the same principles that apply when running to first base also apply when attempting to score from third base. The runner runs hard and in as straight a line as possible; focuses on home plate; maintains a consistent stride and speed; and runs directly over the plate, being sure to touch it before slowing down. The runner does not alter his running stride or leap at the plate, as both actions retard forward speed. For the same reason, he does not slide unless it is necessary to avoid a tag. He looks to the on-deck hitter for a signal to stand up or *go down*. If a slide signal is given, the runner glances quickly at the catcher's glove for an indication of the approaching ball's path and slides away from it. Any runner approaching home plate must be prepared for contact and must go in hard; but he must present the catcher with as little surface area to tag as possible.

ROUNDING

If there is to be no play at first base, the runner attempts to progress from home plate to second base, in the shortest possible time. This necessitates the neutralization of centrifugal force, which tends to throw the runner into right field and along a time-consuming, circular path. To execute a more abrupt turn, without undue loss of speed, the runner should use the following technique:

1. Use cleats to prevent slipping.
2. Run straight toward first and then, about ten feet from the base, angle out *slightly* to the right until it is convenient to turn and approach the bag in as straight a line as possible toward second base. (See Figure 10–1.)

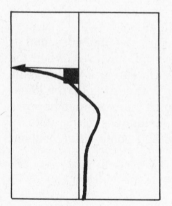

Figure 10-1. Rounding First Base

Figure 10-2. Rounding with a Right-Foot Touch

3. Lean well in toward the diamond, and focus on the bag.
4. Push off the front, inside corner of the base. If contact is with the right (outside) foot, the push-off is directly toward second base (see Figure 10–2). If the contact is with the left (inside) foot, the runner throws his right leg and arm forcefully across his body, steps onto his right foot, and uses a strong push-off inward toward the pitcher (see Figure 10–3).

A runner should follow the basic procedure outlined above when rounding any base. The path for a home run is diagramed in Figure 10–4.

Figure 10-3. Rounding with a Left-Foot Touch

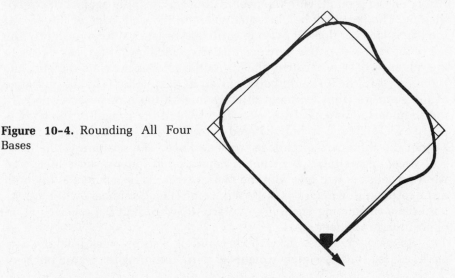

Figure 10-4. Rounding All Four Bases

Figure 10-5. Rolling Start

BREAKING FROM A BASE

There are two methods commonly used by runners to break from a base: a rolling start and a stationary start.

Rolling Start

To execute a rolling start, the runner begins in forward-stride position, with the front foot on the edge of the bag closest to the next base, and the back foot about a half step behind the bag. It is generally advantageous to start with the left foot forward, and on the far side of the bag, so that the right foot will clear to the side of the base when it swings forward. (See Figure 10-5.) The toe of the lead (left) foot should be planted firmly on the ground, with the heel resting comfortably against the top of the bag. The foot may be placed adjacent to the right edge of the base if the bag is loose or doesn't provide sufficient resistance for a push-off. The toe of the rear foot points between forty-five and ninety degrees relative to the advance base or straight ahead. As the pitcher presents the ball, the runner's visual field should be narrowed to the pitcher. The toe and knee of the runner's front leg point directly toward the next base, along with the shoulders. The knees are bent slightly, and the weight of the body is fairly evenly balanced, but centered behind the base. The trunk is flexed so that the shoulders are above the lead knee. The position of the arms will vary, depending upon what is comfortable for a given athlete and what he believes will give him the fastest start. Some runners allow both arms to hang downward in a flexed, semirelaxed manner, while others hold them in running position—one arm forward and the other back, in opposition to the feet.

As the pitcher goes through her windup, a strong push from the runner's rear leg shifts the body weight forward, initiating the action phase of

Figure 10-6. Stationary Start

the break from the base. The body remains low so that the thrust will be as nearly horizontal as possible; and as soon as the center of gravity has moved ahead of the feet, the front foot pushes off against the base. The final push-off is made by extending the hip, knee, and ankle joints of the front leg as the rear (right) leg swings through, and the opposite arm comes forward sharply.

Stationary Start

The stationary start from a base, like the rolling start, begins with a forward-stride position. In this case, however, the rear foot is on the edge of the bag closest to the next base, and the front foot is about a step ahead.

As Figure 10–6 illustrates, the sole of the rear foot is planted firmly against the bag, and the lead foot is a comfortable distance ahead. Both toes and knees point directly toward the next base, along with the shoulders. There is a moderate bend in both knees, and the trunk is inclined forward so that the shoulders are in front of the lead toe, and the weight is centered above the lead leg. The position of the arms will vary. If they are held in running position—one arm forward and the other back, in opposition to the feet—they will be in position to contribute to the forward thrust off the bag. Some runners, however, prefer to allow both arms to hang downward in a flexed, semirelaxed manner. The head is turned slightly, and the eyes focus on the pitcher as he presents the ball and begins the delivery.

As the pitcher goes through the windup, the runner may choose to lean back slightly and then start forward before the ball is released, in order to initiate some forward momentum. As the pitcher completes the windup, the runner's back leg extends and begins to move the center of gravity forward. The primary forward thrust is exerted by the front leg, however, as the weight is on that foot. The hip, knee, and ankle joints of the front leg extend as the rear leg swings through, and the opposite arm comes forward sharply.

Regardless of the method employed, the time of departure of the runner's foot from the bag should coincide with the time of departure of the pitcher's rear foot from the pitcher's plate. This timing provides a little quicker start than leaving the base as the pitcher releases the ball. The rolling start method, if perfected, provides runners with the advantage of more initial momentum for a faster start. A disadvantage is that it takes considerable practice to develop proper timing. Runners must watch the pitcher's windup and anticipate at what point during the windup they must begin to respond in order to be losing contact with the base as the pitcher releases the ball. If the actions of a runner and the pitcher do not coincide, the runner will either lose time by breaking too late and being farther from the next base than necessary or be called out for leaving the base too soon. Differences in pitching styles further increase the runner's difficulty. A second disadvantage of the rolling start is that some umpires have difficulty judging the legality of the break. The preliminary motion of the runner often gives the impression that the runner has left the base, although, in fact, the rear foot may still be touching the bag.

Basing his recommendations on the results of two unpublished studies, Kirby recommends that a runner use a moving start for the quickest break possible.* In recent years, more and more players have adopted the moving, or rolling, start. Whether or not it is the best technique for all players, regardless of skill level and experience, still remains to be seen.

Leading Off

If baserunners choose to use the maximum time allowed by the rules, they will use a rolling start to leave base as soon as the ball is delivered from the pitcher's hand and will run at full speed, without hesitation, directly toward the next base. This technique is usually used when a baserunner intends to advance by means of a steal, run and hit, or suicide squeeze play. The decision to advance has been made before the pitch, and any delay in leaving the base is a waste of valuable time. Starting to leave the base as the pitcher's rear foot clears the rubber, rather than waiting for the ball to leave the pitcher's hand, permits the quickest

*Ronald S. Kirby, "A Pilot Study of Methods of Breaking from the Base in Softball" (Unpublished study, Southeast Missouri State University, 1973), and Ronald S. Kirby, "Analysis of Selected Methods of Breaking from the Base in Softball" (Unpublished study, Southeast Missouri State University, 1975).

Figure 10-7. Set Baserunning Position

possible start because reaction time is taken into consideration. Use of the rear-foot cue will result in the runner's foot leaving the base at the moment the ball leaves the pitcher's hand.

Sometimes a runner's decision to advance will not be made until after the pitch. In this case, after taking as long a lead as the runner deems safe (usually one body length plus one step, to allow for a step and dive back to the base on a pick-off attempt), the runner should stop and set in a balanced position, ready and able to move quickly in any direction. As Figure 10–7 illustrates, the feet should be a comfortable distance apart, with the weight evenly distributed on the balls of the feet. The body is in a slight crouch, with the arms hanging loosely in front of the body. The body faces toward the infield or, on occasion, the outfield, depending upon where the ball is. The eyes must be kept on the ball at all times to obtain information that will enable the runner to anticipate the behavior of the ball and the fielder. A fast reaction is very important. For example, the quicker a runner on first base realizes that the batter has hit the ball on the ground, and reacts by starting toward second, the better his chances of avoiding a force-out or a double play.

Sometimes, a runner may not intend to advance, but merely wish to draw a throw, hoping to force a defensive error. This would require that the baserunner feint a run to the next base. If nothing develops that will permit the runner to advance, he puts on the brakes and scrambles back to his base. At the very least, this will keep the defense guessing, and it may distract them. As a rule, when the ball is in the infield, the runner must take care not to venture further from base than the nearest defender.

Cross-Over Step

Once the baserunner has decided to go on to the next base, the runner may employ the type of cross-over step used when fielding a ground ball to the right. This is executed by pivoting on the front (right) foot and instantaneously pushing off toward the next base with the back (left) foot. The pivot squares the hips, shoulders, and head with the advance base, while the push-off moves the center of gravity forward. As soon as the center of gravity has moved ahead of the feet, the front (right) leg extends, the back (left) leg swings through, and the left arm comes forward sharply. The body remains low so that the thrust of the legs will be as nearly horizontal as possible.

If the baserunner decides to return to the base, the runner should employ the cross-over step (pivot left and push off) used when fielding a ground ball to the left, or cross over and dive back.

Jab Step

A jab step may also be used to move on to the next base. It is executed from the same set position as the cross-over step. In this case, however, the runner takes a step toward the advance base with the front (right) foot, while simultaneously rotating on, and pushing off of, the ball of the rear (left) foot. The rear (left) leg then swings through, past the right foot, as with a cross-over step.

RETURNING TO A BASE

If, after the runner has rounded a base or led off, a throw is made to that base, the runner should return to the bag quickly.

When electing a stand-up return, the runner should tag the corner of the bag farthest from the throw and lean away from the baseman—taking care not to lean too far, however, because a smart baseman will push slightly with the tag. If the runner has leaned too far, this push may cause him to lose his balance and his contact with the base. He may then be tagged out. When a safe return to the base is questionable, or the runner is too far off the base to use the stand-up return, the runner should dive back to the bag head first, touching the bag with the hand. (See Figure 10–8.) The runner starts the dive with a crouch (so that his body is closer to the ground), immediately transfers weight to his left foot, and pivots on the ball of his left foot to face the bag. He uses a cross-over step with the right foot, leans forward until the center of gravity is ahead of the striding foot, pushes off the right foot in the direction of the head, and lies out flat so that the force of impact is absorbed by as much of the body as possible. If the throw is coming from the right, the runner fully extends the right arm so that the right hand touches the front outside corner of the bag. The head and fingers of the right hand point up. The left hand touches the ground, with the fingers pointed toward the outfield. (This position allows the runner to push himself toward the base if the dive leaves him short, and it also reduces the chance of injury to the hand.) If the throw is approaching from the left, the runner should touch the front inside corner of the bag with the left hand and touch the ground with the right hand—

Figure 10-8. Dive Return

fingers pointed toward the infield. Timing of the dive should be such that the base is tagged as the body contacts the ground.

If, after the runner has rounded a base or led off, a throw is made elsewhere, the runner should be prepared to advance should the ball be fumbled or overthrown. A baserunner must never turn his back on a play away from the base to which he is returning. Not only might he miss an opportunity to advance, but a quick throw might catch him completely off guard, and off base.

SLIDING

The ability of a player to slide is a tremendous asset. It may enable the athlete

1. To avoid a tag
2. To avoid overrunning second or third base without undue loss of speed and without discontinuity of motion
3. To break up a double play
4. To avoid a collision with a fielder
5. To gain the confidence necessary to be an aggressive, challenging baserunner who welcomes any opportunity to advance

Sliding, or controlled falling, can be executed headfirst or feetfirst. Of the two, it is generally agreed that a headfirst slide is the quickest way to reach a base, but also the most dangerous. Consequently, the vast majority of coaches encourage their players to adopt a more conventional feetfirst slide. The safest, most effective, all-purpose feetfirst slide is probably the bent-leg. Other types are the pop-up, the double-play, and the hook.

Bent-Leg

The bent-leg slide is usually employed to go straight into a base quickly, to avoid overrunning, or to jar the ball loose from a fielder's hands. It is a versatile method in that it can be used to slide directly into the bag on force plays or to either side of the bag on tag plays. In addition, it is probably the safest slide to execute because the spikes are less likely to be caught in the ground, and the force of impact is distributed over a larger surface area of the body, than with other feetfirst slides. Another reason the bent-leg slide is so popular is that it serves as the foundation for the pop-up slide, which enables the runner to regain his feet and continue running with minimal loss of time. It is recommended that beginners practice and master this slide before progressing to other methods.

The bent-leg slide should be executed without undue loss of speed. Consequently, there should be no discontinuity of motion between the run at full speed and the takeoff into the slide. Continuity necessitates that there be no leap or jump, as such actions retard horizontal speed and increase the time required to reach the base. The timing of the slide is also important. Starting too early (too far from the base) increases the duration of the slide. Friction (the sliding action of the body along the ground) slows down speed for a longer period of time than necessary or desirable. Starting too late (too close to the bag), on the other hand, increases the

Figure 10-9. Bent-Leg Slide

chance of injury—as the slider's body hits the bag with greater force—and increases the danger of oversliding the bag.

Figure 10–9 illustrates the bent-leg slide. The runner runs into the slide and, beginning about eight to ten feet from the base, leans back. She extends the striding foot (whichever one is most natural) *slightly* upward and forward toward the bag. As the center of gravity shifts backward, the runner pushes off the supporting (takeoff) leg, bends it to a forty-five- to ninety-degree angle, and tucks it up under the knee of the extending forward leg. She holds the arms high and out to the side for balance. At this point, the top leg is slightly bent, with the kneecap facing up; the foot is *slightly* off the ground, toes pointing up, so the spikes cannot catch. The bottom leg is bent at the knee so that the lower part, from knee to ankle, is at a ninety-degree angle to the line of forward motion and the bag. The ankle is fully extended so that the laces of the shoe face the base, and the spikes cannot catch. The head is in line with the trunk, or slightly forward, eyes focused on the base. The body is often turned slightly to the side of the bent leg. The force of impact, as the body falls to the ground, is absorbed primarily by the upper part of the bottom leg and the buttocks. By landing so that as much as possible of the leg, hip, and back hit the ground simultaneously, the runner minimizes the danger of abrasions and spikes catching.

Pop-Up

To finish a slide standing up and ready to advance, the runner begins with the bent-leg slide, as previously described. He does not lean back quite as far, however; he is almost sitting down at the start of the slide and keeps the trunk fairly erect. (See Figure 10–10.) He braces the lead leg against the base at contact and simultaneously presses down

Figure 10-10. Pop-Up Slide

against the ground with the bottom, bent leg. The momentum of the body, the push of the bottom leg against the ground, and the extension of the lead leg as the center of gravity moves over it—all combine to get the slider to his feet.

Double-Play

To break up a double play, the runner should move directly toward the striding foot of the thrower, but he should not slide more than three feet out of the base line or an interference call may result. The runner should modify the bent-leg slide by also bending the top knee to a forty-five-degree angle. By approaching in this manner, the slider ensures that if contact does occur, the shin of the slider, rather than the spikes, will hit the fielder. Also, the flexed knees can give to absorb some of the impact force.

The object of this slide is to prevent an accurate relay throw by breaking the fielder's concentration and causing him some anxiety or by upsetting his balance. Any deliberate attempt to injure the fielder is never justifiable and must never be tolerated. It is recommended that the double-play technique be taught and employed with discretion. It is certainly not a priority skill for beginners, and it is not appropriate in all competitive situations.

Hook

The object of the hook slide is to evade a tag or to present the baseman with as small a part of the body as possible to tag. Consequently, the base is contacted with the foot while the rest of the body falls away from the base. The hook can be executed on either side of the body for slides to either side of the base. If the baseman moves to the runner's left to field the ball, the slide is performed on the right side of the body, to the outside of the diamond, with the left foot hooking the bag. The procedure is reversed when the throw approaches from the right. Most players will have a natural preference for a slide on one side, but they must practice both so that they can more effectively deal with attempted tags from any direction. Figure 10–11 illustrates the execution of a hook slide.

The runner must watch the covering baseman's eyes, glove, or body position for clues to help determine which side of the base to touch. To execute a hook slide to the right of the bag, away from the throw and the potential tag, the runner should use the following technique:

1. Approach the base straight on.
2. Fake a lean toward the ball, pointing the left toe in that general direction.

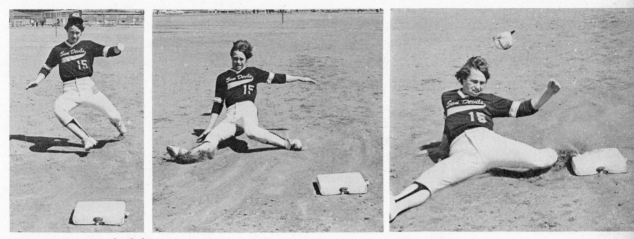

Figure 10-11. Hook Slide

3. With weight on the left foot, lift the right leg forward.
4. Point the right toe, turn the foot so that the outside of the ankle faces the ground, and push the foot diagonally forward to the right as the weight shifts inward on the left ankle to provide the push for the slide on the bone of the turned right ankle.
5. Drop the right shoulder so that the landing force is absorbed along the entire right side of the body.
6. Push the left hip and shoulder down and back to the left, during the slide, so that the body doesn't roll to the right.
7. Turn the head so that the eyes focus on the closest inside corner of the base, and point the left toe toward that corner.
8. Maneuver the left foot slightly, if necessary, to avoid the tag or to try to dislodge the ball.

When teaching the hook slide to beginners, the following progression may be helpful:

1. Have the slider sit and assume sliding position. Check the foot position. It is recommended, at this stage of the learning process, that the right and left legs be kept fairly close together to avoid stretching the groin too far.
2. Have the slider step diagonally forward with his left foot, pointing the toe of the left foot outward. While maintaining this foot position, the slider should bend his knees and place the palm of his right hand and the fingers of his left hand on the ground to either side of his right knee. Keeping his left foot on the ground, the slider lifts his right leg, turns the outside ankle bone to face

the ground, and lifts his left hand up so that body weight is supported by the right arm. At this point the right foot slides through diagonally to the right, with the ankle bone pressing along the ground.

3. Have the slider jump and slide his right leg along the ground, using the hands for support as in step 2.
4. Have the slider jog, push, and slide, using the hands for support as in step 2. Emphasize staying level with the ground—not jumping.
5. Have the slider run, push, and slide.

The first three steps of this progression may be performed on a slick (linoleum) surface, with sneakers. Such a surface offers little resistance, and the feet slide easily. All steps of the progression may be performed on grass, with or without sneakers. Be sure, however, that the area is smooth and clear of rocks, glass, and other obstacles.

Headfirst

The headfirst slide is probably the fastest and most dangerous of all types of slides. It is fastest because during the approach to a base the body is already leaning forward, and the center of gravity is ahead of the striding foot. By shifting the weight farther forward, the runner puts the body in falling position. The direction of force from the pushing (take-off) foot is in the direction of the slide, and the arms also swing forward in the desired direction. This slide is more dangerous than other slides because the head, arms, and hands are placed in a vulnerable position. A throw might hit the runner on the head; a covering baseman jumping for a throw might come down on the head, arms, or hands of the runner; and the runner's fingers or wrists might be jammed by the force of impact with the bag or by slipping under the bag. Although some runners indicate a general preference for the headfirst slide, the vast majority use it primarily to return to a base quickly on a pick-off attempt (see Figure 10–8) or to protect a leg injury.

To execute a headfirst slide directly into the base, the runner starts with a crouch so that the body is closer to the ground and so that the force of the push into the slide will be more nearly horizontal. (See Figure 10–12.) He leans forward until the center of gravity is ahead of the striding foot, pushes off the lead foot, and throws the weight of the body toward the base. The head is up, and both arms extend out in front of the body, fingers pointing up. The slide is made by arching the back slightly and sliding on the lower chest, stomach, and upper thighs. The feet should be kept off the ground so that they do not drag and retard forward speed. The fingers should also be raised.

Figure 10-12. Headfirst Slide

When more evasive action is necessary to avoid a possible tag, and when the throw is approaching from the right, the runner should extend the right arm so that the right hand contacts the front, left side of the bag. He should slide and absorb the impact of the landing primarily on the right side of the body. This action is reversed when the throw is approaching from the left.

Fear of Sliding

A coach can do several things to reduce the anxiety that is frequently associated with sliding.

1. Modify the environment to reduce the chance of injury. A smooth, obstacle-free sliding surface is desirable. There is little chance of injury when sliding, without cleats, on wet grass or in a sand pit. Wet grass is highly favored over a sand pit, however, because an actual *slide* (along the surface of the ground) is possible.
2. Have the slider wear long pants and sliding pads, if they are available, as well as sneakers or two pairs of socks. Do not allow cleats of any kind. Knee and elbow pads are recommended.
3. Have the slider follow a step-by-step progression. For example, to develop a bent-leg slide, the slider may follow these steps:
   a. Assume bent-leg, figure-4 position on the ground.
   b. In slow motion, walk into a controlled fall and assume sliding position.
   c. Run straight through the sliding area.

211

      d. Run, at individual's own set speed, and slide.

      e. Increase speed, and slide.

      f. Slide into loose base.

      g. Slide on dirt infield, without cleats.

      h. Slide on dirt infield, with cleats.

4. Have the player slide while holding handfuls of grass or dirt. This practice combats the player's tendency to use the arms to break the fall.

RUNDOWNS

The following suggestions may prove helpful to a runner caught in a rundown:

1. Use feints, shoulder fakes, changes of speed, and quick changes of direction to draw throws or to force the defender to pump. The more throws and exchanges the defense is forced to make, the greater the chance of error.
2. Try not to commit in any given direction while a defender has the ball in throwing position. Change direction as soon as the ball leaves the player's hand. Try to stay as far away from the ball as possible.
3. Periodically change sides of the base line to obstruct the vision of defenders and to block the potential path of the ball should it be thrown. Aligning one's body with the glove of the target receiver can prevent a throw from reaching the receiver and can, as a result, break up the play. It also makes the tracking of the ball more difficult for the receiver. At the same time, however, the body of the runner is exposed and vulnerable to potential injury.
4. If the opportunity arises, establish contact with a defensive player who is in the base line, but doesn't have the ball (e.g., break toward the rundown player as soon as he releases a throw). This forces an obstruction call against the defender, and the runner is awarded the base he would have reached had there been no obstruction.
5. Dodge the tag, when possible, by dropping down, leaping aside, or, in some cases, diving over the defender. If all else fails, attempt to dislodge the ball during the tag.
6. Stay alive as long as possible, to give other runners more time to advance.

Baserunners must constantly be aware of each other's positions and predicaments if rundowns are to be avoided, or if they are to be planned and executed to offensive advantage. When a baserunner is caught in a rundown, the situation is usually unintentional. Occasionally, however, it may be planned. (See Chapter 10 for rundown strategy.)

FOUR

Team Play

11

Defense

Once the batter makes contact with a pitched ball and breaks through the first line of defense (the battery), the infield and outfield must provide the support necessary to retire the batter-baserunner or to limit his advance. Defensive personnel may be called upon to respond to bunts, steals, hit and runs, run and hits, extra-base hits, etc. Individual actions (e.g., fielding a fly ball, throwing, receiving a throw, tagging a runner) must be executed and, frequently, coordinated in the form of relays, cutoffs, rundowns and pickoffs. Cover and back-up responsibilities must be integrated to provide a comprehensive team defense. A disorganized, inconsistent defense gives up runs through mental and physical errors.

The extent to which an opponent's run production will be limited depends upon the ability of defensive personnel to function effectively as a coordinated unit. All team members must work hard to master fundamental skills, develop appropriate conditioned responses, and enhance their game sense so that they can make decisions and respond to various situations with insight and understanding. Strategies are also an important part of team defense. The particular tactics and strategies that a coach advocates will vary depending upon the coach's defensive philosophy, the game situation, the combination of skills possessed by the members of the team, and the skills of the opposition.

ANALYZING THE SITUATION

To determine the appropriate defensive strategy to employ, coaches should consider the following factors:

1. The game situation (e.g., inning, score, number of outs, home- or visiting-team status)
2. The batter at the plate and on deck (e.g., bat control, power, running speed, strengths and weaknesses, habits)
3. The baserunners (e.g., position on the base paths, speed, judgment, aggressiveness, habits)
4. The offensive team's general philosophy, commonly employed tactics and strategies, past successes and failures, and strengths and weaknesses
5. The pitcher (e.g., how well he is throwing, what he is throwing, his speed and control)
6. The strengths, weaknesses, and abilities of defensive personnel
7. The environment (e.g., temperature, field conditions, wind velocity and direction)

Strategy that is to be used in a game should have a high probability of being executed properly and successfully.

PLANNING DEFENSIVE STRATEGY

After analyzing the game situation and considering the probable action of the offense, the coach should develop a sound defensive strategy that will do the following:

1. *Maximize the strengths of defensive personnel.*
   a. Place better fielders in position to handle the greatest number of balls.
   b. If the shortstop has a significantly stronger arm than the second baseman, or vice versa, assign the player with the stronger arm to make all relay throws.
   c. If an infielder has a very strong arm, gets a quick jump on the ball, and is fast, have that fielder play deeper than usual to increase his fielding range.
   d. When ahead in the late innings of a game, substitute in a player who is a weak hitter but strong fielder.

2. *Recognize opponent strengths, and take advantage of opponent weaknesses.*
   a. Consider moving an infielder to the outfield when a consistent long-ball hitter, but poor bunter, is at the plate.
   b. If the batter is a slow runner, play a little deeper in the infield. There will be more time to make the play at first.
   c. If the opposing team primarily consists of singles hitters who rely on speed and aggressive running to beat out infield hits and to

stretch singles into doubles, pitch high to them, attempting to force them to hit the ball into the air. Move outfielders in a step or two.

3. *Recognize opponent habits and tendencies, and neutralize the effectiveness of anticipated opponent action.*
   a. If it is thought that the offense may be going to attempt a hit and run, run and hit, bunt and run, run and bunt, steal, or squeeze play, call a pitchout. It will reveal the intentions of the offense and will, perhaps, leave a runner vulnerable to being put out.
   b. If the offense likes to take aggressive leads and to get quick starts off base, make discriminate pick-off attempts.
   c. If the opposition likes to bunt, try to discourage or intimidate them by playing the first and third basemen in close to the plate.
   d. If a team consistently sacrifices with a runner on first and no outs, call a pitchout and a pick-off throw to first; or charge with the pitch, field the ball as quickly as possible, and play on the lead runner.
   e. If the opposition likes to advance a first-base runner to third on a bunt, make sure that third base is covered, and prepare to make the play to third or to catch the runner rounding second.
   f. If the offense invariably tries to advance the back runner in a double-steal situation, but does not prepare to score on the play, go for the putout of the back runner.

4. *Meet the demands of the game situation.* Consider carefully the inning, the number of outs, the position of runners on the base paths, and the importance of the runs that the baserunners represent. Adjust the depth and alignment of infielders and outfielders, accordingly. Try to keep runners as far from home plate as possible.
   a. When there is an important runner at third and there are fewer than two outs, and the run cannot be conceded, play the infield in, close enough for the fielder of a ground ball to throw the runner out at the plate. Consider that this tactic limits the fielder's range, however. Too many times, ground balls that could have been played if the infield had stayed at regular depth have been hit through a pulled-in infield. Fielders should know their own maximum effective throwing distance from home and should not pull in farther than necessary. Fielders who are strong enough to throw the runner out after fielding a ground ball behind the base line should not limit their range by moving in too far.
   b. When it is very doubtful that a runner can be thrown out at the plate, concede the run and try to keep other runners from advancing to scoring position.
   c. With fewer than two outs, and a tie or lead runner in scoring position in late innings, do not catch foul pop-ups or foul fly balls while

going away from the infield or deep in the outfield. Allowing the ball to drop sacrifices an out, but ensures that a run will not score. When protecting a relatively large lead in the late innings, take the out and sacrifice the run. This strategy is also recommended when defensive personnel have weak skills and difficulty attaining putouts.

d. With the winning run on third and fewer than two outs in the last inning of the game, move outfielders in close enough to make a play at the plate following the catch of a fly ball. How far each outfielder must move in depends upon that fielder's arm and the speed of the runner at third. The batter's ability and power are irrelevant to the fielder's position in this situation. If outfielders play so deep that they cannot make a strong, accurate throw to home following a fly-ball catch, the run will score whether the batter is put out or gets a hit.

Playing the Batter

A basic plan of attack should be developed for each hitter before the game. It should be based on an analysis of the batter's strengths, weaknesses, habits, and performance history (what, how, and where the batter hits). It should also take into account the pitcher's condition (e.g., speed, control, stuff, best pitch), the weather (e.g., wind speed and direction), the field conditions, and the game situation. All hitters are dangerous and must be treated with respect, regardless of their position in the batting order, but the third, fourth, and fifth batters are usually the stronger, more consistent hitters. In general, pitchers should try to pitch to the batters' individual weaknesses and keep them off balance.

Under some circumstances, the defensive team may choose to give the batter an intentional walk. When first base is open, and runners are in scoring position, a free pass will do the following:

1. Set up a force play and increase the chance of getting an out.
2. Increase the chance for a double play.
3. Simplify the decision-making task of fielders and reduce the potential threat of a squeeze play.
4. Allow the battery to pitch around a particularly troublesome batter who historically hits well off the pitcher of record; who is on a hitting streak; or who is a very good clutch hitter.

This strategy is most appealing when in the late innings of the game, when the winning run is on third base, when there are fewer than two outs, and when the on-deck batter is a relatively weak, less-accomplished hitter. It is rarely used when the walk will advance the tying or winning runner into scoring position.

An alternative to an intentional walk, with first base open, is to pitch to the scheduled batter, but very, very carefully. The batter should not be given anything good to hit. The pitcher should try to keep the ball on the corners of the plate, thereby forcing the batter to go for a borderline pitch. This can be a very effective strategy against an anxious batter or against one who can hit very well but sometimes goes after bad pitches. If the count reaches 3–0, or 3–1, the defense may decide to put the ball in the strike zone or to intentionally throw a ball and put the batter on first base rather than taking the chance that the batter will receive and hit a "fat" pitch.

Throughout the game, fielders should be positioned where the batter is most likely to hit the ball. They must be flexible and make adjustments according to the following variables:

1. The pitch to be thrown. For example, if a batter has been pulling the ball because the pitcher has been consistently jamming him, fielders should shade toward the appropriate field as long as the pitching strategy remains the same.
2. The weather and field conditions. For example, infielders should move in one or two steps toward the plate when the ground is wet and soft.
3. The game situation. For example, at the beginning of a game against an unfamiliar opponent, outfielders should play deep. When ahead in the late innings of a game, first and third basemen guard their respective foul lines, and outfielders play deeper to prevent an extra-base hit or a big inning. Infielders should play as deep as possible under the following circumstances:
   a. There are two outs, regardless of the number and position of runners on the base paths.
   b. There are no runners on base, regardless of the number of outs.
   c. There is a runner on first or second base, representing the tying or winning run.
   d. The defensive team is ahead in the game and can afford to give up a run.
   e. An out is the primary objective.
   f. A double play is an important objective.
   g. The batter is not apt to bunt or has two strikes.
   By playing deep, infielders increase their range and the length of time they have in which to react to a batted ball.

At times, drastic shifts may be used. For example, when a batter rarely, if ever, hits toward a particular field, the fielder in that area can be moved to another area where his defensive skills are more apt to be needed.

Playing the Runner

Occasionally, the defensive team may choose to circumvent the batter and call for a pitchout or pick-off play on a baserunner.

Pitchout

If it is thought that the offense may be going to attempt a hit and run, run and hit, bunt and run, run and bunt, steal, or squeeze play, a pitchout may be thrown by the pitcher. This will reveal the intentions of the offense and will, it is hoped, leave a runner vulnerable to being put out. The pitchout allows covering basemen to cheat, moving toward their bases as the pitcher delivers the ball, without danger of being caught out of position by a bunt or hit. It also allows the catcher to concentrate more fully on the pick-off throw. A ball will be called on the batter, however. Consequently, before a pitchout is called, consideration must be given to the count on the batter and to the question whether the advantage to be gained by the basemen and catcher will contribute significantly to the success of the play.

Pickoff

A pick-off play is a planned maneuver with a quick throw designed to catch a runner off base. Whether or not to call a pick-off play depends upon the following:

1. The ability (skill) of defensive personnel to properly execute a pick-off play.
2. The philosophy of the defensive coach and the degree of confidence the coach has in the team's ability to effectively execute a pick-off play.
3. The offensive philosophy of the opposing coach and the anticipated action of the offense—do they historically attempt to move baserunners on the first or second pitch? Are they more likely to bunt, steal, delayed steal, hit and run, or run and hit? Do they like to run and to draw throws?
4. The game situation—score (importance of the run that the baserunner to be picked off represents), inning, number of outs, count on the batter, number and position of baserunners.
5. The element of surprise, the speed and game sense of baserunners, and the perceived readiness of the baserunners to deal with a pick-off attempt.
6. The next batter and the chance of retiring him.
7. The pitcher's control and present effectiveness.

8. The willingness of the catcher or coach to accept the risks and the potential consequences of the attempt.

A pick-off call is generally recommended under the following circumstances:

1. The catcher has a strong, quick, and accurate pick-off throw.
2. A runner is taking a big lead on the pitch or is not alert when returning to base after the pitch.
3. A bunt or a hit and run is anticipated.
4. The pitcher is struggling.
5. The opposing team is unfamiliar. By showing, early in the game, a willingness to play on runners, the defense may discourage aggressive baserunning, big leads, and testing of defensive personnel.

The preliminary steps in the execution of a preplanned pick-off play are as follows:

1. The catcher gives the pick-off signal (e.g., wipes his forehead, pulls on his mask, rests his glove on his hip). The call may be initiated by a fielder, but this is rare.
2. The fielder who is to receive the throw gives the catcher an acknowledgment signal (e.g., picks up dirt, taps his glove).
3. The catcher may or may not give a pitch-out signal.
4. If a pitchout is not called, the pitcher may throw a strike, but it should be on a corner—preferably high, outside, where it will be hard to hit. The pitch should be easy for the catcher to handle and should not be a change-up. Fielders must not prematurely commit to the pick-off play, or they may be caught out of position by a bunt or hit.
5. The pitcher concentrates on the batter and the pitch—not on the runner—while the catcher concentrates on receiving the pitch.

Defensive personnel should follow through with a called pick-off play unless the following conditions exist:

1. The pitched ball is not caught cleanly and in position for a quick, balanced, and accurate pick-off throw.
2. The target receiver is not in position to catch the throw.
3. There is little or no chance, considering the runner's body position and balance and his distance from his base, to effect a putout. An indiscriminate throw, with little chance of retiring a baserunner, satisfies the runner's objective by enhancing the

possibility that he will advance. The runner may not even have been attempting to advance, but simply trying to draw a throw in hopes of forcing an error.

4. The runner has jumped well off base in an apparent attempt to draw a throw and to execute a delayed steal. In this case the catcher may fake a throw on the runner, run directly toward the runner and force him to commit in a given direction before throwing, throw to the pitcher within the eight-foot circle, or yell delayed steal and follow through with the pick-off throw.

If the risk of a pick-off play is greater than the coach is willing to accept, or if the ability of the defense to successfully carry out a pick-off play is highly suspect, a fake throw may be used by the catcher to keep a runner honest or to drive him back to his base. A defensive player faking pick-off coverage, or cutting behind a runner who has led off base, may also help to keep runners from becoming too aggressive without risking a throw.

The keys to an effective, successful pick-off play are

1. *Confidence* (e.g., being committed to the play, throwing with conviction and without hesitation)
2. *Execution*
3. *Appropriateness* (e.g., keeping the play a surprise, knowing when to throw and when not to throw, anticipating the intentions of the offense and countering their efforts)

Potential pick-off plays vary depending on the number of runners on base and on their positions.

Runner on first base. The pick-off throw may go to the first baseman or the second baseman.

PICK-OFF THROW TO FIRST BASEMAN

The first baseman gives a target between his waist and knees and to the inside of the first-base line. The catcher receives the pitch and, with a quick snap, throws to the glove target of the first baseman. The first baseman receives the throw and tags the runner at the earliest possible moment. The second baseman backs up the inside of the first-base line in case of an errant throw, and the right fielder backs up the foul side of the first-base line. The shortstop covers second base, and the third baseman covers third.

This play may be executed with, or without, a pitchout.

PICK-OFF THROW TO SECOND BASEMAN

The catcher receives the pitch and, with a quick snap, throws to the glove target of the second baseman, who has cut in from behind the runner. The first baseman ducks or moves aside to clear a path for the throw. The second baseman *ideally receives the throw between his waist and knees and to the inside of the base line. He tags the runner at the earliest possible moment. The* right fielder *backs up the play in case of an errant throw. The* shortstop *covers second base, and the* third baseman *covers third.*

This play is particularly effective when the first baseman is pulled in toward the plate in anticipation of a potential bunt. A pitchout should be called so that the second baseman can break early to cover first and to cut the runner off.

Pick-off throws to first should not be done too often, as this plays into the runner's hands. It is wiser for the catcher to ignore the runner and to set him up for one well-timed pick-off throw. The catcher can also set a runner up for a pick-off by calling for the first baseman to cover after the first pitch, and then calling for the pick-off throw to the second baseman at first base on the second pitch. The runner might be caught off base, watching the first baseman. (This same technique can be used at second, with the shortstop functioning as the decoy and the second baseman or center fielder taking the throw, and at third, with the third baseman functioning as the decoy and the shortstop taking the pick-off throw.)

Runner on second base. Pick-off throws may go to the second baseman, the shortstop, or the center fielder.

PICK-OFF THROW TO SECOND BASEMAN

The catcher receives the pitch and throws to the pitcher. The pitcher *receives the throw with both hands, with his right foot forward or even with the left (if a right-handed thrower), and with his weight centered primarily on the right foot. He executes a left rear pivot and a quick, snap throw to the glove target of the second baseman. The* second baseman *ideally receives the throw between his waist and knees and to the third-base side of second. He tags the runner at the earliest*

Runners on first and second; second and third; or first, second, and third. The mechanics of a pick-off throw to first are basically the same whether there are runners on first and second; first, second, and third; or first base only. The difference is that with multiple runners the receiver of the pick-off throw must be alert for a potential play elsewhere. This is true for pick-off throws to second and third, as well.

A pick-off play with multiple runners on the bases should be called only after careful consideration, as a mistake could give the opposition a big inning. If a pick-off attempt is to be made, the defense should consider playing on the back runner, for the back runner frequently feels that the defense is concerned principally with the lead runner. This presumed preoccupation often gives the back runner a sense of security and the temptation to become more daring.

Runners on first and third (double-steal situation). The pick-off throw may go to the pitcher, the second baseman, the shortstop, or the third baseman.

PICK-OFF THROW TO PITCHER

The catcher receives the pitch and throws to the pitcher at about shoulder height so that it looks like a throw to second. The pitcher catches the ball and listens and looks for an opportunity to play on either the lead or the back runner. A quick, snap relay throw to third or first occasionally catches the runner off guard or leaning in the wrong direction. The runners must commit to advance or return to their bases as soon as the pitcher receives the throw within the eight-foot circle. The first baseman covers first, the shortstop or second baseman covers second, and the third baseman covers third. The right, center, and left fielders back up first, second, and third base, respectively.

This is an extremely conservative play that has a low success/attempt ratio. It is basically a token play, although its use may be justified for very young, inexperienced players who have limited throwing and catching skills. It has the greatest chance for success when used against players who lack game and baserunning sense. It may also be appropriately used when the baserunner at third is hyper and appears almost overanxious to score.

PICK-OFF THROW TO SECOND BASEMAN (IN BASE LINE)

The second baseman moves into the base line, about fifteen to twenty feet from second base. He gives a target at chest height.

OPTION 4

The second baseman an
The second baseman to
handed batter at the pla
event of a bunt, a fake bu
the shortstop can take t
move into coverage or ba
fielder backs up the cat

We recommend option
most circumstances—particu
shortstop is in the best positic
apply the tag to the runner.
confusion, especially if the of
improved at first base becau
and the pitcher can be reliev
the coach desires.

Third base. Coverage o
ond, varies. There are three

OPTION 1

The third baseman cov
or not the batter bunts
bunts toward the left-f
shows no intention to
second baseman covers
first. If, on the other ha
shortstop takes the ba
moves into coverage or
center, and left fielders
respectively.

This coverage can be u
a left-handed batter at the p
the mound; and when a bun
is only one receiver for the
should be no confusion at th
is that there are only three
handling bunts, as opposed
backup at third is limited to

b
fi
ca
co

sa
ba

opt
cou
fro
rur
bat
bui
qui
goc

The catcher receives the pitch and, with a quick snap, throws
to the glove target of the second baseman. The second baseman
receives the throw and (1) makes a play on the back runner by
personally applying the tag, throwing to the shortstop covering
second, or forcing the runner to commit to first and throwing to
the covering first baseman or (2) makes a play on the lead run-
ner by throwing to the catcher covering home plate (if the run-
ner is attempting to score), running directly at the runner (if he
is well off third base but is not committed in any direction), or
throwing to the third baseman covering third (if the runner can
be caught off base). The third baseman must assist the second
baseman by watching the lead runner closely and calling (1)
"Home!" if the runner breaks for the plate; (2) "Hey!" if the
runner is well off base but not committed in any direction; or
(3) "Three!" if the runner has led off sufficiently that a throw to
third can catch him off base. The right, center, and left fielders
move into position to back up potential throws to first, second,
and third base, respectively.

If the second baseman has a strong, accurate arm, this play can be
very effective. It is recommended when the runner at first is slow, or when
the defense anticipates that the back runner might try to get caught in a
rundown in an attempt to distract the defense in order to give the lead
runner a chance to score. By receiving the catcher's throw in the base line
the second baseman is in position to apply a possible tag to the back runner, while at the same time being closer to home for a possible throw to
the plate should the lead runner be drawn off third.

PICK-OFF THROW TO SECOND BASEMAN
(IN CUT-OFF POSITION)

Same as the pick-off throw to the second baseman in the base
line, except that the second baseman moves to a position in
direct line between home plate and second base, about fifteen
to twenty feet from the pitcher's plate. The shortstop covers
second and backs up the catcher's throw to the second base-
man. If the lead runner is not going on the throw, the second
baseman may allow the ball to go directly through to the short-
stop for a play on the back runner at second base.

This play is recommended when it is anticipated that the offense's
primary objective is to score the runner at third. The throw to the cutoff
becomes a decoy to draw the lead runner off base. The second baseman
must have a good arm if the lead runner is to be prevented from scoring. It
is also important that the second baseman move into position close to the

coverage (
situations
tions.

Defe

A ru
and run,
and back
option the

Stra

Seco
There are

OPT

The
whe
cent
base
the
first

OP

The
one
whe
cov
fiel

OP

The
one
is
bu
or
ba
up
de
rig

OPTION 2

The third baseman and shortstop cooperate for the coverage of third. The third baseman usually takes the bag; but, if a fake bunt is employed by the batter, and the third baseman is assigned to handle bunts down the third-base line, he may be pulled in toward the plate and be unable to recover in time to get to the bag in position to receive the throw and to apply a tag to the oncoming runner. In this case, the third baseman ducks, as necessary, and gives the catcher a clear path for the throw to the covering shortstop. If the third baseman is able to read the steal quickly enough, and time permits, he may call off the shortstop and cover third personally. The shortstop's responsibility would then be to back up the inside throwing angle from the catcher to third base. The second baseman covers second, the first baseman covers first, and the pitcher handles all bunts toward the right-field side of the diamond. The right, center, and left fielders back up first, second, and third base, respectively.

This coverage is particularly good when there is a left-handed pull hitter or a right-handed batter at the plate; when the pitcher is a good fielder; and when a bunt is not likely. It provides for flexibility at third and adequate backup at each base. The disadvantage of this coverage option is that there may occasionally be confusion at third between the third baseman and shortstop—they may not know who should make the catch and the catcher may not know who the target receiver is. Communication is essential. In addition, if the runner gets a good jump off second with the pitch, and the defenders are caught off guard and do not respond quickly to the steal, or the shortstop is deep in the hole to begin with and the third baseman requires assistance, the covering baseman will very likely present the catcher with a moving target. In fact, the baseman may still be moving as he catches the ball and attempts to tag the runner. This significantly increases the difficulty of the play, reducing the chance for a successful tag-out at third. Another disadvantage is that there are only three fielders (catcher, pitcher, third baseman) for handling bunts, rather than four (first baseman is missing).

OPTION 3

The third baseman and shortstop cooperate for the coverage of third, as in option 2, but the responsibilities of the second baseman, the first baseman, and the pitcher vary, depending upon the actions of the batter. When there is no indication that the batter intends to bunt, the second baseman *covers second. If the batter bunts or fakes a bunt, the* second baseman *moves into coverage or back-up position at first base. Either the* pitcher *or the* first baseman *handles bunts down the right-field line, depending upon the relative fielding abilities of each player and the bunt defense selected. The* center fielder *is left to cover second base, with no backup.*

This coverage can present problems if the runner at second aborts the steal attempt and tries to return to second, or if he is caught in a rundown between second and third. Otherwise, coverage is more than adequate. Four fielders (catcher, pitcher, first baseman, third baseman) are in position and available to handle bunts, and a back-up infielder is present and can offer assistance when necessary at first and third. If coverage assistance is not needed, there is double backup at both first and third. With a sole runner at second, this coverage option is recommended because of its flexibility and depth of backup at the bases where plays are most likely to be made.

Delayed Steal

Steal on the battery. A baserunner executes a *delayed steal on the battery* by taking off for the advance base as the ball leaves the catcher's hand for the return throw to the pitcher. The runner depends upon the element of surprise for offensive success. If the defensive players are caught off guard, they will be slow to respond to the steal attempt and will very likely be out of position. When they do become aware of the baserunner's advance, they will all too frequently panic and overreact. The pitcher, in his haste to make a quick play on the runner, may throw the ball erratically; throw it before the covering baseman is in position to receive it; or throw it too hard for the baseman to handle. Even if the ball is thrown well, the baseman, in his haste to tag the runner, may take his eyes off the ball and fail to make the catch. To insure that these things do not happen, the defense must attend to the runner. The catcher must consistently check the runner before returning pitched balls to the pitcher. Infielders must try to force the runner back to base between pitches, and to limit his lead, by taking steps toward the runner or by covering bases and being a threat to receive a pick-off throw. As soon as the pitcher receives the ball from the catcher or a fielder, he must routinely check the progress of the runner.

An alert defense will very likely discourage any attempt at a delayed steal. If, however, a runner decides to challenge the defense, his intent should be picked up early enough for the principals involved in the play to respond with control. Those who read the steal first should alert the pitcher by yelling "Going!" As soon as he hears the warning, the pitcher should turn to face the advance base of the runner, sight the covering baseman and give him time to get into position, set, and throw with a step and follow-through in the direction of the target receiver.

Coverage is basically the same as for a straight steal. If the runner is attempting to advance to second, the shortstop receives the throw from the pitcher, and the second baseman backs it up. The first and third basemen cover first and third base, respectively. The right, center, and left fielders back up first, second, and third, respectively. If the runner is attempting to advance to third, either the third baseman or the shortstop receives the throw, and the left fielder backs it up. The first baseman again covers first, and the second baseman covers second. Right and center fielders back up first and second, as usual. Coverage is the same whether there is a sole runner on second or runners on first and second attempting a double steal. If the runner is on third and is attempting to score, positioning is the same as for a steal of third. The only exception is the first baseman, who should move quickly to back up the catcher at the plate. The pitcher's throw will be to home.

Steal on the defense. A baserunner executes a *delayed steal on the defense* (catcher and a baseman) by drawing a pick-off throw and taking off for the advance base as soon as the catcher's arm starts forward for the throw to the baseman or as soon as the ball leaves the catcher's hand. Again, the offensive success of the play is dependent upon the element of surprise. The safest and surest way to prevent the delayed steal is to not throw to the bases. Such conservatism can allow the runner to take an extensive lead, however. To keep the runner close, the catcher can return pitches to the pitcher immediately. Once the pitcher receives the ball while standing within an eight-foot radius of the pitcher's plate, the runner must immediately proceed to the next base or return to his base. He cannot delay, fake, or reverse his direction in an attempt to draw a throw. He is forced to commit himself immediately, and in full view of the pitcher, so there are no surprises. Another option the catcher has is to fake a throw. This could force the runner into premature disclosure of his intentions. If the runner breaks too soon, the catcher and fielders can respond as for a straight steal.

If the catcher does attempt a pick-off throw, and the runner takes off immediately for the next base, those who initially read the steal play should yell, "Going!" As soon as he hears the warning, the baseman who receives the catcher's throw should turn to face the advance base of the runner, sight the covering baseman, give him time to get into position on the same side of the runner as the ball, set, and throw with a step and a follow-through in the direction of the target receiver.

If the pick-off throw is to first with a sole runner on the bag (the most common delayed-steal situation), the second baseman backs up the throw, while the shortstop covers second and the third baseman covers third. The right, center, and left fielders back up first, second, and third, respectively. The coverage is the same when the pick-off throw is to first with runners on first and second, but the first baseman should try to make the play on the lead runner at third, whenever possible. If the pick-off throw is to third, the receiver can be the third baseman or the shortstop, with the left fielder backing up. The catcher covers home, and the first baseman or pitcher backs up. The second baseman covers second, and the right and center fielders back up first and second base, as usual. Practice and experience in handling all types of delayed steals can result in their becoming low key, routine plays. They should almost invariably result in a putout.

Double Steal

Runners on first and second base. Coordinated team response to a double steal with runners on *first* and *second* is the same as with a sole runner on second. The defense should make the initial play on the lead runner, but should be alert to shift to the back runner if the opportunity presents itself.

Runners on first and third base. The double-steal situation with runners on *first* and *third* is particularly challenging because of the variety of options available to both the offensive team and the defensive team. The success of the defensive team in executing a pick-off play in this situation will depend largely upon the players' ability to guess the intentions of the opposition. Are the opponents going to try to score the lead runner? to advance the back runner to scoring position? to play it safe and stay put—perhaps attempting to force an error by drawing a throw while not placing either runner in too much jeopardy? Guessing right is not easy. Some questions to ask when using logic to anticipate what the offense will do in a double-steal situation are as follows:

1. How fast are the runners at third and first?
2. How alert and aggressive is each runner? Does he get a good jump off base with the pitch?
3. How many outs are there? What inning is it? What is the score? Are we ahead? behind? how far?
4. Is the batter a good or weak hitter? Can he bunt, slug, or push bunt well?
5. Do the runners like to run? to draw throws? to delayed steal? to bunt or run and hit in this situation?

In general, the more the defensive players know about the habits and abilities of the opposition, the more apt they will be to correctly anticipate the opposition's actions, and the greater will be the success/attempt ratio of their pick-off plays.

The opposition will probably try to score the runner at third when he is fast; when the runner represents the tying or winning run, it is late in the game, and there is one out; when the batter is a weak hitter; when the catcher or the second baseman and the shortstop have weak or erratic arms; when the catcher throws through to second base; or when the back runner is involved in a rundown. The opposition is likely to try to advance the back runner to scoring position when he has adequate speed, but the runner at third is slow; when the back runner represents the tying or winning run; or when the batter is a weak hitter and there are no outs or one out. The opposition will probably play it safe and stay put when both runners are slow; when the catcher, second baseman, and shortstop have strong, accurate arms; or when the defense has a reputation and history of picking off runners in this situation.

If it is anticipated that the lead runner will try to score, the following offensive tactics can be expected:

1. The back runner uses a straight steal to draw the long throw from the catcher to second base. The lead runner breaks for the plate as soon as the catcher's actions indicate that he intends to throw to second or as soon as the ball leaves the catcher's hand.
2. The back runner breaks for second, stopping short and getting caught in a rundown. The lead runner breaks for the plate as soon as the defense's attention is drawn to the rundown.
3. The lead runner attempts to score on an infield hit or in delayed response to defensive action.
4. The lead runner coordinates his actions with those of the batter and attempts to score as the result of a suicide or safety squeeze. Such a play is risky in this situation, however, because of the danger of a pitchout.

The defensive counteraction to prevent the lead runner from scoring is a pick-off throw to the pitcher, to the second baseman in the base line or in cut-off position, to the shortstop in cut-off position or at third base, or to the third baseman. A pitchout is essential.

If it is anticipated that the back runner will try to advance to scoring position at second base, the following offensive tactics can be expected:

1. The back runner uses a straight steal while the runner at third takes a short lead and then fakes a break toward home in a protective effort to draw the throw or to delay the throw to second.

2. The batter and back runner team up with a run and hit, a run and bunt, or a safety or sacrifice bunt. The lead runner again takes a short lead before breaking toward home in a protective effort to draw the throw.
3. The lead runner stays close to third base, and the back runner attempts a delayed steal on the catcher's return throw to the pitcher.

The defensive counteraction to prevent the back runner from advancing to scoring position at second base is a pick-off throw to the second baseman in the base line or to the shortstop at second base. A pitch-out is recommended.

If it is anticipated that the opposition will play it safe and that neither runner will attempt to advance by means of a steal, the following offensive tactics can be expected:

1. Both runners take leads and attempt to draw a throw or force an error, but are very careful not to be picked off.
2. The batter fakes a bunt while the back runner fakes a break toward second and the lead runner stays close to third.
3. The batter takes a pitch and observes the movement of the defense.
4. The batter hits away as usual.

The defensive counteraction to the conservative play of the offense can be a pick-off throw to the first baseman, to the second baseman at first, to the shortstop at third, or to the third baseman. The defense can also pitch to, and play for, the batter, with a follow-up pick-off throw to first only if the pitched ball is caught by the catcher.

The primary objective of the defense, when faced with a double-steal situation, is to prevent the lead runner from scoring. The secondary objective is to prevent the back runner from advancing to scoring position. A pre-planned, well-executed pick-off play can achieve both objectives and result in a putout as well. The intention is usually to draw the lead runner off third while placing the defense in position to make the play on the back runner at second if the lead runner doesn't commit to home. Under some circumstances it might seem wise not to throw at all. By opting not to make any pick-off throw, the defense virtually eliminates the possibility of the runner's advancing from third, but concedes the advance of the back runner to second. Such lack of action might be warranted if the runs are relatively unimportant (e.g., the defense is ahead by a large margin in the late innings of the game) or if the risk of the pick-off attempt is significantly greater than the threat of facing the batter with two runners in scoring position rather than one. It should not be done routinely, however, or opponents will take undue advantage of the free pass. (See the pick-off section earlier in this chapter for a detailed analysis of pick-off throws in a double-steal situation.)

Handling Rundowns

If a runner is picked off base or otherwise caught between two bases, a rundown play is used to put out the trapped runner.

One Baserunner

The steps in the execution of a rundown play with a sole runner on base are as follows:

1. *The play is set up.* The player with the ball must first make sure that the runner is indeed trapped. To do this he may position his body so that the runner's return to base is cut off, or he may throw to the baseman closest to the runner and have him cut the runner off. The next step is to start the runner moving. The ball is thrown to the covering baseman ahead of the runner, and the rundown play is begun. (*Note:* Some coaches prefer to have the fielder who has the ball when a runner is trapped chase the runner immediately, regardless of the direction. Others prefer to always have the runner chased back. Most coaches agree, however, that a runner trapped between third base and home plate should be forced back, away from the plate—never toward home.)

2. *Players move into position.* As the rundown play is set up, the closest players on each side of the trapped runner must immediately react and move into coverage and back-up position as shown in Figure 11–1. It is recommended that there be three players on each side of the runner. The covering baseman with the ball is the chaser, or rundown player. The covering baseman without the ball is the target receiver and tag player. The remaining two defenders on each side of the runner back up the play, handle errant throws, and participate in the rundown if necessary (e.g, when several throws are required for the putout).

3. *The chaser runs hard, directly at the trapped runner.* By running at full speed toward the runner, the chaser forces him to commit in a given direction and makes it difficult for him to stop or to change direction quickly. While running, the chaser holds the ball behind his ear and out to the side, in cocked position, so that it is clearly visible to the target receiver and ready to be tossed. He neither fakes a throw nor pumps, as these actions often confuse the receiver as much as the runner. He positions his body to the right or left side of the runner so that his view of the

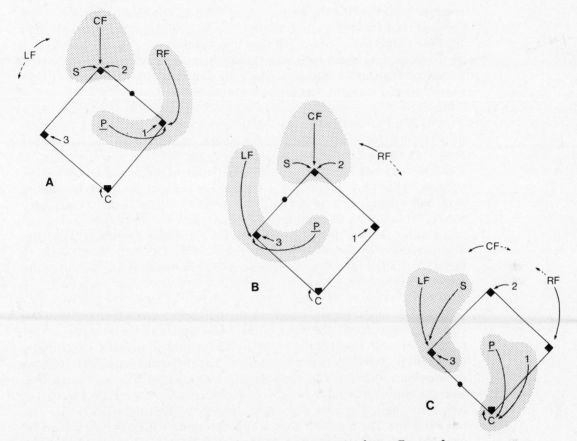

Figure 11-1. Rundown Coverage and Back-Up Assignments when a Runner Is Caught Off Base between (a) First and Second, (b) Second and Third, and (c) Third and Home.

target receiver is not obstructed by the runner. A right-handed thrower usually shifts to his right, or ball side.

The primary objective of the chaser is to catch and tag the runner. The resultant putout is fast and relatively safe. The chance for error during an exchange is eliminated.

4. *The target receiver prepares to catch a potential toss from the chaser.* If the chaser is unable to catch and tag the runner, he will toss to the target receiver. The receiver must prepare accordingly. He should move forward so that he is between the runner and the base he is responsible for covering. He should also shift to the side of the runner to be in direct line with the chaser. It is important that the chaser and receiver be aligned on the same side of the runner so that the glove target of the

receiver is clearly visible to the chaser, the ball is clearly visible to the receiver, and there is a clear path for the potential throw. Throws across the base path are dangerous, as they may hit the runner or be mishandled by the target receiver if he is screened by the runner. Shifting to the side of the oncoming runner also minimizes the extent of body contact with the runner should a tag by the target receiver be necessary.

5. *If the chaser is not able to run down and tag the runner, he tosses to the target receiver.* Although the chaser may be running fast at the time, his throw to the target receiver must be soft and accurate. A forearm-snap toss is recommended. The timing of the toss is critical to the success of the play. If it is too soon, the runner will probably be able to stop and retreat. If it is too late, the runner will probably reach base safely. To facilitate the timing of the play, the receiver may step forward and call for the ball (e.g., "Now!" "Here!" or "Ball!") when, in his judgment, it must be thrown to effect the putout. The ball should not be thrown or called for unless the runner is committed in the direction of the target receiver.

6. *The target receiver catches the ball and tags the runner, and the chaser quickly clears the base path.* While awaiting the toss, the target receiver should stand with his knees bent and his weight distributed evenly on both feet so that movement in any direction is possible without compensatory action. His arms should be extended toward the chaser, with the glove chest high and the pocket facing the chaser. As the chaser tosses the ball, the receiver's eyes should be focused directly on the release point. The receiver must watch the approaching ball as closely as possible and concentrate first on the catch, then on the tag. The tag accomplishes nothing if the ball is not in the glove.

If not in position to receive the chaser's throw, the target receiver should clear out of the way, immediately. He should not try to make the catch while backpedaling, for instance, if there are teammates in back-up position.

If the timing of the play is good, and the target receiver catches the ball just before the runner arrives, the runner will have time only to stop and, perhaps, turn around before the tag is applied. If the throw is released too soon or the runner is not committed at the time of the throw, he will be able to recover and retreat in the opposite direction. In this case, the target receiver may catch the ball, but he will probably not be able to reach and tag the runner.

It is important that the chaser clear the base path as soon after throwing as possible in order to eliminate the possibility of contact with the runner. Some runners are coached to attempt to establish contact with any defensive player who is in the base line but doesn't have the ball. Contact could result in an obstruction call, which would nullify the rundown attempt. The chaser should go to the end of the back-up file at either base, depending on the technique adopted by the team.

7. *If the target receiver catches the ball, but is unable to tag the runner, he has two options.*

   a. He can become the chaser and run hard, directly at the runner, thereby forcing him to run toward the advance base.
   b. He can head the runner toward the advance base and then make a quick throw to the covering baseman, who will chase the runner back toward the base farthest from home.

The advantage of course *a* is that the runner can be put out in a shorter period of time, with fewer throws. The chance for error during a throwing exchange is potentially eliminated. The disadvantage of course *a* is that a misplay at either end of the rundown would very likely enable the runner to advance. Course *b*, on the other hand, increases the chance for a ball-handling error and increases the time required to complete the play; but it decreases the penalty for error. A misplay might allow the runner to return to his base safely, but it should not allow him to advance.

Multiple Baserunners

When dealing with situations involving multiple baserunners, the defense should think ahead and plan a course of action to counter potential offensive efforts. When the back runner is caught in a rundown, the defense should take action that will, at the very least, maintain the status quo. If possible, the defense should achieve a putout—preferably of a lead runner. Good timing, execution, and judgment can even result in two putouts. The key to a successful conclusion of the play is frequently the chase player in the initial rundown. He must decide appropriately when to pursue the putout of the trapped runner, when to shift play to another runner, and when to hold the ball or give it to the pitcher within the eight-foot circle and let things stand—preferably with no advance of any runner. He cannot carry out the play by himself, and he will have difficulty making a wise decision if he receives no feedback from teammates. Communication, teamwork, and control are essential if any rundown play is to be of benefit to the defense.

The steps in the execution of a rundown play with multiple baserunners and a trapped *back* runner are as follows:

1. Defensive players must maintain control, patience, and calm. They should place pressure on the runners, not themselves or their teammates.
2. Players must trap the back runner and must not let him escape.

3. Players must move into coverage and back-up positions to put out the trapped runner as quickly as possible. They must concentrate on the rundown of the trapped runner, but must also be alert for an opportunity to shift play to a lead runner. As long as the back runner is in jeopardy, and the ball is in play, lead runners are a threat to advance.

4. All bases must be covered. The baseman covering the lead runner's bag can assist the chase player in the rundown play by watching the lead runner and calling "Going!" if the runner breaks for the next base; "Hey!" if the runner is well off base but not committed in any direction; and "Two!" or "Three!" (depending upon the initial position of the runner) if he has led off sufficiently that a throw to that base can catch him off the bag. Saying nothing indicates that the runner is not going and is not playable.

5. The chase player in the rundown of the trapped runner makes a play on the back runner by tagging him or by forcing him to commit and then tossing ahead to a covering teammate for the tag-out. Every effort should be expended to put the runner out as quickly as possible so that lead runners have little opportunity to advance.

6. If a teammate calls "Going," "Hey," or a base number, the chase player may concede the advance of the back runner and shift his attention to the lead runner. He may throw one base ahead of the lead runner (if the call was "Going!"), run directly at the runner (if the call was "Hey!"), or throw to the covering baseman at a specific base (if the call was a bag number).

7. If the play shifts from the rundown of the back runner to that of a lead runner, the nearest back-up players must shift accordingly. Each player must make a conscious effort to contribute to the play in some way. There should be no spectators on the playing field. Any player who is not the chaser or the target receiver directly involved in the rundown should stay well away from the runner.

8. The play should end with the rundown and putout of the lead runner. Defensive personnel must be alert, however, for potential subsequent play on a back runner. It is likely that back runners will try to advance while the lead runner is receiving primary attention. It is even possible that two runners will end up on one base. If this happens they should both be tagged. The umpire can sort things out. He will rule that the runner who originally occupied the base is entitled to it, and he will call the other runner out.

9. If there are two outs when the back runner is trapped, the defensive players may choose to pursue the putout of the back runner,

but they should be aware that he must be retired before a lead runner touches home plate or the run will count. There are times (e.g., when the defensive team is ahead by a relatively large margin in the last inning of a game) when an out is more important than the prevention of one run.

COVERING AND BACKING UP

Each player will have a role to play, regardless of the specific action that follows the delivery of the ball to the batter. It will be to field or catch the ball, to cover a base, or to back up. From an off-field position, all nine defensive players should be seen to move in unison.

Table 11–1 summarizes coverage responsibilities of players for each base. Coverage must be coordinated so that no base is ever open. Table 11–2 summarizes the back-up responsibilities of each player.

Table 11-1. Covering First, Second, Third, and Home Plate

Where	Who	When
First Base	First Baseman	For all plays to first, except when the first baseman is drawn away to field the ball
		For all pick-off plays, except when it's been prearranged that the second baseman is to cover
		When a runner is caught off base between first and second
	Second Baseman	When the first baseman is assigned to field bunts
		When the pick-off play called requires that the second baseman cut behind the runner for an attempted tag-out at first
		When the first baseman is drawn away to field a batted ball
	Pitcher	When both the first and second basemen are pulled away from the bag—a rare occurrence
	Right Fielder	When the first baseman is serving as the cut-off player
Second Base	Second Baseman	For all hits to the left side of the field
		When assigned to cover second on a steal
		When the pick-off play called requires that the second baseman cut behind the runner for an attempted tag-out at second

Table 11-1. Covering First, Second, Third, and Home Plate (*continued*)

Where	Who	When
	Shortstop	When a runner is caught off base between first and second or between second and third (If the shortstop gets there first, he may cover.)
		For all hits to the right side of the field
		For all bunts with a sole runner on first
		When assigned to cover second on a steal
		When the pick-off play called requires that the shortstop cut behind the runner for an attempted tag-out at second
		When a runner is caught off base between first and second or between second and third (If the second baseman gets there first, he may cover.)
	Center Fielder	For all bunts with runners on first and second; first and third; or first, second, and third
		When the pick-off play called requires that the center fielder cut behind the runner for an attempted tag-out at second
Third Base	Third Baseman	For all plays to third, except when the third baseman is drawn away to field the ball
		For all pick-off plays, except when it's been prearranged that the shortstop is to cover
		When a runner is caught off base between second and third or between third and home
	Shortstop	For all bunts (if so assigned), or shallow hits to third, with a runner on second
		When a runner is attempting to steal third, and the third baseman is unable to cover
	Left Fielder or Pitcher	For bunts to third with a runner on first (Coverage responsibility depends upon the bunt defense being employed at the time.)
Home Plate	Catcher	For all plays at home, except when the catcher is drawn away to retrieve a wild pitch, passed ball, or errant or misplayed throw
		When a runner is caught off base between second and third or between third and home
	Pitcher	When the catcher is drawn away to retrieve a wild pitch, passed ball, or errant or misplayed throw—if so assigned
	First Baseman	When the catcher is drawn away to retrieve a wild pitch, passed ball, or errant or misplayed throw—if so assigned
		When both the catcher and the pitcher are pulled away from the plate—a rare occurrence

Table 11-2. Back-Up Responsibilities of Each Player

Player	Responsibilities
Catcher	*Throws* to first from right field or the infield when there is no runner in scoring position
	Throws to second and third from the outfield, provided home plate is not left unattended with a runner in scoring position
Pitcher	*Throws* from the catcher to the first baseman covering home (if so assigned) when the catcher has left the plate to retrieve a wild pitch or passed ball, to catch a foul fly, or to field an errant throw
	Throws to all bases from the outfield
First Baseman	*Throws* from the catcher to the pitcher covering home (if so assigned) when the catcher has left the plate
	Throws back to the pitcher from the left side of the infield
	Throws to second base from left and left-center field
	Throws to the relay when the first baseman is functioning as the cutoff (if so assigned)
Second Baseman	*Throws* from the catcher to the pitcher
	Pick-off throws from the catcher to the first baseman at first
	Throws from the catcher to the shortstop covering second (if so assigned) on a steal attempt
	Hits to the pitcher, first baseman, and shortstop (in the hole)
	Throws to the relay (shortstop) following an extra-base hit to left or center field when the second baseman is functioning as a double cutoff
	Throws to first base following bunt pick-ups, with the first baseman covering first
Third Baseman	*Throws* back to the pitcher from the right side of the infield
	Throws to second base from right and right-center field—provided no runner is attempting to advance from second to third
Shortstop	*Throws* from the catcher and first baseman to the pitcher
	Pick-off throws from the catcher to the third baseman at third
	Throws from the catcher to the second baseman covering second (if so assigned) on a steal attempt
	Hits to the pitcher, third baseman, and second baseman (in the hole)
	Throws to the relay (second baseman) following an extra-base hit to right field when the shortstop is functioning as a double cutoff
Left Fielder	*Hits* to the left side of the infield
	Hits to the center fielder in left- or straight-away center field
	Throws from the right side of the field to second or third base
Center Fielder	*Hits* up the middle—to the second baseman and shortstop
	Hits to left and right field

Table 11-2. Back-Up Responsibilities of Each Player (*continued*)

Player	Responsibilities
Right Fielder	*Throws* from infielders to second base
	Hits to the right side of the infield
	Hits to the center fielder in right- or straight-away center field
	Throws from the left side of the field to first or second base

12

Offense

Batters can earn their way on base through a hit or bunt, or they can be given entry to the base paths through an error (e.g., fielding, throwing, catching, mental), a base on balls, being hit by a pitch, or catcher interference.

ADVANCING THE RUNNERS THROUGH THE USE OF PLAYS

Once runners get on base, they must be moved around the bases and, ultimately, across home plate. The batter and runners must coordinate their actions if they are to accomplish that goal. Plays are sometimes communicated to both the batter and the runners by means of signals. (See the section on offensive signals in Chapter 14.) Among the most common offensive plays designed to advance a runner are the run and hit, the hit and run, the run and bunt, the bunt and run, the safety bunt, the sacrifice bunt, the sacrifice fly, the straight steal, the delayed steal on the battery, the delayed steal on the defense, and the double steal.

RUN AND HIT

The runner takes off for the advance base as the pitcher releases the ball. If the pitch is a strike, the batter attempts to hit it—on the ground, preferably behind the runner. If it's a ball, the batter takes the pitch, and the runner follows through with a straight-steal attempt.

A run-and-hit play is used to advance a runner without sacrificing the batter. It is an aggressive play that puts the runner in motion as the pitcher releases the ball. Consequently, there is less chance that the runner can be forced out and that a double play can be executed. In addition, depending upon where the ball is hit and how it is fielded, the runner may be able to advance two bases rather than one. Furthermore, the runner gets a fast start off the base and may draw the attention of a defender. If the defender pulls out of position, he will leave a hole through which an accomplished place hitter can attempt to put the ball. At the very least, the defender may lose his concentration or become anxious.

The advantage of a run-and-hit play is that it affords the runner two methods of advancing—on the hit, if the pitched ball is a strike, and on a steal, if the pitch is a ball. The runner's advance is not dependent upon the batter's hitting the ball. If the batter hits a ground ball and is put out at first, the play is no less effective than a successful sacrifice-bunt play. The risk lies in the danger that the batter may hit an aerial ball that can be caught by the defense. If the ball is fielded and thrown to the runner's base before he is able to return, a double play will result.

Not every batter is a good candidate for a run-and-hit play. Hitters of fly balls, line drives, and long balls, for instance, are usually ruled out. The ideal run-and-hit batter is a good hitter who can get the ball down consistently, has good bat control, and can hit the ball to right field. A left-handed batter has an edge because his power field is usually right. The run-and-hit batter must realize and accept that his primary responsibility is to advance the runner. Hitting the ball on the ground must be his major objective. If the batter hits a ground ball, places it behind the runner, and obtains a base hit, too, he will have accomplished all that can have been asked of him, and more than is usually expected.

A run-and-hit play is most likely to be called when there is a potential force play in effect, when there are fewer than two outs, and when the baserunner is fast. The runner will need speed because the batter will take the pitch if he does not consider it good enough to be hit with control (e.g., on the ground, behind the runner). The runner, then, is on his own to steal. Depending upon the count, the location of the pitch, and the game situation, the batter may swing and miss in order to afford the runner some protection.

Most run-and-hit plays are called when the pitcher is behind in the count (e.g., 2–0, 2–1, 3–1, 3–2) and is, therefore, more likely to try to throw a strike. A 3–2 count is ideal when there is a runner on first. The runner is off and going with the pitch. If it's a strike, the batter has a good pitch to hit. If it's a ball, the runner is awarded second base anyway, without liability to be put out, by virtue of the batter's receiving a base on balls and becoming a runner at first. As a rule, all runners go with the pitch when a force is in effect, there are two outs, and the count on the batter is 3–2.

A run-and-hit play is not usually advised when there are two outs, when the baserunner is slow, and when there is a runner on third base. If there are runners on first and third, the run-and-hit play can be called, but with the general understanding that it applies to the batter and first-base runner only.

HIT AND RUN

The runner takes off for the advance base as the pitcher releases the ball. If the pitch is a strike, the batter attempts to hit it—on the ground, preferably behind the runner. If the pitch is a borderline ball, the batter must protect the runner by attempting to hit the pitch or by swinging and missing to prevent the catcher from jumping out on the ball and making a snap play on the runner. If the pitch is bad or wild (e.g., in the dirt, very high), the batter protects the runner as necessary. With a runner on third, the only time the pitch may be taken is when it is obvious that the catcher will not be able to handle the ball and keep it in front of his body.

A hit-and-run play is used to advance a runner one or more bases and to afford protection from a double play, without necessarily sacrificing the batter. It is generally called under the same conditions as the run and hit, except that the baserunner usually possesses fair-to-average speed, rather than good speed. Consequently, the steal is not a viable option. To protect the runner, the batter must try to make contact with the pitched ball if it is anywhere near the strike zone. As a result of the need to protect the runner, this play is more dependent upon the batter's receiving a pitch that he can get his bat on. It is not advised when the pitcher has questionable or poor control or when the pitcher is ahead in the count (e.g., 0–2, 1–2). In the latter case, the batter is at a disadvantage because the pitcher will most likely try to keep the ball close to, but out of, the strike zone. When the pitcher is behind in the count (e.g., 2–0, 2–1, 3–1, 3–2), he is more likely to throw a strike.

If a hit-and-run play is to be properly executed, the batter must be able to make contact with the ball. The batter may not be the best hitter on the team, but he will be counted on to get a piece of the ball and to keep it down. Coaches should watch hitters in batting practice. Normally hitters will swing at a wider variety of pitches under practice conditions than during a game. The coaches should try to identify prospective hit-and-run candidates—those batters who go after a wide variety of pitches and who make contact with almost everything they attempt to hit. They should look, too, for batters who consistently hit ground balls and can go with the pitch. The ideal hit-and-run batter has good bat control and can place the ball to right field. A left-handed batter, because he normally hits to right, has an edge in this regard. Fly-ball, line-drive, and long-ball hitters are usually ruled out, as are batters who strike out frequently.

A hit-and-run play may be called with the team's best hitter at bat. Consider that the main objective of the play is to advance the runner. A .400 hitter will still be put out more often than he obtains a hit. He will, however, probably hit the ball well a higher percentage of the time than a weaker hitter would. In terms of achieving the team objective, he is a good hit-and-run prospect. Players who are accomplished hitters because they are selective in the pitches they go for, however, may be unhappy about receiving a hit-and-run signal and losing the flexibility to pick the pitch *they* want to hit. Those players need to be reminded that individual goals are subordinate to team objectives.

A hit-and-run play may also be called when the batter at the plate has a relatively low batting average. The critical question is whether the batter can make contact with the ball and hit it down. Getting a base hit is secondary. If the batter hits a ground ball and is put out at first, the play is no less effective than a successful sacrifice-bunt play.

Like the run-and-hit play, the hit-and-run play puts the runner in motion as the pitcher releases the ball; lessens the chance of a force-out at the advance base and a double play; and takes the chance that the batter will not hit an aerial ball that can be caught and turned into a double play. If the defense anticipates either play and calls for a pitchout, the runner is in jeopardy.

Unlike the run-and-hit play, the hit-and-run play may be called with a runner on third. The advantage is that the runner will get a quick start and will be better able to score on an infield hit. It is not recommended, however, because it is usually not worth the risk when there are so many other safer ways that the runner can score (e.g., wild pitch, passed ball, sacrifice fly, hit, error, illegal pitch).

RUN AND BUNT

The runner takes off for the advance base as the pitcher releases the ball. If the pitch is a strike, the batter attempts to bunt it—on the ground, between fielders or in front of a deep-playing fielder. If it's a ball, the batter takes the pitch, and the runner follows through with a straight-steal attempt.

The run-and-bunt play is similar to the run-and-hit play. The notable dissimilarity is, of course, that a strike will be bunted, rather than hit. If the pitch is a ball, the batter—depending upon the count, the location of the pitch, and the game situation—may swing and miss in order to afford the runner some protection for the steal. A fake bunt and take is not recommended because it would alert the defense. The shortstop, in moving to cover second for the bunt, would be in position to cover the steal. A fake bunt followed by a fake slug could be effective because the potential slug would at least momentarily freeze the shortstop and the second baseman.

Because the run-and-bunt play is used to advance the runner and to afford protection from a double play without necessarily sacrificing the batter, some thought must be given to the type of bunt to be executed. The most appropriate bunt will depend upon the game situation (e.g., count on the batter, number of outs, score) and the position of the defense. For instance, with two strikes, the batter is automatically out if he bunts foul. This risk may be eliminated by using a slug or slap bunt. If there are two outs, the batter cannot sacrifice. If he doesn't go for a base hit, he can be put out at first to end the inning. In this case, a slug, push, surprise, drag, or knob bunt may be used. If a defender is playing deep, the ball may be bunted gently in his direction. If the defenders are shallow, in anticipation of a bunt, a fake sacrifice followed by a slug or push bunt can be very effective. Occasionally, the defense can be frozen by using a fake sacrifice and fake slug before laying the ball down gently.

Some batters may find it easier to bunt than to hit. Younger, less-experienced batters in particular frequently lack the bat control necessary to execute a run and hit. The success of a run-and-bunt play is not as dependent upon accurate placement of the ball. Bunting down, and fair, is often sufficient to severely test the skill and poise of any defense. Experienced and inexperienced defenses can be affected by the pressure of fielding a bunt and coordinating defensive action when several options are presented and when the runner is in motion, challenging the defense and perhaps threatening to score. The advantage of the run and bunt over the run and hit, especially when used as a surprise tactic or at lower levels of play, is that the run and bunt is more likely to force errors and to advance the runner. The disadvantage is that the batter is more likely to be put out, particularly if the defense reads the play and responds as for a typical sacrifice bunt.

Most run-and-bunt plays are called when there is a potential force play in effect, when there are fewer than two outs, when the baserunner is fast, and when the batter is more likely to get the ball down on the ground with a bunt than with a hit. If there is a runner on first and the third baseman is not alert in covering his base, a fast runner may be able to advance from first to third. Chances of this happening are increased if the third baseman is forced to field the bunt and he and his teammates are slow to cover third and if the arms of defensive personnel are relatively weak or inaccurate. If there is a runner on first, and the second baseman covers second on steals, the fast start of the runner off base may draw the attention of the baseman and lead him to believe that an attempted steal is in progress. If he pulls out of position, and the ball is bunted to the first baseman, forcing him off base, first could be left uncovered. If the opposition likes to play on the runner advancing from first to second, his quick start off base could allow him to reach second safely. In addition, time taken by the defense to make the initial play to the lead base could afford the batter the time he needs to reach first base safely.

A run-and-bunt play is most likely to be called when the pitcher is behind in the count (e.g., 2–0, 2–1, 3–1, 3–2) and is, therefore, more likely to try to throw a strike. It is not recommended for use when there are two outs, when the baserunner is slow, and when there is a runner at second with a left-handed batter at the plate. (A left-hander usually hits to right field. The second-base runner has a good chance of advancing on a hit to the right side because the throwing distance for the fielder is greater, and because the runner can take off immediately.) A run-and-bunt play should not be called with a runner on third. If there are runners on first and third, the run-and-bunt play can be called, but with the general understanding that it applies to the batter and the first-base runner only. The third-base runner can score on an error or on the play to first or second.

BUNT AND RUN

The runner takes off for the advance base as the pitcher releases the ball. If the pitch is a strike, the batter attempts to bunt it—on the ground, between fielders or in front of a deep-playing fielder. If the pitch is a borderline ball, the batter must protect the runner by attempting to bunt, or by either swinging and missing or faking a slug, to prevent the catcher from jumping out on the ball and making a snap play on the runner. If the pitch is bad or wild (e.g., in the dirt, very high), the batter protects the runner as necessary. With a runner on third, the only time the pitch may be taken is when it is obvious that the catcher will not be able to handle the ball and keep it in front of his body.

The bunt and run is generally called under the same conditions as the run and bunt, except that the baserunner usually has fair-to-average speed rather than good speed. Consequently, the steal is not a viable option. To protect the runner, the batter must try to make contact with the pitched ball if it is anywhere near the strike zone. As a result of the need to protect the runner, this play is more dependent upon the batter's receiving a pitch that he can get his bat on. It is not advised when the pitcher has questionable or poor control or when the pitcher is ahead in the count (e.g., 0–2, 1–2). In the latter case the batter is at a disadvantage because the pitcher will most likely try to keep the ball close to, but out of, the strike zone. When the pitcher is behind in the count (e.g., 2–0, 2–1, 3–1, 3–2), he is more likely to throw a strike.

Like the run-and-bunt play, the bunt and run can be executed with a variety of bunt techniques. The most appropriate bunt to employ will depend upon the game situation and the position of the defense. The object is to take advantage of the opposition. This can be done through surprise, deception, and accurate placement of the ball. Ideally, the runner will be advanced, and the batter will become a baserunner. Of the two objectives, however, it is most important that the runner be advanced. If the batter bunts fair and is put out at first, the play is at least as effective as a successful sacrifice-bunt play.

The key to a successful bunt-and-run play, like that of a hit-and-run play, is the batter. He must be able to make contact with a wide variety of good and bad pitches, and he must be able to get the ball down, in fair territory. The placement of the ball is not as important as when executing a hit and run, but it is still essential that the batter get a piece of the ball and direct it down. A pop-up or miss would quite likely result in a double play. Whether to call for a bunt and run or a hit and run will depend upon the offensive skills of the batter, the speed and position of baserunners, and the position and expectations of the defense.

A bunt and run executed with a runner on third base is called a *suicide squeeze*. It is appropriately named because of the risk involved. If the batter or runner gives the play away, or the defense anticipates the play and calls a pitchout, the runner will very likely be tagged out at the plate or caught in a rundown. Similar results will almost invariably occur if the batter fails to pick up the signal for the play. Because of the potential harm caused by a failure to communicate and to coordinate action between the batter and the baserunner, the batter is usually required to acknowledge receipt of the signal before the squeeze play is considered to be on. The batter may acknowledge the signal by picking up dirt, adjusting his clothing, touching the end of his bat to home plate, wiping his forehead, etc. Having accepted and acknowledged the signal, the batter must concentrate intently on making contact with the ball and bunting it down, in fair territory. Missing the ball or bunting into the air could produce disastrous results.

If a suicide squeeze is to have a good chance for success, the runner at third must have good speed and must get a quick start off the base. Surprise and the pressure of a potential score are additional factors in favor of the offense. The placement of the bunt is not particularly important, except that it should not be hard and directly to the pitcher. If the first and third basemen move in to discourage a potential bunt, but no pitchout is anticipated, the batter may use a slug or push bunt. If the risk is considered to be too great, the play may be called off or replaced with a hit and run. To eliminate the chance of being hit by the ball, the runner must be sure to remain in foul territory when advancing toward the plate.

Few plays, if any, are as exciting, and as stressful for the defense, as the suicide squeeze. Successfully executed, it can demoralize the defense and shift momentum to the offense. It must not be used indiscriminately, or overused, however. It is recommended that the suicide squeeze be called in the late innings of a close game, preferably with one out. It may be called with two out, but only if the play is completely unexpected or if there is an exceptionally good bunter (drag) at the plate who has demonstrated the ability to bunt for a base hit. When a suicide squeeze is called with runners on second and third, the back runner should be alert to advance from second to home on the play if the opportunity should arise.

SAFETY BUNT

As the pitcher releases the ball, the runner takes an aggressive lead and watches the ball's approach to the batter. If the batter tries to bunt the pitch, the runner takes off for the advance base as soon as it is evident that the ball has been directed downward or that it cannot be caught in the air. If the batter takes the pitch, misses it, or bunts into the air, the runner returns to base. Occasionally, the runner may bluff a break for the next base in an attempt to draw a throw, and to force an error.

A safety-bunt call takes some of the pressure off the batter by affording him the flexibility to choose the pitch to be bunted. As a good pitch is the easiest to bunt, the batter should wait and try to contact the first pitch that enters the strike zone. A pitch outside the strike zone should be taken for a ball. This strategy places pressure on the pitcher and reduces the chance that the batter will miss the ball, pop up, or bunt foul. A batter who fails to effectively contact good pitches will invariably have similar or greater difficulty with bad ones. If a run and bunt or a bunt and run were called, failure would place the runner in jeopardy. A safety bunt takes some responsibility away from the batter by restricting the advance of the baserunner until he sees the bunted ball heading directly toward the ground, or until it is evident that an aerial bunt cannot be caught. This conservative approach eliminates the danger that a ball bunted into the air can be caught and turned into a double play. It also protects the runner from a pitchout and pick-off attempt and from the danger that the batter may miss the bunt attempt completely, thereby permitting the defense to play on the runner. At the same time, however, the runner has only one option for advancement. He is dependent upon the batter's bunting the ball to move him along the base path. Furthermore, by waiting to be sure that the ball is directed downward before committing to the advance base, the runner gets off to a late start. If the bunt is hard and directly to the pitcher, the first baseman, or the third baseman, or if the runner is slow, a double play can result, even though the batter manages to get the ball down, in fair territory. The conservatism of the play protects the runner from the potential failure of the batter to execute the bunt, but, at the same time, it increases the vulnerability of the runner should the batter get the bunt down—particularly if a force is in effect. If no force is in effect, the runner may choose to go on the bunt, or he may wait and go when the fielder throws to first in an attempt to retire the batter.

A safety bunt is most likely to be called when the batter's ability to make contact with the pitched ball, and to direct it down, is suspect; when the baserunner has average-to-good speed; or when the defense is conservative—rarely attempting to play on a lead runner, preferring instead to attempt to put out the batter at first base. The play may also be called when competing with younger, less-experienced defensive players who are not always alert for subsequent play or who have weak arms. A runner at third, for instance, may occasionally be able to go home on the throw to first following the fielding of a bunt by the third baseman. When the third baseman is forced to field the bunt, his task is made more difficult by the fact that the runner is behind him and out of sight. The baseman needs practice and experience to be able to effectively hold a runner in this situation and to draw him off base so that a play can be made on him. The threat of the lead runner's scoring places added pressure on the defense. Anxiety levels are likely to rise, and if not controlled, they can lead to errors.

A safety bunt is not recommended for use when there are two outs; when the defense is aggressive and likes to play on the lead runner; when defensive personnel have good gloves, strong arms, and game sense; when the batter is a good hitter and bunter; and when the baserunner is either very fast (run and bunt) or relatively slow (bunt and run). If a safety sacrifice bunt is anticipated, fielders can be right on top of the batter when the bunt is laid down. A double play or putout of the lead runner could result. Therefore, it is necessary to remember that any type of bunt (e.g., slug, push, drag, knob, surprise) may be used when a safety bunt is called. Surprise and deception are essential; they can contribute significantly to the success of the play.

A safety bunt with a runner on third base is called a *safety squeeze*. It is appropriately named because it is a very conservative play that minimizes the danger of the lead runner's being put out at home or doubled off base as the result of a caught aerial bunt. If the safety squeeze is to have a good chance for success, however, the runner at third must have good speed and must get as quick a start as possible. It will help if the defense can be caught off guard. It will also help if the first and third basemen have weak arms or have difficulty handling the stress that bunt plays create. The best place to bunt is probably down the third-base line because the third baseman will have his back to the runner and will be dependent upon his teammates to tell him what the runner is doing. If the baseman throws to first, the third-base runner may have time to score before the first baseman can relay the ball to home plate. If the baseman makes his first throw to home, the runner may retreat to third, draw the attention of the defense, and give the batter more time to reach first base safely.

A safety squeeze is recommended for use almost solely at lower levels of play. The reason for this is that the runner at third will usually not be able to score unless the defense commits an error or the fielder's arms are weak. At higher levels, if a squeeze play is considered, it should be a suicide. The risk to the runner is greater, but so, too, is the runner's chance of scoring if the batter gets the bunt down in fair territory.

SACRIFICE BUNT

The runner responds as for a safety bunt or a bunt-and-run play, depending upon the pitcher's control, the count on the batter, and the demonstrated ability of the batter to bunt the ball. The batter attempts to place the ball on the ground strategically, in fair territory, so that the fielder's only play will be on the batter. The batter "sacrifices" himself to move the runner and to increase the runner's chance of scoring.

The sacrifice bunt is described, in detail, in Chapter 9, "Bunting." It is a relatively safe way to avoid a force-out at an advance base or a double play. Consequently, it is customarily employed when the game is close and when there is a runner on first, or on first and second, with no outs. It is occasionally used as a surprise tactic to force an error with runners on first and third, no outs. It may be used, too, when there is a runner on second, no outs, because there are several more ways to score from third than from second. The appropriate time to sacrifice will vary to some extent, depending upon the condition of the infield, the hitting and bunting prowess of the batter at the plate and on deck, and the strength of the opponent's bunt defense. The appropriate place to direct the bunt will also vary, depending upon the bat control of the bunter; the position, depth, and defensive skills of opposing infielders; the position of the baserunner; and the bunt defense that the opposition is expected to employ. For example, the batter may bunt to a deep infielder, to a weak fielder, between fielders, to the spot vacated by a covering fielder, or to third if there is a runner on second (to draw the third baseman away from the bag). The batter (right-handed) may also go with the pitch (e.g., outside pitches to first, inside pitches to third).

Because the batter anticipates being put out, he is usually more concerned about effective performance than pretense. Consequently, the batter may use a completely overt sacrifice-bunt technique. The rationale supporting this technique is that most teams know when a sacrifice bunt is in order, and it is highly unlikely that they will be totally deceived by a change in the batter's position within the box. In addition, many times it doesn't matter whether or not the defense is aware of the batter's intent. They must still make the play. A well-executed, appropriately placed bunt will put pressure on the defense and will make the play on a lead runner difficult. Furthermore, if the commitment to sacrifice is made early, the defense may doubt its sincerity and disregard the obvious cues. By assuming a squared-around set position as the pitcher releases the ball, the batter can concentrate and attend fully to the execution of the bunt. This is the easiest sacrifice-bunt technique for most batters.

To some extent, the rationale for an overt sacrifice bunt is sound. If it is used indiscriminately or overused, however, the defense may read the play, charge, and be right on the batter as he bunts. By getting to the ball so quickly, a fielder will be able to catch the ball shortly after it hits the ground or even while it is still in the air. There is a good chance that a play can be made on the lead runner and that a double play can be completed. Therefore, it is recommended that some action be taken periodically to keep the defense honest. Some batters, given a sacrifice-bunt signal, will attempt to maintain a hitting pretext for as long as possible before shifting into bunt position. Others will fake a slug before laying the ball down. Deceptive action should be encouraged provided that it does not detract from the batter's ability to execute the bunt.

Occasionally a push or slug may be substituted for the traditional sacrifice bunt. These techniques are particularly recommended when there is a runner on first and the infield is playing in, anticipating a sacrifice. As the batter squares around, the third baseman pulls in, and the shortstop moves to cover second. This opens up the left side of the infield for the slug or push. With a runner on second, the angles up the middle of the diamond are recommended because the shortstop moves to cover third, and the second baseman moves toward first. When bases are loaded, no bunt is recommended because each fielder knows that the best play is to home. There is no need to check or hold runners.

SACRIFICE FLY

This play occurs when there is a runner on third base, with fewer than two outs. The runner takes a normal lead, in foul territory, as the pitcher releases the ball. He watches the ball's approach to the batter. The batter attempts to hit the first good pitch, into the air and deep into the outfield. If the ball is hit and directed up, the runner returns to third and tags up. This is standard procedure regardless of the direction (fair or foul) and probable depth of the hit. The runner may advance, with liability to be put out, when a legally caught aerial ball is first touched, provided he has simultaneously or subsequently tagged his base. The batter attempts to place the ball in the air in such a way that a fielder may be able to catch the ball, but will not be able to throw home in time to put out the advancing runner. The batter "sacrifices" himself to score the runner.

Whether or not the runner will be able to tag and reach home safely will depend upon the speed of the runner and the timing of his takeoff from the bag, the depth of the hit and the distance of the fielder from home, the body position and balance of the fielder as he catches the ball, the speed with which the fielder gets rid of the ball, the strength and accuracy of the fielder's arm, the effect of wind on the ball's flight, and the ability of the catcher to both handle the ball and apply a tag to the runner. If the ball is caught, it doesn't matter whether it is fair or foul.

Coaches sometimes disagree on the best technique to use to tag up, but they agree on the desired end result—as early and fast a start off base as the runner can legally attain. Some coaches suggest that the runner assume traditional lead-off position, with the back (usually the left) foot on the bag and with the front (usually the right) foot closer to, and pointing toward, home. Both knees are bent, and body weight is centered over the front foot. The first step is forward with the rear foot. Other coaches suggest that the runner assume position as for a rolling start, with his strongest foot on the front of the bag and with his weakest foot a comfortable distance behind the bag. This position requires that the runner initiate forward movement just before the ball touches the fielder's glove. In both cases, the runner should start low, with short, gradually increasing strides. The runner may turn his head so that he can see the catch and time his departure from the base himself, or he may keep his eyes focused on home plate and rely on the third-base coach for instruction. When the third-base coach assumes full responsibility for timing the runner's departure from the bag, he yells "Tag up!" as soon as the fly ball is hit, watches the ball while the runner focuses on home plate and prepares to take off, and yells "Go!" some time before the ball contacts the fielder's glove. The technique used by the runner to leave the bag will affect the timing of the coach's directive to go. In addition, there will be some variation in lag time between when the coach says go and when the runner translates the message into action. The response time of some athletes is quicker than that of others. Therefore, it is imperative that the third-base coach practice this play over and over again with each runner, to establish proper timing. If a baserunner leaves his base to advance to home before a fly ball has been initially touched, the defensive team may appeal the play, and the runner may be called out.

If the runner returns to third as soon as it becomes evident that the ball has been hit into the air, he will be in position to advance whether the batted ball is caught or fumbled or whether it falls in for a hit. If, on the other hand, the runner maintains a normal lead on the hit, he can only advance if the ball is dropped or falls in for a hit. If the ball is caught, he must go back to third and tag (thereby losing precious time) before he can advance once more. It stands to reason that a runner who can score from a tag when the ball is caught can certainly score from a tag when the ball is fumbled or drops for a hit. Consequently, it is suggested that when the ball has been directed into the air, the runner always return to third and commit himself to scoring from a tag. The question whether or not the ball will be a base hit becomes irrelevant.

The only time the tag approach may be costly is when the ball is popped up or hit shallow. By going back to tag, the runner is unlikely to be picked off base, but he is also highly unlikely to score, whether the ball is caught or not. By taking a lead on the hit, the runner is closer to home and can conceivably score if the batted ball is dropped. If it is caught, however, the runner can be put out if he is legally tagged while off base or if the ball is legally held on his base before he is able to return to tag. The shorter the throwing distance of the fielder from third, the more vulnerable the runner is. Whether or not the chance of a lead is worth the risk depends upon the game situation and the probability of a defensive error. A less risky alternative might be to tag and fake a break for home, hoping to draw a bad throw.

The ideal batter in a sacrifice-fly situation is a strong, powerful, fly-ball hitter. He may choose to sacrifice some power and place hit to a fielder whose throwing arm is weak or inaccurate, or he may choose to go for the long ball. The runner is dependent upon the batter's hitting the ball, but he may score on either a hit or a caught fly. The sacrifice fly is not recommended under the following circumstances:

1. When the batter is a weak hitter
2. When the batter tends to hit line drives or ground balls
3. When a strong wind is blowing in toward the plate

STRAIGHT STEAL

The runner takes off for the advance base as the pitcher re-leases the ball. If the pitch is a strike or borderline ball, the batter fakes a bunt, swings and misses, or takes any other action short of contacting the ball that can help to protect the runner. If the pitch is a ball or a wild pitch (e.g., in the dirt, very high), and no play on the runner is likely, the batter should take the pitch. The runner prepares to slide away from the attempted tag. He remains alert to get up quickly and to advance should the opportunity arise.

A straight steal is used to advance the runner without the aid of a hit ball, without sacrificing the batter, and without giving up an out. The most the batter gives up is a pitch. Because the pitch could be a strike, however, the count on the batter must be considered before the play is called. It is not appropriate to employ a steal when the batter has two strikes, because he cannot afford to take another strike or borderline ball; nor should the play be called when the count is 0–1, or 1–1. Taking a strike would put the batter in a hole. When the batter has no strikes or is ahead in the count (e.g., 0–0, 1–0, 2–0, 3–1), he is hurt less by taking a strike. Some compromise may be necessary, on occasion, to promote the essential element of surprise. The runner's vulnerability to being put out increases significantly when the defense is able to anticipate, and prepare for, the steal. This is especially true if it responds with a pitchout. The defense is less apt to call for a pitchout when the pitcher is behind in the count.

Not every runner is a good candidate for a steal. The ideal base stealer is a smart, aggressive runner who is able to get a quick start off base, has good-to-excellent speed, uses good running technique, and can slide away from a tag. (See the sliding section of Chapter 10, "Baserunning.") He recognizes, and takes advantage of, opportunities to advance.

A straight steal against highly skilled teams with hard-throwing pitchers and strong, accurately throwing catchers is difficult and, for the most part, dependent on the pure speed of the runner and the element of surprise. It should be noted, however, that steals are not made on the catcher alone. A baseman who is slow to cover the advance base, and a "junk" pitcher, increase a team's vulnerability to a steal.

The batter can contribute to the potential success of the steal play by subtly moving a little more toward the rear of the batter's box when assuming hitting position. This forces the catcher to move back a little and increases the distance that both the pitch and the pick-off throw must travel. The batter may also fake a bunt, pulling his bat back directly behind the pitched ball without contacting it. This action may prevent the catcher from continuously tracking the ball, thereby making the catch more difficult. It also freezes the catcher momentarily and prevents him from jumping out to catch the ball and making a quick, snap, pick-off throw. At the same time, however, the batter's action alerts the defense that a play is in progress. With a runner on first, for example, the short-stop, in moving to cover second for the bunt, would be in position to cover the steal. A full swing and miss is a good alternative to the fake bunt.

A number of variables must be considered before attempting a steal play:

1. Score of the game
2. Speed of the baserunner
3. Position of the baserunner
4. Number of outs
5. Count on the batter
6. Hitting and bunting prowess of the batter at the plate and on deck
7. Quickness of the catcher's release
8. Speed and accuracy of the catcher's pick-off throw
9. Unexpectedness of the play
10. Position of the defense

The following examples illustrate how these variables interact to create circumstances that will influence the desirability of a steal:

1. Close game, runner on first, two out, good hitter at bat—steal. *Rationale:* The batter cannot be sacrificed, because an out will end the inning. By stealing, the runner will be in scoring position, and there is a chance that he can be hit in by the batter. If the steal is unsuccessful, the good hitter will lead off the next inning. The steal is not advised when there is a weak hitter at bat because even if the steal is successful, the batter may not be able to drive the runner in. If the steal is unsuccessful, the weak hitter will lead off the next inning. That is not desirable.
2. Close game, runner on second, one out, right-handed batter at the plate, a fair hitter—steal. *Rationale:* There are many more ways to score from third than from second (e.g., wild pitch, passed ball, sacrifice fly, infield hit). With zero or two out and a good hitter at bat, the steal will not be worth the risk, as the runner is already in scoring position. With a left-handed batter at the plate the steal is also not advised because the catcher has a clear view of the play and an unobstructed throw to third. These conditions decrease the chance for successful execution of the steal.

Most steals are of second base because of the long throwing distance from the plate. Stealing third, however, is possible—particularly if the third baseman is playing in. A fake bunt will draw the attention of the third baseman and force the shortstop to cover the bag. If the fake is delayed until the last moment, as when attempting to disguise a bunt as a hit, the shortstop will have little time to react and get into position to handle the catcher's throw and tag the oncoming runner. In fact, the shortstop will often have to catch the ball on the run. This can be very difficult. If the third baseman charges as soon as the batter squares to bunt, and the batter fakes a slug, both the baseman and the shortstop may momentarily freeze. Third base could be left uncovered.

A steal should be attempted only under the following circumstances, when the chance for success is good:

1. A steal is not expected. (*Rationale:* The defense may fail to, or be slow to, cover.)
2. The catcher has a weak arm, an inaccurate throw, and a slow release; or the catcher has the time-consuming habit of taking steps before throwing.
3. The runner has good-to-excellent speed, has a quick start off base, and can slide away from a tag.
4. The pitcher throws a lot of change-ups, knuckleballs, and other off-speed pitches. (*Rationale:* The longer it takes for the pitch to reach the catcher, the more time the runner has to advance.)

A steal may also be used to get the defense thinking about runners; to put added pressure on the defense, raise their anxiety levels, and force errors; to distract the pitcher and upset his concentration; and to challenge and test the catcher.

A steal is not advised under these circumstances:

1. The defense is cheating in obvious anticipation of the steal. (*Rationale:* It may be more effective to catch the defense off guard by calling a play that can take advantage of the shift in the position of defensive personnel.)
2. The pitcher has control problems, or the catcher is having difficulty handling pitches. (*Rationale:* The risk of the steal is not worthwhile if the runner is likely to advance on a wild pitch or passed ball.)
3. There is a runner on third. (*Rationale:* If the pitch were caught by the catcher, the runner would advance directly into an obvious tag-out.)

The runner should not follow through with a steal attempt if he fails to get a good jump on the pitch. The attempt should also be aborted when it becomes evident that the defense has anticipated the play and called a pitchout.

DELAYED STEAL ON THE BATTERY
(PITCHER AND CATCHER)

The runner takes a normal, not particularly aggressive, lead as the pitcher releases the ball. He watches the ball's approach to the batter, but tries not to draw the attention of the catcher. He may maintain his position or even fake moving back to his base. The safest time to take off for the advance base is as the ball leaves the catcher's hand for the return throw to the pitcher. However, by watching the catcher's eyes and throwing hand and noting his general body position, the runner may pick up valuable cues that will enable him to break for the advance base as the catcher starts his throwing motion.

This play may be called in conjunction with a take signal. The batter allows the pitch to pass by without a fake or any other action that might place the defense on alert. The runner takes off for the advance base on the catcher's return throw to the pitcher. The advantage of calling the take is that the play is definitely on. The disadvantage is that the batter may have to take a strike. Careful consideration must be given to the count on the batter when the play is called.

A delayed steal may be called with no directive to the batter. In that case the batter is free to respond to the pitch as if no play were called at all. If the pitch is good, the batter may go for it. If the ball is contacted, the runner responds in normal fashion to the subsequent action. If the pitch is swung at and missed, or taken, and if the element of surprise is still in the runner's favor, he carries out the delayed-steal attempt. If attention is focused on the runner, the play is aborted and the runner returns to his base. The advantage of not calling a take is that the batter is free to hit the pitch if it is a good one. The disadvantage is that the opportunity to employ the delay may be lost as the result of the batter's hitting into a force or double play, flying out, etc.

A delayed steal is an excellent surprise tactic when the pitcher routinely fails to look the runner back, when the catcher consistently fails to check the runner before returning throws to the pitcher, and when infielders rarely move to cut off a runner's return to base or to hold him close to base after pitches. A fast runner can take advantage of even occasional lapses by the pitcher, catcher, or covering baseman. If the delay is to succeed, however, it must catch the defense off guard. The acting of the principal players (batter and runner) and the timing of the play must be good. If the runner breaks too soon, the catcher can respond to the play as to a straight steal. If the runner breaks too late, the defense will have a greater chance of reading the play and of alerting the pitcher, perhaps in time for the pitcher to throw to the advance base for a play on the runner.

A delayed steal is sometimes used when there are two outs, because the defense is more apt to become lax in this situation. Unlike the straight steal, the delay may also be used by a runner at third. This is a rare and daring play, but if it is successful, it can ignite the offense and totally demoralize the defense. Whether successful or not, a delayed-steal attempt establishes that the offensive team is aggressive and willing to take chances on the base paths. This philosophy can be threatening to a defense, placing added pressure on defensive personnel. They must pay closer attention to runners than they might like. This can upset their concentration, raise their anxiety level, and divert their attention from the batter. At this point, what the offense does becomes somewhat less important than what the defense thinks the offense might do. A successful delayed steal exposes the vulnerability of the defense. Remember, however, that the play is risky and dependent upon the element of surprise. Therefore, it should not be overused or used indiscriminately.

DELAYED STEAL ON THE DEFENSE (CATCHER AND BASEMAN)

As the pitcher releases the ball, the runner takes a very aggressive lead to draw a throw from the catcher. The batter responds to the pitch like a hitter with a green light. If it is a good pitch he may go for it. If it is not, he takes it. If the batter contacts the ball, the runner responds in normal fashion to the subsequent action. If the batter swings at the pitch and misses, or takes the pitch, but the catcher shows no sign of making a pick-off throw, the runner simply returns to his base. If, on the other hand, it appears that the catcher may attempt a pickoff, the runner takes off for the advance base as soon as the catcher's arm starts forward for the throw to the baseman or as soon as the ball leaves the catcher's hand. The latter option is recommended when the catcher is known to fake throws.

A delayed steal on the defense is most commonly used as a surprise tactic when the catcher attempts frequent or indiscriminate pick-off throws. The opportunity to use the play is most apt to arise when there is a runner on first, because less risk is involved with the throw and, consequently, the catcher is less hesitant to throw. The play is rarely called with a runner on second, because most catchers realize that a direct throw to second has little chance of retiring any but the most inattentive, foolhardy, or slow runners. It is not recommended for use with a runner at third because of the risk involved. There are many other ways to score that are safer and have a greater chance for success. Furthermore, most catchers exercise special caution when considering a pick-off throw to third because precise timing and execution are required, and an error will very likely allow the runner to score. Similar caution usually prevails when there are multiple runners on the bases.

The delayed steal on the defense cannot be carried out if the catcher doesn't attempt a pick-off throw. Because there is no way of telling, in advance, whether or not the catcher will "cooperate" and throw, the batter should not be given a take. In fact, there is no reason for the batter to concern himself at all with this steal. It is best left to the fast, aggressive, alert runner who has good judgment on the bases and can pick the appropriate time to attempt it. The success of this steal, like that of the delayed steal on the battery, is dependent upon surprise. The play must not be overused or used indiscriminately. The chances for its success increase when the defensive personnel involved have relatively weak or inaccurate throws, are inexperienced, have questionable game sense, or are highly anxious and stressed.

The benefits to be gained from a delayed steal on the defense are the same as those to be gained from a delayed steal on the battery. In addition, the steal on the defense may discourage the catcher from making throws to the bases. Runners may be able to take advantage of the catcher's hesitancy and conservatism by taking more aggressive leads off base.

DOUBLE STEAL

A double steal, as the name implies, is performed with runners on any combination of two bases (i.e., first and second; first and third; second and third). All the aforementioned straight- and delayed-steal tactics can be used, but each runner should have some idea of what the other one intends to do so that there will be no confusion between them. They will each have a better chance for success if their actions are coordinated.

The double-steal situation with runners on first and third is particularly challenging because of the variety of options available to both the offensive team and the defensive team. From an offensive standpoint, the first step in planning a course of action is to determine the primary objective. It may be one of the following:

1. To advance the third base (lead) runner and score
2. To move the first base (back) runner into scoring position, to remove the potential force at second, and to decrease the probability of a double play

3. To maintain the status quo, relying on a defensive error, or the action of the batter, to move the runners

The next step is to determine how the primary objective can best be achieved. As a part of the decision-making process, consideration must be given to the following variables: score, inning, number of outs, count on the batter, hitting and bunting prowess of the batter at the plate and on deck, lead and back runners' speed, skill and position of defensive personnel, and anticipated defensive response to the situation (see the section covering double steals in Chapter 11, "Defense.")

Defensive coverage of the double-steal situation is becoming increasingly sophisticated. (See the pick-off section of Chapter 11, under the heading "Playing the Runner," for a detailed analysis of pick-off throws with runners on first and third.) Although there are still some teams, particularly at lower levels of play, who seem to give the back runner a routine "free pass" to second, it is generally unwise to respond to the double-steal situation in the same offensive manner each time. The back runner is usually the catalyst. He makes things happen. He may advance to second or sacrifice himself to score a run, but he should never allow himself to be picked off. He should be more conservative with two outs than with none because the catcher is more apt to play on him. If the attempt is successful, and the putout is obtained before the lead runner legally touches home plate, the run does not count and the inning is over. The lead runner must concentrate on the catcher because the runner is most vulnerable to a snap pick-off throw from the catcher to a covering baseman at third. Throws from the catcher elsewhere will usually give the runner at third more time to decide on a course of action and to respond accordingly. Knowing something about the defense's tactical preferences in this situation can better enable the runners to correctly anticipate the opposition's actions and to increase their chance of responding appropriately to counter those actions.

ADVANCING RUNNERS THROUGH REGULAR OFFENSIVE ACTION

When plays are called, the baserunners gain advantage from knowing what the batter intends to do. When plays are not called, the batter is free to respond to the pitch as he sees fit, and the runners must be prepared for anything.

A team's chance of scoring is greatest when runners are on base with no outs. Consequently, it is generally recommended that such runners be relatively conservative, avoiding unnecessary risk. With one out, most coaches favor more aggressive play. With two outs, most coaches recommend a return to more conservative baserunning. One more out will end the offense's chance of scoring.

In general: (1) the more risk the defense is ready and willing to take, the less risk the runners should take hoping to draw throws and force errors; (2) no runner should take a lead farther from his base than the closest defender; and (3) the runner at third should not take such a big lead that he has to start back toward his base before the catcher receives the pitch, or he will forfeit a quick jump on a wild pitch or passed ball. Good baserunners take maximal leads off base, and draw throws, without being picked off. They are prepared to seize any opportunity that affords them a reasonable chance to advance.

When starting from third, the runner should stay in foul territory as he advances toward the plate, and in fair territory as he returns to his base. This practice ensures that a fair hit ball will not strike the runner. If a foul-hit ball strikes him, he is not out. In addition, a throw from the catcher to third will be as difficult as the runner can make it. At no time, while off base, should the runner take his eyes off a ball that is in the hands of a defender.

Responding to a Wild Pitch or a Passed Ball

If the pitch to the batter is wild or becomes a passed ball, the runner must be sure that the ball has gotten a safe distance away from the catcher before committing to the next base. There must be no hesitation or change of mind. If the runner fails to get a good start off base, he should stay.

Most coaches allow their players to decide for themselves whether to advance or not on a wild pitch or passed ball. The reason for that procedure is that by the time the base coach determines that the runner has a good chance to advance and gives instruction to the runner, and the runner receives the message, the opportunity to move ahead safely may have passed.

Responding to a Hit

If the pitch to the batter is hit, and there are two outs, the runner should immediately (at bat-ball contact) break for the advance base. If there are fewer than two outs, the runner should concentrate on the ball as it comes off the bat, trying to judge the future flight of the ball from its initial direction and speed. The ball may be directed up or out (aerial ball) or down (ground ball).

Aerial Ball

The primary responsibility of a runner who is on first or second base with fewer than two outs when an aerial ball is hit is to ensure that he cannot be picked off base. The runner is most vulnerable when a line drive is hit. Consequently, as soon as it becomes evident that the ball has been directed out, toward an infielder, the runner must get back to base quickly and tag. The shorter the throwing distance of the fielder from a runner's base, the more vulnerable the runner is. When a pop-up or fly ball is hit, the runner usually has more time to respond and to decide on a course of action. Once out of immediate danger, the runner is free to direct his attention and energy toward advancement. The first factor usually considered is Will the ball be caught? If the answer is obviously no, and the ball has been hit into fair territory, the runner can immediately start for the next base.

If it is reasonable to assume that the batted ball (fair or foul) will be caught while still in the air, the runner can expect to have to tag before advancing. If there is a good chance that he can tag and reach the next base safely, he should commit himself to the attempt. If a safe advance is doubtful, the runner may try to force play (i.e., draw an errant throw) by taking an aggressive lead off base with the hit or by tagging and faking a start for the next base on the catch.

When there is doubt regarding the "catchability" of the batted ball, runners have three options.

1. They can assume that the ball will drop, take off immediately for the next base, and advance as far as possible with the hit.
2. They can assume that the ball will be caught and tag.
3. They can take a lead and watch what happens. This is a compromise that requires no decision regarding the "catchability" of the ball. If the ball is caught, the runners, by virtue of having taken a lead, will lose time by having to return to their bases to tag; but they will not lose as much time, and will not be as vulnerable to being picked off, as they would have been if they had taken off with the hit. If the ball is dropped, the runners, by virtue of having taken a lead, will be closer to the next base than they would have been if they had tagged, but not as close as if they had started on the hit.

A third-base runner responds a little differently to aerial hits. As soon as it becomes evident that the ball has been directed into the air, he should immediately return to third and commit himself to scoring from a tag. A runner who can score from a tag when the ball is caught can certainly score from a tag when the ball is fumbled or drops for a hit.

If there are multiple runners on the base paths, and an aerial ball is hit, back runners should be alert to tag and advance when it becomes evident that a play will be made on the lead runner. The back runner must also keep an eye on the lead runner in case he aborts his advance and returns to third or the ball is cut for a play on the back runner.

Ground Ball

If a force is in effect (i.e., runners on first; first and second; or first, second, and third), the runner must take off for the next base as soon as it becomes evident that the batted ball has been directed down or that it will not be caught in the air. If a force is not in effect (i.e., no runner on first), the runner has the flexibility to stay at his base or to advance. If there is a good chance that he can take off on the hit and reach the next base safely, he should commit to the attempt. If advancement is not feasible at that point (because, for example, the ball is hit in front of the runner and cuts off his path to the next base; or the fielder has the ball, is checking the runner, and has the option of making the initial play on the runner or the batter), the runner may take a lead and wait to see what happens. An opportunity to advance may arise.

The following are offered as suggestions to guide the runner when a ground ball is hit.

1. Know the position of each defender when the ball is hit.
   a. Take off immediately for the next base if it is obvious that the ball will go through the infield.
   b. If the fielder of the batted ball is deep or does not charge, and the ball is hit slowly, consider advancing.
   c. If the infield is playing in (e.g., to make a potential play at the plate), and no force is in effect, make sure that a sharply batted ball is through the infield before committing to the next base.
   d. Advance on ground balls hit behind you if the infield is at regular depth or back and the probability of reaching the next base safely is high.
2. Do not hinder a defensive player attempting to field the ball.
3. Coordinate action with other baserunners. Protect them when possible.
4. If no force is in effect, and you were not able to advance on the hit, be prepared to break for the next base as the ball leaves the fielder's hand for the throw to first.
5. If no force is in effect, but you attempted to advance on the hit and it is obvious that the ball will reach the target base before you, stop and try to get caught in a rundown.

Responding to a Rundown

When a baserunner is caught in a rundown, it is usually unintentionally. Occasionally, however, it may be planned.

a. A baserunner may allow himself to be caught in a rundown in order to pressure the defense and to force them to commit an error that will permit his advancement.

b. When there are multiple runners (e.g., first and third, second and third, bases loaded), the back runner may make himself vulnerable in an attempt to draw the attention of the defense. The back runner may well sacrifice himself in order to help score the runner from third. If there are two outs at the time, however, the "caught" runner must do everything he can to delay the putout, as the lead runner must touch home plate before the tag of the back runner if the run is to count.

    If there are multiple runners and it is the lead runner who is caught, a back runner should jump off base to try to draw the play. If the attempt fails, as it probably will when playing a well-drilled team, the back runner should try to advance to the lead runner's base. The trapped runner must try to stay alive as long as possible in order to give his teammate more time to advance. Should the lead runner be tagged out, the back runner is as close to home as he can be. The back runner must keep his eyes on the play, however, and be alert to jump back off base should the lead runner escape a tag or otherwise be able to return safely to his base. In that case, the back runner would be vulnerable and would most likely be caught off base. If the defense shifts its attention to the back runner, the lead runner should try to take advantage of the situation and score. A rundown play is often accompanied by heightened anxiety levels. Trying to run down one player while keeping another from advancing is a difficult task that requires communication, timing, and errorless play. Consequently, under these circumstances, intentionally allowing oneself to be caught in a rundown can be good strategy.

MAKING DECISIONS ON THE BASE PATHS

The freedom baserunners have to make their own decisions on the base paths depends upon the philosophy of their coach. Some coaches, particularly those whose players are beginners, prefer to control all movements of runners. The first and third base coaches instruct each player to stop, round and hold (take a turn), round and advance, or return

quickly to a base. This practice places full responsibility for the consequences of decisions on the shoulders of the coaches, who are ultimately
accountable for what takes place on the playing field. At the same time, it
relieves the players of the anxiety that often accompanies the decision-
making process and frees them to concentrate on technique. Also, some
players lack softball insight and the ability to make sound baserunning
judgments. Others must analyze the situation and frequently lose the edge
that self-determination should provide—conservation of time! The
assistance of a base coach in such instances is a necessity. The disadvantage of exercising a high degree of control over a baserunner's movements
is that the player may become totally dependent and never develop a
"baserunning sense." Also, it takes time for the coach to decide what the
runner is to do and then communicate that decision to the runner. In addition, misunderstandings can have serious consequences.

Baserunners must run the bases on their own and should, ideally,
know better than anyone else whether they should attempt to advance.
Consequently, many coaches believe that there are situations in which
decisions can and should be made by the runners themselves. As a rule,
such coaches leave runners on their own when the play is in front of them.
A runner, then, becomes either more or less dependent upon the first- and
third-base coaches for assistance and information, depending upon the
position of the ball and whether or not it is in the runner's field of vision
as he advances. The success of this more flexible approach to coaching
baserunners will depend upon the ability of each baserunner to assess the
game situation and to make quick, sound judgments. Coaches can help
athletes develop this ability by (1) providing them with periodic skill
evaluations and self-testing activities and (2) sharing scouting reports with
them so that they will know, for instance, the strength and accuracy of opponents' arms and the defensive playing tactics of opponents.

Between pitches the coach can do the following:

1. Remind runners of the game situation (count on the batter,
   number of outs, inning, and the importance of their run).
2. Inform them when the infield-fly rule and third-strike rule are in
   effect.
3. Help them to keep track of the ball.
4. Provide them with such directives as "Tag up on a deep fly ball,"
   "Run on a ground ball," or "There are two outs—run on any hit."

Runners can help themselves by the following actions:

1. Watch the coach, between pitches, for signals to the batter and
   the baserunner.
2. Watch the runner ahead and respond to his actions.

3. Prepare mentally. Anticipate what might happen and think about the appropriate response.

GENERAL STRATEGY

When attempting to determine the appropriate offensive strategy to employ, coaches should consider the interaction of the following factors:

1. The game situation (e.g., inning, score, number of outs, count on the batter).
2. The opposition's tactical preferences, past successes and failures, strengths and weaknesses.
3. The opposing pitcher's speed, control, habits, and tendencies.
4. The alignment and depth of defensive personnel.
5. The environment (e.g., temperature, field conditions, wind velocity and direction).
6. The strengths, weaknesses, and abilities of offensive personnel (i.e., batter at the plate and on deck, runner). What plays, if any, are they capable of executing?

A sound plan of attack attempts to do the following:

1. *Take advantage of apparent weaknesses of opponents.*
   a. Narrow the strike zone and be selective when facing a pitcher who has little control. If the pitcher is strong, try to get on base any way possible (e.g., hit the ball on the ground, bunt, walk).
   b. Steal on a catcher whose throwing arm is weak or inaccurate.
   c. If the infield is weak, or the ground is rough, try to hit the ball down or bunt to the weakest position.
   d. Try to place hit to an outfielder whose fielding or throwing arm is weak.
   e. Be prepared to take an extra base on fielders who have weak arms. Force them to throw.
   f. Delayed steal if the pitcher fails to check the runners between pitches.
   g. Advance on infield hits if the defense fails to hold the runners.
   h. Look for an opportunity to advance from first to third on a bunt if the defense is lax in covering third.

2. *Take advantage of opponent's habits and tendencies.*
   a. Advance the back runner in a first-third situation when the defense routinely chooses not to throw toward second.
   b. Delayed steal when the catcher attempts frequent or indiscriminate pick-off throws.

3. *Neutralize the effectiveness of the opponent's strategy.*
   a. Bunt when the infield is playing deep.
   b. Slug or push bunt when the defense is primed to charge in anticipation of a bunt.

4. *Utilize the unique abilities of offensive personnel.*
   a. Give a green light to a good hitter to go for a 3–0 or 3–1 pitch, but give a weak hitter a take.
   b. Call a suicide squeeze with a good bunter at the plate and a fast runner at third, but go for a sacrifice fly or base hit with a long-ball hitter at bat.
   c. Bunt and steal to advance runners into scoring position, rather than waiting for a big hit, when the team is composed of fast runners who are relatively weak hitters. Scrappy, aggressive baserunning can turn a weak-hitting team into a giant killer. When the team is composed of strong hitters, on the other hand, work for a big inning. Use bunting as a surprise tactic, on occasion, but rely principally on hitting.
   d. Insert a pinch runner to decrease the chance of a double play; to increase the chance to score from third on a wild pitch or passed ball, caught fly ball, or infield hit; to increase the chance to score from second on a single or double; and to put more pressure on the defense by having more speed on the base paths.
   e. Insert a pinch hitter if there is one available who can better meet the demands of the moment (e.g., bunt, advance a runner, hit a long ball) than the scheduled batter. Choose the pinch hitter carefully, considering the score and inning. As a player can only pinch hit once, be sure that he is called on at the right time.

5. *Meet the demands of the game situation.*
   a. Consider having the batter take the first pitch under the following circumstances:
      (1) The pitcher is having obvious control problems.
      (2) The previous batter was hit by a pitch.
      (3) Previous batters have been retired on one or two pitches.
      (4) The pitcher is throwing very hard in the early innings, particularly on a hot, muggy day.
      (5) One's own pitcher can use a little extra time to rest following a stint on the bases.
      (6) The batter appears to be anxious or overactive.
      (7) You want to see how the defense will respond to the situation.
      (8) You want to call a play, but not on the first pitch.

b. Consider having the batter hit the first good pitch under the following circumstances:
   (1) Previous batters have been defensive or overly selective, have been taking too many pitches, or have been routinely getting behind in the count.
   (2) The pitcher has good control, likes to get ahead in the count, and can then pick and hit his spot.
   (3) Runners are in scoring position.
   (4) The batter is a pinch hitter.
   (5) The batter is the first to face a relief pitcher who is known to have, or appeared in warm-up to have, pretty good control.

c. In the early innings of the game, with a runner on second and fewer than two outs, consider the following:
   (1) Calling for a bunt if there is a weak hitter at the plate who has good bat control.
   (2) Calling for a steal of third if the runner is fast and the defense is inattentive.
   (3) Letting the batter swing away if he is a good hitter.

d. Be conservative in baserunning if one run won't tie or win the game.

e. When ahead or tied in the late innings of a close game, with two outs and no one on base, go for a long hit.

f. In the late innings of a close game, with a runner on first, consider the following:
   (1) Calling for a bunt if there is a weak hitter at bat.
   (2) Calling for a hit and run if there is a strong hitter at bat and a slow runner on base.
   (3) Calling for a steal, run and hit, or hit and run if there is a strong hitter at bat and a fast runner on base.

g. If the pitcher is tiring or in trouble, try to keep the pressure on. Curtail free swinging at the plate, and eliminate the calling of plays that are high risk (e.g., hit and run, bunt for a base hit, steal of third).

Although the primary offensive objective of each team is to score runs, the beliefs and attitudes of the coaches of each team relative to how this objective can best be achieved, will vary considerably. Consequently, a team's offensive strategy will often reflect the coach's philosophy.

Some coaches are extremely aggressive and encourage their players to test and challenge defensive personnel. They like to surprise the defense and are not discouraged from calling for a low-percentage play if they believe that the time is right and that it can succeed. Actions reflective of aggressiveness include (1) hitting the first good pitch; (2) going for a

3–0 or 3–1 pitch frequently; (3) preferring to advance runners through the use of steals, hit or bunt and runs, and run and hit or bunts; (4) doing the unexpected (e.g., bunting for a base hit, trying to squeeze a runner home, delayed stealing).

A coach with an aggressive offensive philosophy tends to try to make breaks rather than waiting for something to happen. A coach with a conservative philosophy, on the other hand, tends to wait for the defense to make a mistake and then tries to capitalize on it. As a rule, teams composed of inexperienced, lesser skilled players would be wise to adopt a more conservative style of play at the plate, while being very aggressive on the bases. At higher levels of play, most coaches would probably describe their philosophy as somewhere between liberal conservatism and pronounced aggressiveness.

An acceptable offensive philosophy guides action and results in the production of runs. Toward this end, the following suggestions are offered:

1.   *Encourage and reinforce place hitting, particularly to right field.* The ability to control the direction in which the ball will go when it leaves the bat gives the batter the flexibility he needs to (a) adjust to defensive alignments and depths, (b) exploit specific defensive weaknesses, and (c) maximize offensive potential.

With a runner on first, a place hit toward right field is recommended because it makes a double play more difficult to turn. (The runner may cross the path of the batted ball or limit throwing angles to second. Furthermore, to play on the lead runner a right-handed thrower who fields the batted ball must either turn to his right, with his momentum moving away from the direction of the throw, or use a backhand flip. It takes practice and experience to be able to make an accurate, timely, appropriately paced throw to the covering shortstop at second base. In addition, there are more options for the right-side fielder to choose from. It is possible to turn a double play by tagging the runner advancing toward second and throwing to first to force the batter; by throwing to second and then to first to force out the runner and the batter; by tagging the batter and throwing to second for the tag of the runner; or by forcing the batter at first and then throwing to second for the tag of the runner. The fact that there are so many options, and potential distractions, increases the chance for error and the difficulty of the play.) Another advantage of a place hit toward right field with a runner on first is that it will advance the runner to second more often than will a ground ball to the left side. Also, if the ball does go through to the outfield for a base hit, the runner has a greater chance of advancing to third because the throw to third base from right field is much longer than from center or left field. If the hit is in the air, it is apt to tail away from the fielder, toward the right-field foul line. This increases the difficulty of the fielder's throw, particularly if it is right-handed. The runner may be able to tag and to advance, even from first, on a caught fly ball.

With a runner on second base, a place hit toward right field is also recommended. The second-base runner has a better chance of advancing on a hit to the right side than to the left, because the throwing distance for the fielder is greater and because the runner can take off immediately. When the ball is hit to the left side of the diamond, the path of the runner to third is cut off. The runner must delay his advance until the fielded ball has left the defender's hand for a play at first, or until the batted ball is through the infield.

With a runner on third base, a place hit toward right field is recommended for several reasons. First, the shorter the throwing distance of the potential fielder from third, the more vulnerable the runner. Because the right-side fielders are far from third, the third-base runner can take a more aggressive, longer lead when a ground ball is hit in their direction. If the infielders are playing deep, the ball is hit slowly, and the fielder does not charge, or the ball is misplayed, the runner may be able to score. When the ball is hit to the left side of the diamond, the runner must immediately break for home or return to his base on the hit. If he maintains his lead, he risks drawing the play and being caught in a rundown. Second, when a very shallow fly ball or infield pop-up is hit, the runner will probably not be able to score unless the ball drops in fair territory and he has a lead. If the ball is hit toward right field, the risk of taking a lead off third is diminished. Third, when a normal fly ball is hit to right field, rather than left, the runner tagging at third has the play more directly in front of him. He can use his own visual cues to supplement the verbal cues of the third-base coach and to time his departure from the bag.

2. *Always work to get runners into scoring position (e.g., second base with no outs, third base with fewer than two outs).* The closer a baserunner gets to home, the more pressure he can put on the defense, the more ways he can score, and the more likely it is that he will score. Consider, for instance, that a runner may score from third, with two outs, as the result of a wild pitch, a passed ball, an illegal pitch, an infield hit, an infield error, a delayed steal, an attempted pickoff at third, an obstruction during a rundown, or a sacrifice fly. Under the same circumstances, a runner on second is not likely to, and in some cases cannot, score. Therefore, even the better hitters on the team may, on occasion, be called upon to sacrifice.

3. *Look ahead.* For example, with two out, a runner on first, and a weak hitter at bat, think hard before calling a steal. If the runner is put out, the weak hitter will lead off the next inning. This should be avoided, when possible. If the runner is safe at second, the hitter may still not be able to drive him in.

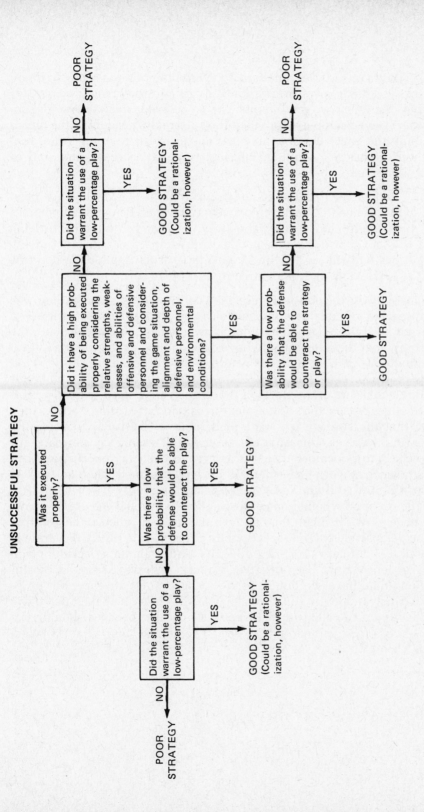

Figure 12-1. Analyzing and Evaluating Unsuccessful Strategy

4. *Build a lead!* Don't be satisfied with it and don't protect it. If you open up a big lead, however, refrain from using surprise tactics. Why, for example, show off a good bunter or a delayed steal when it's unnecessary? Save such plays for when they are really needed. In the meantime, play the game up front and try not to press. Rely on basic, fundamental offense (e.g., hitting, bunting, running) to score runs and to retain momentum.

5. *Remember that the game isn't over until the last out has been made.* If you are behind early, chip away at the lead. Be patient, and don't press too hard to come back right away. If what you have been doing hasn't worked, consider changing your approach. Do not give up quickly on what has worked for you in the past, but, at the same time, don't be afraid to be flexible and innovative if warranted.

The chart presented in Figure 12–1 is offered as a tool to help the coach analyze and evaluate selected strategy after it has been used in a game and has failed. The chart emphasizes the need to consider both the probability that the offense could have executed the strategy properly and the probability that the strategy would have worked if it had been executed properly. Too often, in retrospect, coaches look to the end result for a direct measure of the worth of the strategy they chose to employ. If it worked, they reason that the strategy was good; if it didn't work, they reason that the strategy was bad. This logic is analogous to using the game's final score as a measure of the quality of a team's performance. It is important to remember that just as a team can play poorly and win, poor strategy can work—especially if it is well-executed. Then too, just as a team can play well and lose, good strategy can fail.

The question whether or not a situation warranted the use of a low-percentage play is difficult to answer. If the strategy failed, coaches often become defensive or rationalize, thereby attempting to justify the strategy decision. It is not easy to remain objective and evaluate a decision when its consequences have been negative. Coaches who have been successful for a long time have, no doubt, used low-percentage strategy, but probably sparingly, and with full knowledge of the risks involved. Such plays rely heavily on the element of surprise. Generally, coaches should take fewer chances as a runner gets closer to home and more chances when ahead.

FIVE

Coaching

13

Team Management

The first step in selecting a team is determining how many players to carry. The number will vary depending upon the philosophy of the head coach and the athletic administration, the number and organizational abilities of coaches on the staff, the amount of money in the budget, the extent of the schedule, and the level of competition. Too many players can cause problems. Individuals may not receive the playing time or individual instruction that they may desire. There may not be enough space for individual practice or enough time for the batting practice each player may require. Internal competition for starting positions and playing time can break down team cohesion. Supervision is also difficult. Too few players, on the other hand, can also cause problems. Lack of depth can reduce the coach's flexibility in terms of strategy. There may not be offensive (pinch hitters, runners) or defensive specialists to call upon. Consideration should be given, too, to the fact that injuries and normal attrition will very likely reduce the number of active players on a roster as the season progresses. In summary, it seems apparent that coaches should select the greatest number of players that they can reasonably and effectively handle within their budgets. Some thought should also be given to the versatility of extra players. A utility player can be extremely valuable.

Once the coach has decided on the size of his team, his next step is to determine needs. Where are the team weaknesses? Who has graduated, or is not returning to the team for other reasons? How many upperclassmen or older players are there on the team? Does the team need hitting, pitching, speed, a utility infielder? Needs should be listed in order of priority.

At this stage in the selection process, it might be wise for the coach to engage in a little introspective analysis. He might ask himself, "What are my strengths and weaknesses?" A coach whose strength is defense, for example, might select hitters, reasoning that he might be more successful teaching hitters to field than teaching fielders to hit. The coach might also examine his ability and willingness to help a potential player overcome psychological problems. It would not be wise to select a player that the coach may not be able to handle, even if the player has considerable skill.

The next step is to develop a list of selection criteria. Suggestions are as follows:

1. *Individual physical endowment* (e.g., height, weight, speed, quickness).
2. *Individual physical fitness* (e.g., strength, endurance, flexibility, agility).
3. *Individual skill* (e.g., ability to hit, bunt, field, throw, run). Coaches may base their evaluation of specific skills on the following.
   a. *Hitting*—consistency, power, placement, judgment or "batting eye
   b. *bunting*—consistency, placement, sacrifice, base hit
   c. *fielding of ground balls*—range, hustle, diving, charging
   d. *fielding of short hops*—aggression, courage, confidence
   e. *fielding of fly balls*—good jump, judgment, diving, coming in and going back
   f. *throwing*—speed, distance, accuracy, short release time, appropriate delivery
   g. *running*—judgment on bases, aggression, sliding
4. *Versatility* (e.g., ability and willingness to play more than one position).
5. *Psychological state* (e.g., drive, determination, coachability, leadership, aggression, and game sense). Game sense is largely a result of experience and may take a long time to develop. Coaches, especially at higher levels of competition, may use it as a major selection factor because of its significant relationship to good performance. Intelligence will aid a player in developing game sense more quickly and should be taken into account with less-experienced athletes.
6. *Individual and team goals* (e.g., are they consistent with those of the coach? of other team members?).

Players should be ranked from 1–10 (1 being low, 5 average, and 10 high), within each of the above categories. Weigh each category as desired.

Questions to ask about prospective players include the following:

1. Has the player had sound coaching?
2. Has the player had much competitive experience? at what level?
3. How does the player compare with other players of comparable background and experience?
4. How quickly does the player learn?
5. How willingly does the player try new things? play a new position?
6. Does the player appear to be self-motivated, or will I have to push constantly?
7. Does the player give up or accept a challenge?
8. How does the player react to winning and losing?
9. Can I communicate with the player?
10. Can I handle the player?

In order to answer some of these questions, the coach might do the following:

1. Administer a background questionnaire, or have prospective players write an autobiographical sketch of their softball experience.
2. Place prospective athletes in realistic game situations and observe their responses.
3. Present new material to prospective athletes and observe their responses.
4. Suggest that prospective athletes change their batting, throwing, or fielding technique and observe their responses.
5. Involve prospective athletes in physically demanding situations and observe their responses.
6. Present prospective athletes with a challenging situation, and observe their responses.
7. Involve prospective athletes in a competitive event and observe their responses.
8. Criticize a prospective athlete and observe the response.

The more players a coach must choose among, the more difficult the selection process becomes. It is usually fairly easy to differentiate between the top 10 percent and the bottom 10 percent, but selecting a few out of the average is very hard. Following are some suggestions:

1. Hold tryouts over a two-week period. Those who are not particularly interested will very likely drop out, since they will not want to make such a time commitment. Also, individual performance may vary from day to day. By observing players over a longer period of time, the coach is apt to gain a more reliable and valid picture of their ability.

2. Make the tryout relatively severe. Those who do not want to work will very likely drop out. Those who stick through the entire tryout period will gain some conditioning.

3. Allow the candidates to try out, at least part of the time, at the positions they believe they play best.

4. Make a preliminary cut after the first three days. Focus on skill. Eliminate the bottom 10 percent or more. By reducing the number of potential candidates, you can spend more time observing those who are in contention.

5. If the number of potential players is still too large to deal with effectively, make a second cut at the end of the week, or break the group up into smaller groups and assign them to different time periods.

6. If a choice must be made between an upperclassman and a freshman, all things being fairly equal, favor the freshman, who will have more years in which to develop and to contribute to the program.

7. Compare upperclassmen to upperclassmen, and compare freshmen and sophomores to their peers.

8. If one player has a little less skill, but a better attitude, than another, select the player whose weakness you can best rectify. Can you best deal with the mind or the body of the athletes in question? If one athlete is a weaker hitter and the other a weaker fielder, select the one you can help more considering your own strengths and weaknesses.

9. If it comes down to a couple of candidates and it is impossible to differentiate between the two, or you are unwilling to pick one above the other, encourage both to attend and to participate in team practices even after the tryout period has ended. Injury, sickness, or normal attrition may open up a spot for an extra player. If a spot doesn't open up, the extra practice will, at the very least, improve the player's chances of making the team the following year.

10. Discuss candidates with assistant coaches, or enlist the aid of a qualified observer.

When possible, the coach should talk with each player who does not make the team, although that practice can be very time-consuming. The purpose of this session should be to minimize the trauma involved, if there is any, and to point out the reasons for the cut. Suggestions for improvement should be given to the player, along with encouragement to try out again in the future. Ideally, all candidates should feel that they have received a fair chance to show what they can do. The tryout experience should be as positive as possible.

PRACTICING

The year of the softball player is usually divided into three distinct phases, as follows:

1. *Pre-Season.*   The first part of the pre-season is almost invariably devoted to physical conditioning. When the pitchers start throwing, the second part of the pre-season program has begun. At this time, remaining team members may start batting practice, hitting off a pitching machine. The general weight-training program may be modified to include more softball-specific activities. The last part of the pre-season program begins when the entire team reports for routine practice. Emphasis is primarily on conditioning and the development of individual offensive and defensive skills, although team offensive and defensive techniques are also practiced.
2. *Competitive Season.*   Throughout the season, primary emphasis is on team offensive and defensive play, with drills designed to correct weaknesses and to prepare for specific, upcoming opponents. Conditioning maintenance drills are also included.
3. *Post-Season.* The first part of the post-season should be devoted to evaluations of team and individual performance throughout the pre-season and competitive season. The second part should include a period of time away from softball, although a planned program of daily exercise is recommended.

Practices are held at various intervals throughout the pre-season and competitive season. They are generally planned to help each athlete to (1) get in shape, (2) improve offensive and defensive skills, (3) develop proper responses to game situations, (4) increase knowledge of the game and both offensive and defensive strategy, and (5) develop softball concepts, insights, and *game sense.*

Following are six steps for planning any practice schedule:

1. Determine the most appropriate length and number of practices per week for the athletes involved. Obtain class and work schedules from players. On the basis of this information, develop a master practice schedule with set dates, times (beginning and

end), and places. Distribute this schedule to players, support staff (e.g., managers, trainers, supervisory personnel), and parents (if so desired).

2. Decide what you want to do, and develop an organized, detailed plan to do it. Try to include a balance of instruction in the following subjects:
   a. Fundamental individual defensive skills (e.g., throwing, catching, covering bases, backing up plays)
   b. Position play
   c. Basic team defense (e.g., executing rundowns, pickoffs, relays and cutoffs; handling straight, delayed, and double steals; handling bunts with runners in various positions on the bases)
   d. Fundamental individual offensive skills (e.g., hitting, bunting, baserunning, sliding)
   e. Basic team offense (e.g., drawing throws and forcing errors, receiving and responding to offensive signals, base stealing, place hitting, executing hit-and-run and bunt plays)

   Also include a warm-up designed to prepare the athletes, mentally and physically, for the practice; conditioning drills; strategy sessions; and drills designed to help the athletes learn to handle stress and situational anxiety. Because it will not be possible to cover every aspect of the game in each practice session, plan several practices at one time to ensure that no important facet of the game is inadvertently left out.

3. Arrange for access to the necessary areas (e.g., field, locker room, training room, equipment room) and to lights.

4. Be sure that all necessary equipment is available and ready for use.

5. Develop a plan for handling equipment in order to prevent loss and injury. Determine who will take what to practice, where it will be kept, who will collect it and account for it at the end of practice, and who will return it to its storage place.

6. Check to be sure that each player has transportation to and from practice.

The uniqueness of each coach and team and their situation precludes the development of a master practice regime that is applicable to all. There are, however, some basic principles that are recommended to make practices efficient and productive:

1. Start on time.
2. Give the athletes a brief overview of the practice plan, and set the tone for the workout.

3. Conduct warm-up (jogging; stretching; throwing and catching for at least five minutes without gloves, if early in the season; and throwing and catching for up to ten minutes with gloves). Observe the athletes closely during this period. Talk to them and try to ascertain their readiness for practice. Do they appear tired or edgy? Have they been staying up late with mid-terms or working extra hours? Are they tight from the previous practice, or is someone nursing a sore arm? Is there a special event that they are missing because of practice? Take these factors into account, and be flexible with your practice plan.

4. Balance game situations and drills. Try to develop and use drills that are realistic (match as closely as possible the sights, sounds, stresses, and movements of actual competition). When athletes can grasp the significance and relevance of a drill, it becomes more effective.

5. Accept the challenge to present the same old fundamental skills in new and different ways (e.g., varied order, new drill). Overlearning and retention are important, but it is not necessary to do the same thing the same way over and over again.

6. Build success into the practice, even if the primary focus must be on subordinate (but meaningful) goals. Provide a positively reinforcing environment, and minimize reactions to failure.

7. Pay attention to what is going on, and become a part of the practice. Provide immediate feedback and constructive criticism, as appropriate, but try not to hold up several players to help one. Each player should be involved in practice to the greatest extent possible. Players who are not kept busy may gather in groups or lose interest. That is when valuable time is often wasted, and discipline problems frequently arise.

8. Although you may criticize a player, do not do so in public. Furthermore, allow no player to criticize another. Peer criticism undermines the leadership of the coach, decreases team morale and cohesiveness, and can cause confusion (e.g., player says one thing, coach says another). Head and assistant coaches must communicate to be sure that players are receiving consistent, constructive criticism. If punishment is necessary, describe the appropriate behavior; administer the punishment with as little emotionality as possible; make the punishment relatively severe; and be consistent in the application of the punishment.

9. Try to communicate with each player at every practice. Often the better players receive the most help because the coach feels (consciously or subconsciously) that they can benefit more from instruction (e.g., "Why waste my time with Jim? He'll never be very good"). Consequently, the good tend to get better, and the

weak may fail to improve, or even get weaker. Plan to spend time with less-skilled players.

10. Try to accomplish as much as possible in as short a time as possible. Tolerate no outside interference or inattention. Plan a space for everything, and move quickly from one activity to another. Plan for the productive use of every minute of practice time. Leave nothing to chance.

11. Keep in mind that what you (the coach) know is only important to the extent that it contributes to increased team and individual knowledge and to improved team and individual performance.

12. Evaluate and sum things up at the end of practice.

13. Try to end at the designated time. Timing depends on the organizational skill of the coach. If the practice is to be extended, tell the athletes why. Communication frequently helps to allay confusion and frustration.

14. Try to be organized, objective, fair, supportive, helpful, receptive to suggestions and criticism without defensiveness, and progressive in the presentation of activities so that athletes can experience some degree of success. No activity should be a part of practice without prior consideration of its purpose and its potential contribution to the attainment of team and individual goals.

Batting Practice

Batting practice is a significant part of most general practice sessions. Unfortunately, it is also very time-consuming and boring if it is not carefully planned and conducted.

It is extremely important, when conducting any batting practice, to (1) keep every player busy, (2) keep the practice moving, (3) allow no player to monopolize time at the plate, (4) see that pitchers and catchers receive their fair share of batting time, and (5) stress the need for everyone to remain alert throughout the practice. Players must be required to consider the safety and welfare of others at all times. If any player is in danger of being struck by a batted or thrown ball, those who see the situation develop should yell, "[player's name], duck!" If there is no immediate threat, everyone should remain silent.

If pitchers are throwing to batters out-of-doors, a ball shagger should be used. All throws from the infield and outfield should be made to the shagger—not to the pitcher. Balls should not be scattered around the pitching area, because stray balls can be very dangerous. The pitcher may inadvertently step on one; or a batted ball may strike a stray ball, and the rebound may hit the pitcher.

Each time a ball is delivered to the plate, the batter should have a specific objective in mind—to hit a ground ball, fly ball, or line drive; to pull, hit up the middle, or go to the opposite field; or to bunt to first, to third, or out in front of the plate. Time should also be spent working on weaknesses—high, low, inside, or outside pitches; fastballs, change-ups, rises or drops.

When pitching batting practice, pitchers should be encouraged to balance their own needs with those of the batters they face. There are times when either may need the help or the challenge that the other can present.

Care should be taken during every practice, but especially during batting practice, to be sure that balls that leave the playing area are retrieved immediately. Delay can be costly, as players may forget about them or not be able to find them later.

When the weather necessitates indoor batting practice, a number of problems arise. One problem is space. The stronger and more powerful the hitters, the greater the need for an enclosed batting cage. Another problem is time. If there are twenty team members and one cage, and practice is scheduled for 2 hours, each player will receive a maximum of 6 minutes of hitting. This means that there are 114 minutes of each player's practice time not accounted for. Without organization, chaos will invariably result, with much wasted time.

How each coach chooses to use indoor practice time will depend upon the equipment and the facility available. If a batting cage is available, and there is activity space nearby, players may be rotated in and out of the cage in specific time intervals or after a set number of hits or pitches. Players should be assigned to a position in the batting-cage rotation so that they know who they follow and when they must move to the on-deck area to prepare for their turn at bat. When not in the cage or on deck, players may perform drills as listed and posted by the coach. If two batting cages are available, rotate players in and out of each cage at specific time intervals or after a set number of hits or pitches. Use pitchers in both cages, pitching machines in both cages, or a machine in one cage while pitchers alternate in the other. One cage may be used for hitting and the other for bunting. There are numerous options. Again, it is important to assign players to a position in the rotation at each cage. When not in a cage or on deck, players may perform drills as listed and posted by the coach. If one or more batting cages are available, but there is no space for activity outside the cages, players can be assigned to hit during a set time period. They will report to practice in staggered shifts and leave when they are finished.

Pitching Practice

Pitchers and catchers should begin practice at least two weeks before the rest of the team. The additional time will allow the pitchers to get their arms in fair shape before the rest of the team reports and batting practice begins. Practice usually contains jogging and stretching activities, physical conditioning drills (particularly those that will enhance cardio-vascular endurance and leg strength and endurance), and pitching. Actual pitching practice during the first couple of days is usually very light, although the amount will depend to some extent on the condition of the individual pitcher. Work demands may be measured according to the length of time spent throwing or the number of pitches thrown. For the first couple of days, five minutes of throwing, or about twenty pitches, is probably sufficient, as it is important to minimize the amount of soreness the pitchers experience. Catchers may experience some discomfort and tightness from assuming the crouch position.

Work loads should be gradually increased in duration and intensity as the pitcher's strength and endurance increase. Heavy, moderate, and light workouts, and days off, must be scheduled at periodic intervals and carefully balanced.

The key to any practice schedule for pitchers is progression. Do not try to do too much, too soon. Arm problems, once developed, can become chronic and take a long time to heal.

The pitchers' objectives during the first couple of practices may be to increase their range of motion and to develop a comfortable pitching rhythm. The next step is to work on speed. When a sufficient degree of velocity has been attained, emphasis shifts to fastball control. A stand-up batter (non-swinging) is used when a pitcher has reasonably consistent control. At that point, the pitcher may be called upon to pitch batting practice. The next step in the pitcher's progressive schedule is to work on various types of pitches—first trying to make the ball move, and then working on control. By the time the competitive season begins, the pitcher should be throwing about 300 to 350 pitches in practice.

Many coaches limit their pitchers' first couple of competitive game stints to three or four innings, even if they are pitching well. Subsequent starts may be progressively extended until pitchers are allowed to complete full seven-inning games.

Table 13-1 presents a sample pitching practice.

Table 13-1. A Pitching Practice

Time	Activity
3:00–3:05	Jog
3:05–3:15	Static stretches
3:15–3:25	Leg conditioning (e.g., sprints, jump rope, pick-ups)
3:25–3:30	Loose, easy, *relaxed* throwing (overhand or underhand)—approximately 20 pitches
3:30–3:35	Throwing for *speed*—approximately 20 pitches

Table 13-1. A Pitching Practice (*continued*)

Time	Activity
3:35–3:45	Throwing for *control*—approximately 10 pitches at each of 4 different targets (high-inside, low-inside, low-outside, high-outside) *Note:* A pitcher who has a rise, drop, or curve may throw that pitch during spot-control practice.
3:45–3:50	Throwing for *movement*—approximately 20 pitches that move in one way or another *Note:* It doesn't matter how the ball moves, or whether or not it is a strike.
3:50–3:55	Throwing *types of pitches*—approximately 5 of each pitch in the pitcher's repertoire
3:55–4:05	Throwing *innings*—3 *Note:* Catcher calls balls and strikes.
4:05–4:10	Throwing with a *full count* (3 balls and 2 strikes)—sprint 25 yards for 2 walks in a row
4:10–4:15	Throwing for *speed*—approximately 20 pitches at 10 second intervals
4:15–4:20	Loose, easy, *relaxed* throwing—approximately 20 pitches
4:20–4:30	Stretch *Note:* At the conclusion of the stretches, the pitcher should put on a jacket.
4:30–4:40	70-yard sprints—5, with 30 seconds in between
4:40–4:50	Fielding fungoed grounders
4:50–4:55	Throwing balls in the dirt to the catcher and covering home plate
4:55–5:00	Catch-up time, warm down

Pre-Game Practice

Most teams have a set pre-game practice routine. Players gain some sense of security from the ritualization of the routine despite varying opponents, environments, and weather conditions. Table 13–2 is a sample schedule for a pre-game practice without batting.

Table 13-2. A General Pre-Game Practice

Time	Players	Activity
12:30	All	Arrival at ball park
12:40	All	On field, ready to play
12:40–12:45	All	Jog
12:45–12:55	All	Stretch
12:55–1:05	Infield and Out-field	Throw and catch

Table 13-2. A General Pre-Game Practice (*continued*)

Time	Players	Activity
12:55–1:05	Pitchers and Catchers	Loose, easy, relaxed throwing (overhand or underhand)
1:05–1:35	Infield and Out-field	1. Fungo fielding
		2. Leg conditioning (pick-ups, sprints)
		3. Dry swinging
		4. Tee swinging or ball-toss hitting
	Pitchers and Catchers	Warm-up
1:35–1:45	All	Pre-game huddle (review of signals, statement of game plan)
1:45–1:55	Starting Line-Up, Minus Pitcher	Pre-game infield:

Round 1—Infield catch
   Infielders move in close to home.
   Catcher exchanges throws with 3B, SS, 2B, and 1B, respectively.
   Outfielders back up.

Round 2—Hits for out at first; bunts for double play; outfield backup
   a. Ball is *hit* to *3B*; 3B makes play to first; ball is returned to catcher.
   Catcher tosses *bunt* out in front of plate, fields it, and goes for double play; ball is returned to catcher.
   b. Ball is *hit* to *SS*; SS makes play to first; ball is returned to catcher.
   Catcher tosses *bunt* to *3B*; 3B goes for a double play; ball is returned to catcher.
   c. Ball is *hit* to *2B*; 2B makes play to first; ball is returned to catcher.
   Catcher tosses *bunt* to *1B*; 1B goes for double play; ball is returned to catcher.
   d. Ball is *hit* to *1B*; 1B makes play to first; ball is returned to catcher.
   Catcher throws to second as for a steal putout; SS returns ball to catcher via 1B.

Round 3—Hits for double play; bunts for out at first; outfield backup
   a. Ball is *hit* to *1B*; 1B goes for double play; ball is returned to catcher.
   Catcher tosses *bunt* out in front of plate, fields it, and makes play to first; ball is returned to catcher via 2B and 3B, respectively.

b. Ball is *hit* to *2B*; 2B goes for double play; ball is returned to catcher.

Catcher tosses *bunt* to *3B*; 3B makes play to first; ball is returned to catcher via 2B and 3B, respectively.

c. Ball is *hit* to SS; SS goes for double play; ball is returned to catcher.

Catcher tosses *bunt* to *1B*; 1B makes play to first; ball is returned to catcher via 2B and 3B, respectively.

d. Ball is *hit* to *3B*; 3B goes for double play; ball is returned to catcher.

Round 4—Bunts for out at third and home

a. Catcher tosses *bunt* to 1B; 1B goes for out at 3B; ball is returned to catcher.

b. Catcher tosses *bunt* to 3B; 3B goes for out at home.

c. Catcher tosses *bunt* to 1B; 1B goes for out at home; 1B returns to position at 1B.

d. Catcher tosses *bunt* to *3B*; 3B goes for out at 3B; ball is thrown to first.

Round 5—Outfield throws to bases

a. 1B throws to RF; *RF* throws to *1B*.

1B throws to CF; *CF* throws to 2B,

2B throws to LF; *LF* throws to 3B.

b. 3B throws to RF; *RF* throws to 2B (SS).

SS throws to CF; *CF* throws to *3B*.

3B throws to LF; *LF* throws to *2B*.

c. 2B throws to RF; *RF* throws *home*.

Catcher throws to 2B; 2B throws to CF; CF throws *home*.

Catcher throws to 3B; 3B throws to LF; *LF* throws *home*.

d. Catcher throws to 1B; 1B throws to RF; *RF* throws to *3B*.

3B throws to CF; CF throws to *2B*.

2B throws to LF; *LF* throws to *3B*; 3B throws to first.

Round 6—Relays

a. 1B throws to RF; RF allows ball to pass, chases ball, and throws to relay (2B); relay throws home; cutoff (1B) intercepts ball and throws to second.

b. 2B throws to CF; CF allows ball to pass, chases ball, and throws to relay (SS); relay throws home; cutoff (1B) intercepts ball and throws to third.

c. 3B throws to LF; LF allows ball to pass, chases ball, and throws to relay (SS); relay throws home.

Round 7—Sprints

As the last relay play is being executed, players form a

Table 13-2. A General Pre-Game Practice (*continued*)

Time	Players	Activity
		line between second and third (if their bench is along the first-base line) or between first and second (if their bench is along the third-base line). Once the relay has been completed, and all players have fallen into line, the team sprints to touch the opposite foul line (in front of their bench); sprints back to touch an imaginary line through the pitcher's plate, and sprints back to their bench.
1:45–1:55	Starting Pitcher and Second Catcher	Warm-up
1:55–2:00	All	1. Individual mental preparation for the game
		2. Ground rules
		3. Team cheer
2:00		Scheduled start of the game

If batting were to be included in this practice session, it could take place between 1:05 and 1:30. More time might be required, depending upon the size of the team, the number of pitchers available to throw to batters, and the amount of space available in which to set up stations.

There are several ways in which pre-game batting practice can be conducted. One example follows:

1. Number off.
2. Split into two halves (e.g., odd-even, low number–high number).
   a. Players in one half warm up their arms by throwing and catching and by fielding fungoes.
   b. Players in the other half bat, in assigned order. (Note: Allow each batter one bunt, one slug, and five hits or contacts—depending on the time available.)
3. Switch groups.

Try to structure batting practice so that players are kept active and involved. At times, it may be necessary to set up a station-rotation system. For example, players may number off and move through the following progression:

1. Fielder No. 1
2. Fielder No. 2

3. Fielder No. 3
4. Fielder No. 4
5. Shagger (for the pitcher)
6. Pitcher (underhand; overhand if necessary; or machine ball dropper)
7. Backstopper (well behind the batter)
8. Dry swinger
9. Weighted-bat swinger
10. Fence-ball tosser
11. Fence-ball hitter
12. Tee-ball setter
13. Tee-ball hitter
14. On-deck batter
15. Batter

Throwing and catching warm-up activities could be built into the above progression, if so desired.

Table 13–3 is a sample schedule for a pre-game pitching practice.

Table 13-3. A Pre-Game Pitching Practice

Time	Activity
12:30	Arrival at ball park
12:40	On field, ready to play
12:40–12:45	Jogging with team
12:45–12:55	Stretching with team
12:55–1:05	Loose, easy, relaxed throwing (over or underhand)— approximately 30–40 pitches
1:05–1:10	Batting practice
1:10–1:15	Warm-up pitches—approximately 15
1:15–1:20	Throwing for speed—approximately 20 pitches
1:20–1:25	Throwing for control—approximately 20 pitches, 5 at each of 4 targets
1:25–1:30	Throwing types of pitches—approximately 5 of each pitch in the pitcher's repertoire
1:30–1:35	Practicing pitches that aren't working
1:35–1:45	Pre-game huddle
1:45–1:55	Throwing types of pitches—2 or 3 of each pitch, followed by a double rotation of pitches in the pitcher's repertoire and ending with 3 hard strikes

Table 13-3. A Pre-Game Pitching Practice (*continued*)

Time	Activity
1:55–2:00	Ground rules, team cheer
2:00	Scheduled start of the game

NOTE: Because some pitchers take longer to warm up than others, the pre-game schedule should be fairly flexible. It is recommended that starters and relievers be slightly fatigued at the beginning of the game. Pitchers who consistently lack control through the first couple of innings are encouraged to warm up to a greater extent.

14

Game Coaching

One way of dealing with the assignment of pitchers is to adopt a fixed rotation schedule. If there were three pitchers (A, B, and C), for example, A would start the first game, B the second, C the third, A the fourth, and so on. Each pitcher would start every third game. An alternative plan would be to place the two better pitchers on rotation, with the third pitcher being used in relief, or as a spot starter. The alternative to using a rotation system is to consider each assignment individually.

DETERMINING THE STARTING LINE-UP

The coach's responsibility is to sort out the strengths and weaknesses of each player in such a way that he can put on the field the strongest possible composite of individuals who have the greatest potential to become a solid *team*.

Some suggestions that may be of help when attempting to identify a starting line-up are as follows:

1. Analyze your own personnel. Develop a tentative line-up.
2. Slot in your starting battery, and adjust your tentative line-up if necessary.

315

3. Consider your opponents.
   a. Kind and speed of pitching they typically face.
   b. Type of hitters (e.g., lookers, bunters, power hitters, pull hitters, place hitters).
   c. Offensive philosophy (e.g., aggressive vs. conservative baserunning, lookers vs. swingers).
   d. Past performance.
   e. Abilities of starting pitcher (e.g., speed, control, stuff).
4. Try to match your pitcher with the opponents in such a way that the pitcher's strengths will be maximized.
5. Make changes in your tentative line-up, attempting to place the better defensive players where the ball is most likely to be hit.
6. Make final adjustments, if desired, and develop a batting order.

DEVELOPING THE BATTING ORDER

At the beginning of a game, each player is assigned a position in the batting order. The objective is to organize offensive personnel in such a way that there is maximum potential for the production of runs. Although there is no one, scientific, foolproof formula for the construction of a batting order, there are some commonly accepted guidelines. It is suggested that the line-up take the following form:

1. The first, or lead-off, batter
   a. Aggressive—willing to try to get on base by any means possible
   b. A good eye—able to discriminate between balls and strikes
   c. A consistent hitter with good bat control
   d. A good bunter—able to bunt for a base hit
   e. Good speed—able to beat out infield hits and to stretch singles into doubles
   f. An aggressive, challenging baserunner—consistently tries to draw throws and to force errors
   g. Highest on-base average
2. The second batter
   a. A left-hander batter, if possible—able to hit behind a runner at first base and able to make the catcher's pick-off throw to first base more difficult
   b. Good bat control—able to execute a hit-and-run play with consistent success
   c. A good eye and a consistent hitter, though not as consistent as the lead-off batter

      d. An excellent bunter—able to advance a runner at first or to bunt for a base hit

      e. Good speed—able to beat out a double-play relay throw

3. The third batter

      a. The most consistent hitter, with the highest batting average

      b. More power than the lead-off batter, but less than the fourth batter

      c. Good speed—more than the fourth batter

4. The fourth, or clean-up batter

      a. A good hitter—less consistent, but more powerful, than the third batter

      b. High slugging and batting averages

5. The fifth batter

      a. A power hitter, with a high slugging average

      b. A fairly good hitter, but not as consistent as the third or fourth batter

6. The sixth batter

      a. The second lead-off—less consistent and less speed than the number one batter, but more power

      b. Left-handed, if possible

7. The seventh and eighth batters

      a. The weaker hitters on the team, but still capable of contributing to the offense—less consistent, less strength

      b. Good bunters

8. The ninth batter

      a. A fairly consistent or powerful hitter, if there is one left after the first five spots have been assigned (If not, place the better of the weakest three hitters here—preferably a fast runner so that the speeds of the ninth and first batters are back-to-back.)

Some coaches determine their batting order on the basis of individual batting averages. The player with the highest average bats first, and the player with the lowest average bats last. Positions in between are filled in descending order.

One of the key points to keep in mind when developing batting orders throughout a season is to *be flexible*. Change the order as necessary to take into account such variables as opposing pitcher, each player's mental and physical condition, individual streaks and slumps, lay-out of the ball park (e.g., presence or absence of fences, distances to fences), and weather conditions (e.g., wind speed and direction). As a rule, try to place the better hitters at the top of the order so that they will go to the plate more times during the course of a game. When you are playing an unfamiliar opponent, however, it might be wise to slip a good hitter into the ninth spot in the order. The pitcher may tend to let up a little, or the defense may move in a little, expecting the batter to be weak. A good hitter may be able to take advantage of this situation. If he has been having some problems at the plate while batting third or fourth, movement to the ninth spot may take some pressure off him and help him to regain his form. Occasionally, allow players the freedom to pick their spot in the order. This can tell the coach something about what they think of themselves and their batting abilities.

CONDUCTING THE PRE-GAME HUDDLE

Before a game, the coach should call players together for a pre-game huddle. The purpose of this meeting is

1. To review opponents' major strengths and weaknesses
2. To explain ground rules
3. To review offensive (batting, baserunning) and defensive (alignment, depth) signals
4. To read off the batting order
5. To answer any last minute questions that players may have
6. To set the tone for the game

At the conclusion of the meeting the coach may make a few statements concerning the task at hand. The huddle usually breaks up with a positive affirmation of team goals or a team cheer.

CALLING OFFENSIVE SIGNALS

Before stepping into the batter's box to receive any pitch, the batter should have a specific objective in mind—to hit, sacrifice bunt, take the pitch (let the ball pass by), or one of a number of other options. Sometimes, the batter's objective and response to a pitch will be affected by the immediate objective of a baserunner. The batter should not attempt to hit the ball, for instance, if the baserunner is trying to steal on the pitch. Signals are frequently used to coordinate the actions of players (batters and baserunners). Most coaches make up their own signals, sometimes in collaboration with team members. The following six signal-calling systems are among the most common. (Examples of signals for each system are given in Table 14–1.)

Table 14-1. Signal-Calling Systems

| Offensive Action Desired | Type of System | | |
	Verbal	Prolonged	Combination
TAKE	Call out player's first name.	Hold hand(s) on hip(s).	Place one hand on hip, and rub chin with the other.
BUNT	Call out player's last name.	Hold hand(s) in pocket(s).	Place one hand in pocket, put opposite foot forward.
STEAL	Call out team name (e.g., "Let's go Bears").	Fold arms and hold them across chest.	Walk toward home while clapping hands.
HIT AND RUN	Call out desired action (e.g., "Give it a ride," "Just meet it").	Hold hands together, or clench a fist.	Clench both fists.
	Series	Missing Link	Flash
TAKE	Touch shoulder, elbow, wrist— in order.	Leave out touching the forehead.	Touch the thigh.
BUNT	Touch wrist, shoulder, elbow— in order.	Leave out touching the chin.	Touch the belt.
STEAL	Touch shoulder, wrist, elbow—in order.	Leave out touching the ear(s).	Touch the skin (e.g., chin, hands, forehead).
HIT AND RUN	Touch the wrist, elbow, shoulder— in order.	Leave out touching the elbow(s). Set Series: Touching the forehead, chin, one or both ears, one or both elbows.	Touch the hip(s). KEY: Clapping hands together.

1. *Verbal.* Calling the signal is the simplest system. It is frequently used with young, inexperienced players. Usually the coach will go through a series of visual body signals while calling out to the batter to confuse or distract anyone who may be trying to steal the sign. The disadvantage of this system is that noise and wind may make the sign difficult for the batter or baserunners to hear.

2. *Prolonged.* This system is also recommended for younger, less-experienced players. Because each sign is held for a few moments, timing is not a factor. The batter or baserunners have an opportunity to think about the sign and to get it straight in their minds. The duration of the signal can also be a disadvantage, however, as opponents have a better chance to steal the sign. For this reason the sign should appear as natural and inconspicuous as possible to the uninformed observer. The sign should also be mixed with decoy signals. The coach may specify that the real sign is the first, second, or last one given.

3. *Combination.* Two motions are combined to form a sign. Each motion by itself or in combination with an unspecified motion means nothing. This system is a little more complex than the first two because the batter and baserunners must be alert to the total body action of the coach. The signs are more difficult to steal, however.

4. *Series.* Several motions are made in a specified sequence. The series of signals may be given on one side of the body only or with a random shift from one arm to the other at any time. It makes no difference, for instance, whether the right or left elbow is touched. What is important is the series, or the order in which the parts are touched. If any unspecified motion (e.g., touching the ear or hip, clapping the hands) interrupts the series, the sign is off. Decoy signals may precede or follow the series.

5. *Missing Link.* A set series of signals is established (e.g., touching the forehead, chin, one or both ears, one or both elbows). To call for a specific offensive action, the coach leaves out the appropriate motion in the series. When using the missing link signals shown in Table 14–1, touching the forehead, both ears, and one elbow would call for a bunt. Decoy signals should precede or follow the series. This system is difficult for the opposition to pick up, but the signs may also be confusing to one's own players—especially those who lack experience.

6. *Flash.* This is probably the most popular and deceptive signal-calling system. The key, or indicator, is a critical part of the system because it alerts the batter or baserunners that the real sign is forthcoming—usually immediately after the key. No signal means anything unless it immediately follows the key. The batter or baserunners must watch the coach attentively as he flashes signs in order to pick up the key and the sign that follows it. For example, when a coach is using the flash signals shown in Table 14–1, the coach may touch his thigh, touch his belt, clap his hands, and touch his ear. The ear means nothing, so the batter is on his own. If the coach had touched his hip instead of his ear, a

hit-and-run play would have been on. Decoy signals may precede or follow the key. The key may be changed without changing the signals.

To assure that the batter and baserunners have received a sign, the coach may require an acknowledgment (e.g., clenching the fists, nodding the head, picking up dirt, wiping the hands on the shirt or pants). That is particularly important when a hit-and-run or squeeze play has been called, because coordination of offensive effort is essential to the success of those plays.

The list that follows contains guidelines that may be of help to coaches when calling offensive signals.

1. Keep in mind, when developing signals, that they are sometimes easier to remember if they are associated with something. For example, refer to Table 14–1 and compare the flash signs to the offensive actions they represent. Notice that the sign for "Take" is touching the Thigh; for "Bunt," Belt; for "Steal," Skin; and for "Hit and Run," Hip(s). The first letters of the corresponding words are the same.
2. Keep in mind, too, that any signal-calling system may use a key, or indicator. Use of a key is recommended because the batter and baserunners can look specifically for the key as signs are flashed. If no key is given, there is no message. Decoy signals and extraneous movements can easily be disregarded. Also, the key can be changed without changing the signs.
3. Include a take-off signal (sometimes referred to as a rub-off, forget-it, or start-over signal) in your signal-calling system. It cancels all previous signs.
4. Use an ignore signal, on occasion, to confuse the opposition or to bait them into a particular defensive position.
5. Adopt a system of signal-calling that is appropriate for the players who will use it. Make the signs as simple as possible so they can be easily understood and readily picked up.
6. Use motions that are natural so that they are less obvious to those who might try to steal the signs.
7. Emphasize that batters are at the plate to hit, and that they should attempt to do just that unless a sign directs them to do otherwise.
8. Give signals on almost every pitch so that batters will develop a habit of looking for the signs, and opponents will not know, by the timing of signal-calling, when a special play is forthcoming.
9. Insist that batters and baserunners watch each complete set of

signals before turning away. Those who look away immediately following the actual sign may give it away.

10. Be sure that both the batter and the baserunners can see or hear the signs. They should be looking for the signs while they are out of the batter's box or on base, respectively.

11. Do not start giving signs until you have the attention of both the batter and the baserunners.

12. Give the signals as clearly and distinctly as possible.

13. If the batter or a baserunner appears confused, call time and tell him directly what you want him to do. A batter or baserunner who thinks he may have missed a sign, or isn't sure that he has the right sign, should call time and either have the signals given again, or talk to the coach personally.

14. If a sign must be repeated, change it if desired, or give it again, but in a slightly different way.

15. Practice giving signals in front of a mirror and then with players. Signals should be overlearned.

16. Make players accountable for missed, misread, and disregarded signals.

17. Add signs (e.g., bunt to first or third, slug bunt, suicide and safety squeeze, delayed steal) to the team's signal-calling system as players' skills improve.

18. Periodically review the meaning of each sign in the team's signal-calling system. Be sure to do it with discretion—away from nonteam personnel.

BASE COACHING

Batter

When the catcher fails to handle a pitched ball, the batter may be of assistance to baserunners by using the following signals:

1. Hold one hand up, to indicate "stop" or "stay." This signal is usually given when the batter believes that the catcher is likely to recover the ball too quickly for the runner to advance successfully.

2. Swing one hand in a series of clockwise circles, or extend the arm and point to the advance base. This signal is usually given when the ball passes behind the catcher's body. It indicates that the batter believes that the runner has a good chance to advance successfully.

Often, verbal cues ("Go!" "Stay!") accompany the visual signal.

Any time a baserunner advances toward home from third, the batter is responsible for clearing the base path and for verbally and visually telling the runner whether to stand up or slide.

On-Deck Batter

When the batter has become a batter-baserunner, and a lead runner is approaching home, the on-deck batter assumes responsibility for clearing the base path and telling the advancing runner, both verbally and visually, whether to stand up or slide.

Base Coaches

The ability of the first- and third-base coaches to provide leadership, encouragement, and responsible direction to runners can positively or negatively affect a team's offensive performance. Players are expected to comply with the directives of base coaches. Lack of confidence in them can lead to independent, uncoordinated action. Confusion, hesitation, and even injury can result if a base coach takes too long to give a signal, changes his mind, or gives contradictory verbal and visual signals. Consequently, base coaches should be selected and assigned with thought and care.

Base coaches must remain calm and objective. They must keep things in perspective. Runners should be advanced only if there is a good chance that they can arrive at the next base safely. They should not be sent on hope, wishful thinking, or fan response.

Base coaches can assist runners by

1. Checking the bases frequently to be sure that they are secure and properly aligned.
2. Watching the opposing pitcher closely to pick up patterns of delivery, etc., and watching for defensive patterns, weaknesses, catcher's signs, etc.
3. Watching for pick-off attempts (e.g., players slipping behind a runner) and warning the runners by yelling "Back!" (The first-base coach watches the second baseman so that the baserunner is free to concentrate on the catcher and the first baseman. The third-base coach watches the shortstop and the outfielders.)
4. Making sure that the runners can see the batter's signal, repeating it if necessary. (If a runner still appears confused, the base coach should call time and talk to the runner. Visual signs should not be given verbally from the coach's box, as they could easily be overheard by opponents.)

5. Reminding the runners of the game situation (e.g., number of outs, count on the batter, inning, and the importance of the run they represent).
   a. As a rule, with two outs, the base coach directs baserunners to take off as soon after bat-ball contact as possible.
   b. When there are two outs, and there is a 3–2 count on the batter, the base coach directs baserunners to take off as the pitcher releases the ball.
6. Informing runners when the infield-fly rule and third-strike rule are in effect.
7. Reminding back runners to be alert to the actions of lead runners and to work with them to protect each other, draw throws, etc.
8. Knowing the playing area (fair and foul) in order to be better able to advise runners if an overthrow occurs.
9. Informing runners as quickly as possible when a ball has been ruled foul.
10. Shouting encouragement and pushing the runners to extend themselves as they advance down the line and around the bases.
11. Directing runners to look ahead when running the bases. (Watching the ball results in loss of speed.)
12. Informing runners of the situation as they approach or round a bag and move on (e.g., "Easy," "Hustle," "Have to hurry," "Going to be close").
13. Helping runners to keep track of the ball.
14. Providing runners with such directives as
    a. "Run out *all* hits with intensity. Anything can happen."
    b. "Tag on a deep fly ball."
    c. "Run on a ground ball."
15. Reinforcing (praising) runners for a hit, effort down the line, alertness on the base paths, etc.
16. Calling "time" if a runner has extended himself physically and is tired. (Taking time to talk to the batter can give the runner an opportunity to collect himself.)
17. Making sure the runner is ready (mentally and physically) to play before time is resumed if he has been hit by a pitch or by a thrown or batted ball.

Once the ball has been delivered to the batter, runners become more or less dependent upon the first- or third-base coach for assistance and information, depending upon the position of the ball and whether or not it is in a runner's field of vision as he advances. The quickest and easiest way to transmit information to runners is through a prearranged set of signals. For example:

1. **Run directly across first base,** being sure to touch it in passing.
   Visual: Extend an arm and point directly to the bag.
   Verbal: "Hustle, hustle, straight over!"
2. **Stop** upright and **stay** on *base.*
   Visual: Extend one arm and point directly to the bag. Raise the other arm in traditional stop-sign fashion, or extend both arms overhead, palms facing the runner.
   Verbal: "Right here!" "Hold up!" "Stay!"
3. **Slide.**
   Visual: Extend both arms, palms facing the ground, for a slide straight into the bag. Sweep to the right for a slide to the infield side of the bag, away from the throw. Sweep to the left for a slide to the outfield side of the bag, away from the throw.
   Verbal: "Down!" "Hit it!"
4. **Round** the bag, hold, and be alert to go on or back, depending upon how play develops.
   Visual: Swing one arm in a series of small, quick, clockwise circles. Raise the other arm in traditional stop-sign fashion.
   Verbal: "Take a turn!" or "Round it!" followed by "Go!" or "Hold up!"
5. **Keep on going.**
   Visual: Extend one arm and point directly to the advance base, or swing the arm vigorously in large, clockwise circles.
   Verbal: "Go for——(base to which the runner may be able to advance)!" "Go, Go!" "All the way!"

Signals should be given to runners as quickly and clearly as possible so that the runners can react without hesitation. The simpler the signals, the better.

Base coaches must never assume that any baserunner is aware of the game situation. Constant reminders, instructions, and encouragement must be provided. If a runner is to stop (e.g., running directly over the base at first, or standing upright or sliding at third), the nearest base coach should position as much in line with the runner's approach as possible in order to be clearly visible to him. If there may be an opportunity for the runner to advance, the base coach should move to the end of the coach's box that is farthest from the approaching runner. This will give the base coach a little more time to decide the appropriate directive to give to the runner. By moving toward home plate as a runner advances from second, for instance, the third-base coach remains in front of the runner for a longer period of time. Both visual and verbal signs can be given even after the runner has passed third.

As soon as the lead runner for whom a base coach is responsible has been committed to an advance base, the coach must immediately direct his attention to back runners. The third-base coach, in particular, must guard against the temptation to watch the play at home when there are back runners to assist.

First Base

The first-base coach encourages and guides the batter-baserunner until he approaches second and is picked up by the third-base coach. Reminders that the coach can give to a runner at first, between pitches, include the following:

1. "There are———outs."
2. "Take off as soon as the ball hits the ground."
3. "Tag up on a deep fly ball; go part way on a short one."
4. "Play it safe" or "Be aggressive [take a chance]."
5. "Watch the catcher's arm. Be alert for a pick-off throw."
6. "Watch the third-base coach as you approach second if there is a chance that you can advance farther; touch second; and pick up the third-base coach again."
7. "Watch the first baseman. I'll watch the second baseman and right fielder for a possible pickoff."

Third Base

The third-base coach controls baserunners at second and third. Reminders that the coach might give to a runner at second, between pitches, include the following:

1. "There are———outs."
2. "Take off as soon as the ball hits the ground [if a force is in effect]."
3. "You don't have to go [if a force is not in effect]."
4. "Tag up on a deep fly ball; go part way on a short one."
5. "Play it safe" or "Be aggressive [take a chance]."
6. "Take as quick and as long a lead as possible on the pitch."

Reminders that the coach might give to a runner at third, between pitches, include the following:

1. "There are———outs."

2. "Take off as soon as the ball hits the ground [if a force is in effect]."

3. "You don't have to go [if a force is not in effect]."

4. "Tag up on *all* fly balls hit to the outfield [if there are fewer than two outs]." If the ball is caught, the runner is in position to take off immediately for home plate with no loss of time. If the ball is misplayed or is a hit, the runner can very likely score anyway. By taking a lead on the hit, the runner is gambling that the ball will not be caught. If it is caught, there will probably not be enough time to retreat to third, tag up, and still beat the throw to home.

5. "Stay in foul territory when approaching the plate and in fair territory when returning to third." This practice ensures that a fair-hit ball will not strike the runner. If a foul-hit ball strikes him, he is not out. In addition, a throw from the catcher to third will be as difficult as the runner can make it.

6. "Play it safe" or "Be aggressive [take a chance]." Remind the runner of the importance of the run he represents.

7. "You're on your own if the ball gets by the catcher on a wild pitch or passed ball," or "I'll tell you whether or not to go on a wild pitch or passed ball."

8. "Watch the catcher's arm. Be alert for a pick-off throw. I'll watch the shortstop and left fielder."

9. "The infield is playing back. Go on an infield hit."

10. "The infield is playing in. Wait until the ball goes through the infield."

11. "Be in motion, toward home, with the pitch."

12. "———has a strong arm. Be alert."

13. "You watch the catcher. I'll watch the pitcher, second baseman, and shortstop [with a runner on first and third—a double-steal situation]." In this situation, the runner needs help. He is most vulnerable to a quick, snap throw from the catcher to the third baseman. Consequently, the runner must watch the catcher's arm and body position and dive back to third if there is reason to believe that the throw is going to third. The base coach can assist the runner by watching and interpreting the relative movement of the pitcher, shortstop, and second baseman. For instance, if the second baseman and shortstop break into the diamond, they are giving up second and committing themselves to the lead runner. The coach should yell "Back" or "No" to the third-base runner. If the second baseman and shortstop move to the bag to cover and back up, the coach should yell "Go!" This is a particularly challenging situation for both the offensive and the defensive teams.

CALLING DEFENSIVE SIGNALS

Many times through the course of a game, a coach has to communicate with players while they are in defensive positions. Usually, verbal signals are used for reminders (e.g., "Hold the runner and get the out," "Force at——base," "——outs," "Cover——on a bunt, steal, wild pitch, or passed ball," "Back up the throw to——") and to alert players to potential offensive action (e.g., "Watch for a bunt," "Be ready for a steal," "Be ready for a tag-up on a fly ball," "Fast runner at the plate," "Long-ball hitter at bat"). In addition, verbal signals are frequently used to coordinate the alignment and depth of defensive personnel (e.g., "First and third basemen move in for a bunt," "Play shallow," "Play half way," "Play deep," "Shade right," "Shade left"). Sometimes visual signals are also used for this purpose. For example:

1. To move the infield (outfield) in for a play at the plate, move both hands (fists) in small circles toward the chest.
2. To move a specific infielder (outfielder) in, point toward the fielder with one hand (fist) and move the other in small circles toward the chest.
3. To move the infield (outfield) in halfway, hold the left arm up above the head and make a cutting motion at the elbow with the right hand (fist).
4. To move the infield (outfield) back into deep position, hold both hands (fists) out in front of the body, palms facing out, and continuously extend and flex the elbows in a repetitive pushing motion.
5. To move a specific infielder (outfielder) back, point toward the fielder with one hand (fist) and move the other in a repetitive pushing motion.
6. To move a specific infielder (outfielder) toward the third-base line, point toward the fielder with the right hand (fist) and to the left with the left hand (fist). Reverse the procedure to move a specific fielder toward the first-base line.
7. To move the first and third basemen in, in anticipation of a bunt, point toward first with the right hand and toward third with the left hand, and then move both hands in small circles toward the chest. Follow the same procedure to move the first and third basemen back, but use a repetitive pushing motion away from the chest, rather than a circular motion toward the chest.
8. To indicate to infielders (outfielders) that they are properly positioned, or that they have shifted far enough, hold both hands (fists) out in front of the body in traditional stop-sign fashion.

Visual signals are usually used when the coach wishes to be subtle, as when calling for (1) a pitchout in anticipation of a steal, (2) a pick-off at first or third, or (3) a specific play in response to a double-steal situation. Most coaches make up their own unique signals for these plays, selecting motions that are natural for them.

MAKING LINE-UP CHANGES

All line-up changes should be made for a reason. They should serve a purpose.

Offensive, task-oriented changes are most frequently made when the team is behind in the later innings of a game. They may also be made for disciplinary reasons (e.g., lack of hustle—a batter not running out a hit; consistent misreading, missing, or disregarding of signals). In addition, injury or sickness may make a substitution necessary. Changes may also be made when there is a wide difference in the score. Younger players can be given an opportunity to gain some game experience.

Defensive changes are often made when a team is ahead in the later innings of a game. Defensive specialists may take the place of offensive specialists in order to decrease the possibility of a big inning for the opponent. Defensive changes may also be made if the opponent successfully identifies defensive weaknesses (e.g., a catcher with a sore or weak arm, a third baseman who is erratic when handling bunts), and begins to exploit them. They may also be made in response to sickness or injury, for disciplinary reasons (e.g., a player is pouting after an error or gave up on a misplayed ball when there was still a chance to effect an out), to rest a player, or to give experience and playing time to nonstarters. It is usually not a good idea to replace a fielder immediately after he has committed a mechanical error, because immediate replacement can contribute to the fielder's loss of confidence and increase the anxiety of his teammates. A change may be made after a mental error, however, as players are expected to know their coverage and back-up assignments. They should plan, in advance, what they will do if the ball is hit or thrown to them.

All line-up changes must be made with objectivity and impartiality. On occasion, they may need to be justified.

Pinch hitters and runners, substitute fielders, and relief pitchers should be told, well in advance, when they are to enter the game. Advance notice is not always possible, however. Consequently, all players on the bench must be ready to play at any time. They must remain alert to what is going on in the game, and they must warm up at frequent intervals throughout the game.

CONDUCTING THE POST-GAME HUDDLE

As soon as a game has ended, players may experience a variety of emotions, depending upon how the game turned out, how the team performed, and how individuals performed. Within one team these emotions may range from euphoria to depression. The post-game huddle provides an opportunity to place the game in proper perspective and to prepare the team for what lies ahead. A few significant points may be brought up by the coach regarding the team's performance, and individual players may be given an opportunity to raise questions or to make statements, but the meeting should be as short as possible. It is not the time to work out offensive or defensive problems, to discuss strategies, or to rehash errors. If a meeting for those purposes is desired, it can be scheduled for later in the day, or the next day, when everyone can be more objective. During the post-game huddle it is probably sufficient to try to restore individuals to some semblance of emotional stability and normalcy before adjourning. The huddle should almost invariably end on a positive note!

15

Evaluating Performance

Coaches and athletes invariably want and need to evaluate individual abilities and team play. Through a systematized assessment process, coaches and athletes should receive information that can help them to profit from their experiences.

Methods of Evaluation

Individual and team play can be examined in a variety of ways, including motion pictures and videotapes, statistics, structured observations, subjective evaluations, conferences, and tests.

Motion Pictures and Videotapes

1. Films of individual athletes performing specific skills can be taken at various points throughout the season. By periodically comparing these performances, the athlete can determine the nature and extent of his progress.
2. Films can be utilized to help athletes realize discrepancies between their actual and perceived performances.
3. Films of the opposing pitcher can be analyzed with emphasis on action that telegraphs pitches and patterns.

4. Films of opposing hitters can be analyzed to determine their strengths and weaknesses and to provide concrete data to support the implementation of specific pitching strategy.
5. Films of experts performing skills (e.g., batting, pitching, throwing, hook sliding) can be used to motivate athletes of lesser skill; to give them a general idea of the action pattern required; and, through comparison with their own films, to guide the revision and improvement of their own performances.
6. Films can allow the viewer to identify the events that precede and follow specific behaviors. Such information is essential when attempting to understand why an athlete behaves as he does, as often as he does.

Statistics

Coaches use stat sheets for the collection, organization, and presentation of data generated in a given game, or throughout the course of the season, by their own team or their opposition.

To assess offensive performance, most coaches compute the following statistics:

$$\text{Batting Average} = \frac{\text{Total number of hits}}{\text{Total official times at bat}}$$

$$\text{Slugging Average} = \frac{\text{Total bases reached safely by hits}}{\text{Total official times at bat}}$$

$$\text{On-Base Average} = \frac{\text{Total times reach first safely}}{\text{Total times at bat}}$$

The most common measure of defensive proficiency is the fielding percentage. It is computed as follows:

$$\text{Fielding Average} = \frac{\text{Total number of putouts and assists}}{\substack{\text{Total number of fielding opportunities} \\ \text{(putouts, assists, and errors)}}}$$

A common measure of pitching proficiency is earned run average/game. It is computed as follows:

$$\frac{\text{Earned Run}}{\text{Average}} = \frac{\text{Total number of earned runs scored}}{\text{Total number of innings pitched}} \times 7$$

Data collected to complete individual stat sheets are primarily used to identify the strengths, weaknesses, habits, and tendencies of players; to obtain measures of their productivity; and to obtain measures of their performance consistency. Team stat sheets summarize data and provide a composite picture of the nature and quality of overall team performance.

Batting, fielding, and pitching statistics may be kept for opponents, but the usefulness of the information will depend upon how often an opposing team will be faced and the stability of that team's composition. Stat sheets used to record the performance of opposing hitters will eventually combine to form a "book." Data contained in this book can be of benefit for the following purposes:

1. Determining what pitch to throw to a hitter (e.g., fastball, rise, drop)
2. Determining where to throw to a hitter (e.g., high, low, inside, or outside)
3. Determining how carefully to pitch to a hitter and whether or not to walk him intentionally
4. Deciding how and where to position defensive personnel
5. Projecting what the batter is likely to do at the plate

Be sure to indicate the pitchers for each game played. Stats can vary significantly with differences in pitching strength.

Structured Observations

Coaches frequently rely on observations as a basis for the assessment of individual and team performance. Unfortunately, however, the feelings and attitudes of the coach toward a specific athlete, and toward the team as a whole, can affect the analysis and can bias results. In addition, the coach may categorize the athlete or team on the basis of a few observations, or may only see what he wants or expects to see. If the coach's focus is too narrow, he may (1) jump to conclusions based on incomplete information and observations, (2) overemphasize one aspect of the athlete's or team's play and fail to see the total performance, or (3) become preoccupied with his own internal reactions to what he has seen and fail to keep up with continuous events. If his focus is too broad, on the other hand, he may become overloaded with irrelevant information and data that he is unable to organize and to handle effectively; and he may miss significant but subtle behaviors that influence performance.

Coaches, as professional, scientific, analytical, objective observers, must screen out external distractions and concentrate on the task at hand. They must target behaviors and events, focus on them, and try not to be distracted by their own internal thoughts and feelings.

Subjective Evaluations

The value of others (e.g., parents, friends, opponents, spectators, sportswriters) as reliable and valid assessors of an athlete's or team's performance is suspect, because the people usually possess some degree of bias; often have a very narrow, limited focus; and frequently jump to conclusions based on incomplete information or observations. There is no doubt, however, that their opinions can affect an athlete's and team's performance. The effect, itself, will depend upon the relationship of the individual athlete to the others, his feelings about them, how much he values their opinions, and how well he can handle their positive or negative comments.

Conferences

Conferences are an important part of an assessment program. The productivity of a conference depends, to a large extent, on how the meeting is conducted, the content of conversation, and the degree of trust and respect between the coach and the athletes. Points to keep in mind when attempting to conduct a productive, constructive conference are as follows:

1. Show genuine concern for the athlete. Let him know that you care about him as a person as well as an athlete. If this is not a genuine feeling, do not attempt to fake it. Be honest and be yourself!
2. Consider individual differences in response to criticism, and deal with each athlete accordingly.
3. Determine how the athlete feels about his performance, and that of the team. Reinforce the athlete's assessment, supplement it with statements of your own, raise questions to stimulate further thought and more in-depth analysis, or point out differences of opinion. Be specific and be able to provide clear examples to support your point of view. Discuss those aspects of performance (physical and psychological) that the athlete can be expected to do something about. Give feedback directly, with respect, and with minimal emotion. Try to be analytical—not judgmental.
4. Ask the athlete to respond to questions related to physical conditioning, goals, anxiety, motivation, individual and team play, discipline, practice regimes, etc. Try very hard not to become

defensive or to attack an athlete on the basis of his response to any question. The willingness of an athlete to answer questions honestly, to communicate with the coach, and to make suggestions, will depend upon the coach's objectivity, openness to criticism, and willingness to consider and to implement suggestions. Let the athlete talk, and listen attentively. Try to keep an open mind and to understand the athlete's point of view. Focus not only on what is said, but also on how it is said. Look for nonverbal cues that signify anxiety, concern, pleasure, anger, avoidance. Consider whether or not the athlete's behavior reflects feelings that contradict his words.

5. If the athlete has a problem, or appears upset about something, let him "get it off his chest."
6. If in doubt about what an athlete is saying, restate what you believe him to have said and ask if you are correct in your understanding. Point out apparent inconsistencies in statements. Try to differentiate between what is said and what is meant.
7. Reassure, encourage, support, clarify, summarize, emphasize, restate, and interpret.
8. Collect information; invite a free exchange of ideas; discuss problems, situations, practices, and specific aspects of individual and team play; and compare views.

Conferences can be held between the coach and an individual athlete, the coach and the team captain, and the coach and the team as a whole. Team members may also meet together, in conference, without the coach.

Tests

Individual players' knowledge and understanding of concepts (e.g., rules, signals, cover and back-up assignments, strategies) essential to positive performance can be examined and reinforced through the use of (a) work sheets, (b) oral quizzes, and (c) paper-and-pencil tests. Physical performance can be assessed through the use of ability or skill tests. Reference to test and measurement books is recommended for detailed explanation of various softball skill tests. These measurement tools are used much more extensively by physical education teachers than by coaches.

Factors Affecting Performance

Evaluate individual and team play with respect to base-line performance and team goals. Try to differentiate between poor performance due to lack of, or limited, ability and poor performance due to faulty execution. Remember, and help each athlete to understand, that performance can be affected by the following:

1. The *physical condition* (e.g., height, weight, speed) of individual team members
2. The *physical fitness* (e.g., strength, endurance, flexibility) of individual team members
3. The ability of individual team members to execute *fundamental skills* (e.g., hit, bunt, run bases, field, throw)
4. The *psychological state* (e.g., anxiety, readiness, aggression, drive, concentration, confidence levels, aspirations, expectations) of individual team members.
5. The *weather* (e.g., temperature, wind speed and direction, sun, rain)
6. The *field conditions* (e.g., length of outfield grass, presence or absence of an outfield fence, hardness or wetness of the infield, distance from home plate to the backstop)
7. The *stage of the season* (e.g., early, middle, late) and the adequacy of mental and physical *preparation* for play
8. The quantity and quality of individual and team *experience*
9. The *schedule* (e.g., playing after a lay-off; playing a lot of games in a short period of time, as when in the loser's bracket of a tournament)
10. *Unexpected events* (e.g., injury, sickness, late arrival at the park, change in starting time due to weather, extra-inning game, etc.)
11. The *opponent* (e.g., pitching, hitting, fielding, psychological state, reputation, record, historical performance in competition with team)

Objective consideration of information related to these factors should be an integral part of any assessment process.

Analyze physical performance, but try also to better understand *why* an athlete behaves as he does—what underlying factors contribute to, or detract from, his performance. Attend primarily to the behaviors of those athletes who are not meeting their own, or your, expectations. To deal with the psychological, as well as the physical, components of an athlete's performance, do the following:

1. Observe the athlete's behavior carefully. Focus, in detail, on actual experiences and situations.
2. Decide and list the desirable behaviors.
3. Decide and list the undesirable behaviors, or those patterns of behavior that detract from performance and are self-defeating to the athlete.

4. Recognize that some behaviors are subtle, disguised, and complex.

5. Consider what took place immediately before, and immediately after, the behavior that is of primary concern. These events can affect the occurrence of the behavior. Behavior is strengthened or weakened on the basis of its consequences in the environment. Assume that all behavior is caused.

6. Attempt to increase your insight and to expand your capacity to understand each athlete, to see things from his point of view, and to broaden your repertoire of constructive responses to the athlete's behavior. Keep in mind that behavior is changeable.

7. Look at problems in a variety of ways, and consider and analyze possible solutions. Determine the behavior or patterns that should replace the negative or inefficient ones. Decide and list the reinforcers that will shape the behavior.

8. Develop a progressive program of behavior change. Keep in mind, however, that under stress, athletes often revert to old habits and behaviors. Consider, too, that the best preparation for stress is experience with the stressor.

SCOUTING

Scouting is the process of critically observing and evaluating a prospective opponent. It is one part of a coach's overall plan to prepare the team, as fully as possible, to meet the challenge of competition.

Deciding What Information to Seek

Information that is frequently sought through scouting pertains to the following:

1. The ability of individual players to execute basic fundamentals.
2. The physical condition of individual players and their ability to meet the demands of play.
3. The psychological condition of individual players and the team as a whole, and their reaction to a variety of stressful situations.
4. The ability of individual players, and the team, to execute offensive and defensive tactics and strategies and the relative frequency with which various tactics and strategies are employed.
5. The competitive environment.

Scouting a Game

The scout for a team may be its head coach, assistant coach, scorekeeper, or manager. Occasionally, it may be the catcher or probable starting pitcher. A qualified scout has game sense, knows what to look for, and has some basic observational skills. Following are a few pointers for scouting a prospective opponent in actual game competition:

1. Determine, in advance, what information you want to obtain, and develop a form on which to record the required observations.
2. Obtain a team roster, if possible, and a line-up for the game (e.g., batting order, defensive positions, uniform numbers).
3. Note the environmental conditions at the time that the game is played.
4. Concentrate on the task at hand and resist distractions.
5. Try to look at behaviors with an open mind. Avoid preconceived notions and stereotyping.
6. Comment on the quality of the scouted team's opposition (e.g., pitching, hitting, general defense).
7. Focus on both individuals *and* situations. Pick out one player at a time and zero in on his behavior for a series of plays. Shift to another target player. If time is limited, pay particular attention to key personnel. For a while, narrow your focus to a specific behavior (e.g., pitching, catching, hitting, backing up, covering), then expand focus to overall play. Observe integrated behaviors (e.g., positions of primary and secondary players, and what each does or doesn't do, in specific situations).
8. Be specific, rather than general, and support statements with clear examples.
9. To obtain psychological information, focus on bench conduct, sideline activity, and athlete's behavior immediately preceding and following a play. Pay attention not only to what an athlete does, but also to how he does it.
10. Jot down anything that might be helpful later, especially those things that the coach and team might be expected to be able to do something about.

Index

8th Batter   O RBIs 1 Game   2 at bat   0 Hits   1 out

6th Batter   2 RBIs 2 Game   4 at bat   2 Hits   2 outs
                                          2 singles

2nd Batter   3 RBIs 3 Game   4 at bat   3 Hits   1 out
                                          1 Home Run
                                          1 thriple
              4 game Noplay   1 single

1st Batter   O RBIs 5 game   4 at bat   3 Hits   No outs
                                          1 Triple
                                          2 Singles
                                          1 walk

                      13 at bat   8 hits   4 outs
                                  1 Home run
5 RBI's   2 triples
                                  5 singles
    8 out of 13   1 walk